INSIDER
POWER TECHNIQUES
for Microsoft® **WINDOWS® XP**

Paul McFedries, Scott Andersen,
Austin Wilson, and Geoff Winslow

PUBLISHED BY
Microsoft Press
A Division of Microsoft Corporation
One Microsoft Way
Redmond, Washington 98052-6399

Library of Congress Cataloging-in-Publication Data
Insider Power Techniques for Microsoft Windows XP / Paul McFedries ... [et al.].
        p. cm.
    Includes index.
    ISBN 0-7356-1896-8
    1. Microsoft Windows (Computer file)   2. Operating systems (Computers)   I. McFedries,
Paul.

    QA76.76.O63I555   2003
    005.4'469--dc21   2002044882

Printed and bound in the United States of America.

1 2 3 4 5 6 7 8 9   QWE   8 7 6 5 4 3

Distributed in Canada by H.B. Fenn and Company Ltd.

A CIP catalogue record for this book is available from the British Library.

Microsoft Press books are available through booksellers and distributors worldwide. For further information about international editions, contact your local Microsoft Corporation office or contact Microsoft
Press International directly at fax (425) 936-7329. Visit our Web site at www.microsoft.com/mspress. Send
comments to *mspinput@microsoft.com*.

Acquisitions Editor: Alex Blanton
Project Editor: Jenny Moss Benson
Technical Editor: Jim Johnson

Body Part No. X09-35335

Contents

Acknowledgments

The gurus keep talking about the coming age of self-publishing, where every Tom, Dick, and Harriet can foist their prose on an unsuspecting world. That's fine, but the gurus never talk about an important corollary: Self-publishing almost always means self-editing, too. And that's a big problem, because even the best writers need editing, and not even the best writers can do it themselves. The world needs editors not only because it's hard to dot every "i" and cross every "t," but because we need experts to look dispassionately at our prose and give us good advice about how to fix it. And we have been fortunate, indeed, that we've had the expert editors at Microsoft Press to help us whip this book into shape. We extend sincere thanks to everyone at Microsoft Press who had a hand in bringing this book to print, particularly those with whom we worked directly: acquisitions editor Alex Blanton, project editor Jenny Moss Benson, technical editor Jim Johnson, copy editor Marilyn Orozco, and project manager Barb Levy.

We also want to thank our family and friends for their support and, well, just for being there.

To Karen and Gypsy
—Paul McFedries

To Barbara, Jaguar, Nick, and Luke
—Scott Andersen

To Laura, Molly, and Chaz
—Austin Wilson

To Carol and Sydney
—Geoff Winslow

Introduction

The great artist Pablo Picasso once said that "the more technique you have, the less you have to worry about it." What does this have to do with Microsoft Windows XP? Well, to paraphrase Picasso, the more Windows XP techniques you have, the less you have to worry about Windows XP itself. The way we see it, *what* a person creates using a computer is a unique expression of who that person is, whether it's a memo, letter, financial model, presentation, e-mail message, or Web page.

On the other hand, *how* the average person uses the computer—or, more to the point, how that person uses Windows XP—probably isn't unique at all. It's likely that most users follow the same Start menu paths to launch programs, use standard techniques in programs such as Microsoft Outlook Express and Windows Explorer, and perform customizations that don't go much beyond changing the wallpaper.

Our goal in this book is to show you that changing the "how" improves the "what." By altering your usual way of doing things in Windows XP—that is, by learning a few "insider" techniques—you can become a faster and more efficient user with an optimized and relatively trouble-free system. What you'll find then is that Windows XP fades into the background, and you'll be able to devote all your precious time and energy into getting your work (or play) done.

What kinds of techniques are we talking about? Here's a sampling:

■ Tweaking Windows XP for maximum performance.

■ Automating Windows XP with script files.

■ Working faster and smarter with a few simple Start menu and taskbar customizations.

■ Boosting productivity with easy file and folder techniques.

■ Getting the most out of online sessions by using the most powerful features of Microsoft Internet Explorer.

■ Preventing Windows crashes with a simple maintenance plan.

- Taking the pain out of troubleshooting Windows XP problems.

- Working with the registry safely and easily.

- Taking the mystery out of setting up and administering a small network.

Some Notes Before We Begin

This book is intended for people who want to get more out of their Windows XP investment. Power users will find plenty of tips and techniques to take their Windows XP game to a higher level. But this is definitely not an Alpha Geeks–only book. Intermediate users or even anyone who is reasonably comfortable with Windows XP will find an abundance of powerful and practical advice aimed at upgrading skills and knowledge. We've tried to shun high-end computing jargon to give you the straight goods on each topic, and we tell you why and how our techniques will make you a better Windows XP user.

We want to note, however, that this isn't a book for novice Windows XP users. We've made a few assumptions throughout the book not only about the minimum level of expertise necessary to use the book, but also about how you use Windows XP. Here are some notes:

- We assume you've used Windows XP for a while and are comfortable with basic techniques such as using the Start menu, working with files and folders, dragging objects, and using Windows XP components such as Notepad and Paint.

- We assume you're using Windows XP Professional. Most of the book's techniques also work with Windows XP Home Edition, but many do not. We've tried to point these out as we go along.

- We assume your computer already has an Internet connection.

- Many of the book's techniques require that you be logged on using either the Administrator account or an account in the Administrators group. This is explained in more detail in Chapter 5, "Managing Logons and Users."

- To keep folder paths generic, we've used certain environment variables as folder placeholders throughout the book. There are three in particular that we use quite often:

❑ **%SystemDrive%** This refers to the drive on which Windows XP is installed, such as C:.

❑ **%SystemRoot%** This refers to the folder in which Windows XP is installed, such as C:\Windows.

❑ **%UserProfile%** This refers to the root folder of a user's profile, such as C:\Documents and Settings\Administrator.

■ As a collection of "insider" techniques, this book isn't meant to be read from cover to cover (although you're certainly free to do so). Instead, each chapter is self-contained so that you can dip into the book as required to get the information you need. The only exceptions to this are the first three chapters, which give you some background on a few tools and techniques that we use in most of the other chapters.

■ You'll see reader aids sprinkled liberally throughout the book. These asides offer extra information that we hope you'll find useful and practical. There are five different sidebars:

❑ **Note** These reader aids give you more information about the current topic. They provide extra insights that give you a better understanding of the task at hand.

❑ **Tip** Tips tell you about Windows XP methods that are easier, faster, or more efficient than standard methods.

❑ **Caution** Here we give warning of accidents just waiting to happen. There are always ways to mess things up when you're working with computers, and these boxes help you avoid at least some of the pitfalls.

❑ **Insider Secret** These reader aids present little-known or undocumented tricks along with powerful techniques we've developed from rooting around in the nooks and crannies of Windows XP.

❑ **Notes from the Real World** These anecdotal sidebars offer detailed, practical know-how based on our nearly 50 years of cumulative experience working with all versions of Windows.

6

I

Mastering Essential Insider Techniques

In Part I, you'll learn insider techniques to help you:

1

Mastering Control Panel, Policies, and PowerToys

In this chapter, you'll learn how to:

- Use Control Panel and understand its icons.

- Work with Control Panel files directly.

- Get easier access to Control Panel.

- Work with group policies.

- Use the various programs that come with the Windows XP PowerToys.

Plain and simple, our goal for this book is to help you get the most that you possibly can out of Microsoft Windows XP. Our premise is that rather than sticking to the obvious, you must go below the surface if you want to fully reap Windows XP's bounty. Throughout this book, we do just that. We show you the numerous insider techniques and secrets that lurk within Windows XP that can help you work faster and more efficiently. As you'll see in almost every chapter of this book, these insider techniques involve not only in-depth examination of numerous topics but also the use of certain tools that Windows XP provides. Some of these tools come up again and again in this book, so it makes sense to learn to use them well, which is what you'll do in this chapter. We'll show you how to get the most out of Control Panel, system policies, and the PowerToys add-ons.

Operating Control Panel

Control Panel is a folder that contains a large number of icons—a couple of dozen of them reside in the default Windows XP setup, but depending on your system configuration, 30 or more icons may be available. Each of these icons deals with a specific area of the Windows XP configuration: hardware, applications, fonts, printers, multimedia, and more.

In most cases, opening a Control Panel icon displays a dialog box containing various properties related to that area of Windows. For example, launching the Add Or Remove Programs icon enables you to install or uninstall third-party applications and Windows XP components. A few icons, such as the Printers And Faxes icon, provide access to a menu of devices and services.

To display the Control Panel folder, use any of the following techniques:

- Select Start, Control Panel.

- In Windows Explorer's Folders list, select the Desktop\My Computer \Control Panel folder.

- In My Computer window, click the Control Panel link.

> **Tip**   You can also display Control Panel in My Computer's contents list by selecting the Tools, Folder Options command, selecting the View tab, and choosing the Show Control Panel In My Computer check box.

By default, Windows XP displays Control Panel in Category View, which divides the underlying icons into various categories. In most cases, you click a category and then click the icon you want to work with. This setup might help novice users, but it just delays the rest of us unnecessarily. Therefore, your first Control Panel task should be to click the Switch To Classic View link, which displays all the Control Panel icons, as shown in Figure 1-1. Note that Windows XP remembers the last view you used, so the Classic View will now appear each time you launch Control Panel.

Figure 1-1   Switch Control Panel to the Classic View to see all the icons
in one window.

Reviewing Control Panel's Icons

To help you familiarize yourself with what's available in Control Panel, this section offers summary descriptions of the Control Panel icons found in a standard Windows XP installation. Note that your system may have extra icons, depending on your configuration and which programs you have installed.

- **Accessibility Options**   Enables you to customize input (keyboard and mouse) and output (sound and display) for users with special mobility, hearing, or vision requirements.

- **Add Hardware**   Launches the Add Hardware Wizard, which searches for new Plug and Play devices on your system and can help you install drivers for non–Plug and Play devices.

- **Add Or Remove Programs**   Allows you to install and uninstall applications, add and remove Windows XP components, and, if you have Windows XP Service Pack 1 installed, change the default programs for the Web browser, e-mail client, instant messaging program, and more.

- **Administrative Tools**   Displays a window with more icons, each of which enables you to administer a particular aspect of Windows XP.

- **Date And Time**   Enables you to set the current date and time, select your time zone, and set up an Internet time server to synchronize your system time.

- **Display** Offers a large number of customization options for the desktop, screen saver, video card, monitor, and other display components.

- **Folder Options** Allows you to customize the display of Windows Explorer's folders, set up whether Windows XP uses single- or double-clicking, work with file types, and configure offline files.

- **Fonts** Displays the Fonts folder, from which you can view, install, and remove fonts.

- **Game Controllers** Enables you to calibrate joysticks and other game devices.

- **Internet Options** Displays a large collection of settings for modifying Internet properties (how you connect, the browser interface, and so on).

- **Keyboard** Gives you the ability to customize your keyboard, work with keyboard languages, and change the keyboard driver.

- **Mouse** Allows you to set various mouse options and to install a different mouse device driver.

- **Network Connections** Enables you to create, modify, and launch connections to a network or the Internet.

- **Phone And Modem Options** Allows you to configure telephone dialing rules and to install and configure modems.

- **Power Options** Gives you the ability to configure power management properties for the following: powering down system components (such as the monitor and hard disk); defining low-power alarms for notebook batteries; enabling hibernation; and configuring an uninterruptible power supply.

- **Printers And Faxes** Allows you to install and configure printers and the Windows XP Fax service.

- **Regional And Language Options** Enables you to configure international settings for country-dependent items such as numbers, currencies, times, and dates.

- **Scanners And Cameras** Enables you to install and configure document scanners and digital cameras.

- **Scheduled Tasks** Displays the Scheduled Tasks folder, which you use to set up any program to run on a schedule.

- **Sounds And Audio Devices**   Allows you to control the system volume, map sounds to specific Windows XP events (such as closing a program or minimizing a window), and specify settings for audio, voice, and other multimedia devices.

- **Speech**   Enables you to configure Windows XP's text-to-speech feature.

- **System**   Gives you access to a large number of system properties, including the computer name and workgroup, Device Manager and hardware profiles, and settings related to performance, startup, System Restore, Automatic Updates, Remote Assistance, and the Remote Desktop.

- **Taskbar And Start Menu**   Enables you to customize the taskbar and Start menu.

- **User Accounts**   Enables you to set up and configure user accounts.

Understanding Control Panel Files

Many of Control Panel's icons are represented by *Control Panel extension* files, which use the .cpl extension. Most of these files reside within the %SystemRoot%\System32 folder. When you open Control Panel, Windows XP scans the registry looking for Control Panel files, and then displays an icon for each one. A few icons are represented by Control Panel application names.

Windows XP offers an alternative method for launching individual Control Panel dialog boxes. The idea is that you run Control.exe and specify a parameter that identifies the specific Control Panel function to open. Control.exe can be run from either the Start, Run dialog box or from the command line. This bypasses the Control Panel folder and opens the icon directly. Here's the syntax:

`CONTROL parameter[, option1[, option2]]`

parameter	The name of the CPL file, including the .cpl extension, or the Control Panel application name.
option1	This option is no longer needed and is included only for backwards compatibility with scripts and batch files that use the Control.exe method for opening Control Panel icons.
option2	Many of the Control Panel icons open a multitabbed window. If you know the exact tab you want to open, you can specify an integer that corresponds to the tab's displacement from the left side of the window (the first tab being 0, the second being 1, and so on) as *option2*, and the window will open with that tab displayed. Note that even though *option1* is not specified, its leading comma is still required when *option2* is specified.

For example, to open Control Panel's System icon, with the Hardware tab selected, use this command:

```
CONTROL sysdm.cpl,,2
```

Table 1-1 lists the various Control Panel icons and the appropriate command line to use. (Note, however, that some Control Panel icons—such as Taskbar And Start Menu—can't be accessed by running Control.exe.)

Table 1-1   Command lines for launching individual Control Panel icons

Control Panel Icon	Command
Accessibility Options	CONTROL Access.cpl
Add Hardware	CONTROL Hdwwiz.cpl
Add Or Remove Programs	CONTROL Appwiz.cpl
Administrative Tools	CONTROL admintools
Date And Time	CONTROL Timedate.cpl
Display	CONTROL Desk.cpl
Folder Options	CONTROL folders
Fonts	CONTROL fonts
Game Controllers	CONTROL Joy.cpl
Internet Options	CONTROL Inetcpl.cpl
Keyboard	CONTROL keyboard
Network Connections	CONTROL Ncpa.cpl
Mouse	CONTROL mouse
Phone and Modem Options	CONTROL Telephon.cpl
Power Options	CONTROL Powercfg.cpl
Printers And Faxes	CONTROL printers
Regional And Language Options	CONTROL Intl.cpl
Scanners And Cameras	CONTROL scannercamera
Scheduled Tasks	CONTROL schedtasks
Sounds and Audio Devices	CONTROL Mmsys.cpl
Speech	CONTROL speech
System	CONTROL Sysdm.cpl
User Accounts	CONTROL Nusrmgr.cpl

> **Note**   If you find your Control Panel folder is bursting at the seams, you can trim it down to size by removing those icons you never use. A number of ways exist for you to do this in Windows XP, but the easiest way is probably via group policies. We discuss group policies in detail later in this chapter, and we include an example technique that shows you how to use policies to configure access to Control Panel. See "Example: Controlling Access to Control Panel," later in this chapter.

Accessing Control Panel More Easily

Control Panel is certainly a useful and important piece of the Windows XP package, and even more useful if you can get to it easily. Here are a few methods for gaining quick access to individual icons and the entire folder.

Opening Control Panel Icons Using Alternative Methods

Access to many Control Panel icons is scattered throughout the Windows XP interface, meaning that there's more than one way to launch an icon. Many of these alternative methods are faster and more direct than using the Control Panel folder. Here's a summary:

- **Date And Time**   Double-click the clock in the taskbar's notification area.

- **Display**   Right-click the desktop and then select Properties.

- **Folder Options**   In Windows Explorer, select Tools, Folder Options.

- **Fonts**   In Windows Explorer, select the %SystemRoot%\Fonts folder.

- **Internet Options**   In Microsoft Internet Explorer, select Tools, Internet Options.

- **Network Connections**   In Windows Explorer, select My Network Places, select View, Explorer Bar, clear Folders (or any other selected option), and click View Network Connections in the Network Tasks list.

- **Power Options**   On a notebook computer, right-click the Power Meter icon in the taskbar's notification area and then select Open Power Meter.

- **Printers And Faxes**   Select Start, Printers And Faxes.

- **Scheduled Tasks**   Select Start, All Programs, Accessories, System Tools, Scheduled Tasks. Alternatively, in Windows Explorer select the %SystemRoot%\Tasks folder.

- **System**   On the Start menu, right-click the My Computer icon and then select Properties.

- **Taskbar And Start Menu**   Right-click an empty section of the task-bar or Start button and then select Properties.

Putting Control Panel on the Taskbar

For one-click access to the icons, create a new Control Panel taskbar toolbar by following these steps:

1.   Right-click an empty section of the taskbar and then select Toolbars, New Toolbar. The New Toolbar dialog box appears.

2.   Select My Computer, Control Panel.

3.   Click OK.

From here, you can customize the Control Panel toolbar to fit all the icons on your screen (for example, by turning off the icon titles). See Chapter 10 "Customizing the Interface," to learn how to tweak taskbar toolbars.

Putting Control Panel on the Start Menu

You can turn the Start menu's Control Panel command into a menu that displays the Control Panel icons by following these steps:

1.   Launch Control Panel's Taskbar And Start Menu icon.

2.   Select the Start Menu tab, ensure that the Start Menu option is selected, and then click Customize. The Customize Start Menu dialog box appears.

3.   Select the Advanced tab.

4.   In the Start Menu Items list, find the Control Panel item and select the Display As A Menu option.

5.   Using this same Start Menu Items list, you can also add the Network Connections icon directly to the Start menu. Find the Network Connections item and select either the Display As Connect To Menu option or the Link To Network Connections Folder option.

6. To add the Administrative Tools icon directly to the Start menu, find the System Administrative Tools item in the Start Menu Items list and choose the Display On The All Programs Menu And The Start Menu option.

7. Click OK.

Implementing Group Policies with Windows XP

Group policies are settings that control how Windows XP works. You can use them to customize the Windows XP interface, restrict access to certain areas, specify security settings, and much more.

Group policies are used mostly by system administrators who want to make sure that novice users don't have access to dangerous tools (such as the Registry Editor), or who want to ensure a consistent computing experience across multiple machines. Group policies also are ideally suited to situations in which multiple uses share a single computer. However, group policies are also useful on single-user standalone machines, as you'll see throughout this book.

Working with Group Policies

You implement group policies by using the Group Policy Editor. To start the Group Policy Editor, select Start, Run and then use either of the following methods:

■ To implement group policies for the local computer, enter **gpedit.msc** and click OK.

■ To implement group policies for a remote computer, enter **gpedit.msc /gpcomputer:"*name*"**, where *name* is the name of the remote machine, and then click OK.

The Group Policy window that appears is divided into two sections:

■ The left pane contains a treelike hierarchy of policy categories, which is divided into two main categories: Computer Configuration and User Configuration. The Computer Configuration policies apply to all users and are implemented before the logon. The User Configuration policies apply only to the current user and, therefore, are not applied until that user logs on.

■ The right pane contains the policies for whichever category is selected in the left pane.

> **Note**   You must be logged on to Windows XP with administrator-level privileges to use the Group Policy Editor.

The idea, then, is to open the tree's branches to find the category you want. When you click the category, its policies appear in the right pane. For example, Figure 1-2 shows the Group Policy window with the Computer Configuration, Administrative Templates, System, Logon category selected.

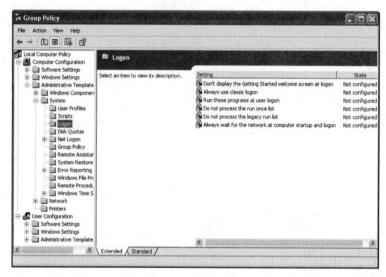

Figure 1-2   When you select a category in the left pane, the category's policies appear in the right pane.

> **Tip**   Windows XP comes with another tool called the Local Security Policy Editor, which displays only the policies found in the Group Policy Editor's Computer Configuration, Windows Settings, Security Settings branch. To launch the Local Security Policy Editor, select Start, Run, enter **secpol.msc**, and click OK.

In the right pane, the Setting column tells you the name of the policy, and the State column tells you the current state of the policy. Click a policy to see its description on the left side of the pane. To configure a policy, double-click it. The type of window you see depends on the policy:

■ For simple policies, you see a window similar to the one shown in Figure 1-3. These kinds of policies take one of three states: Enabled (the policy is in effect and its setting is enabled), Disabled (the policy is in effect but its setting is disabled), and Not Configured (the policy is not in effect).

Figure 1-3   Simple policies are Enabled, Disabled, or Not Configured.

■ Other kinds of policies also require extra information when the policy is enabled. For example, Figure 1-4 shows the window for the Run These Programs At User Logon policy. When Enabled is selected, the Show button appears, which you use to specify one or more programs that run when the computer starts.

Figure 1-4   More complex policies also require extra information such as, in this case, a list of programs to run at logon.

Example: Controlling Access to Control Panel

You can use group policies to hide or display Control Panel icons and to configure other Control Panel access settings. To see how this works, follow these steps:

1.   In the Group Policy Editor, select User Configuration, Administrative Template, Control Panel.

2.   Configure one or more of the following policies:

❑   **Prohibit Access To The Control Panel**   If you enable this policy, users can't access Control Panel using the Start menu, Windows Explorer, or the CONTROL command. This action will also disable the user's ability to access some Control Panel functions through alternative means, such as double-clicking the clock in the notification area or right-clicking the desktop and selecting Properties. Several of these Control Panel functions will not be removed until the user logs off.

❑   **Hide Specified Control Panel Applets**   If you enable this policy, you can hide specific Control Panel icons. To do this, click Show, then click Add, enter the name of the icon you want to hide (such as **Game Controllers**) or the name of the CPL file (such as **Joy.cpl**), and then click OK.

❑   **Show Only Specified Control Panel Applets**   If you enable this policy, you hide all Control Panel icons except the ones that you specify. To do this, click Show, then click Add, enter the name of the icon you want to show (such as **Game Controllers**) or the name of the CPL file (such as **Joy.cpl**), and then click OK.

❑   **Force Classic Control Panel Style**   If you enable this policy, Control Panel is always displayed in the Classic View, and the user can't change to the Category View. If you disable this policy, Control Panel is always displayed in the Category View, and the user can't change to the Classic View. However, when the Not Configured option is selected, the user can change between Category View and Classic View at will.

3.   When you've finished with a policy, click OK or Apply to put the policy into effect.

> **Tip**   Another way to hide and display Control Panel icons is to use Tweak UI, which we describe in the next section. Tweak UI's Control Panel tab offers check boxes for each CPL file (see Figure 1-5 on the following page). Select a check box to display the icon; clear a check box to hide the icon.

Note, too, that group policies also enable you to customize the behavior of some Control Panel icons. When you open the Control Panel branch, you'll see four sub-branches that correspond to four Control Panel icons: Add Or Remove Programs, Display, Printers And Faxes, and Regional And Language Options. In each case, you use the policies in a particular sub-branch to hide dialog box tabs (or "pages," as the Group Policy editor calls them), specify default settings, and more.

> **Note**   Another useful tool that you should know about (and that we use from time to time in this book) is the Computer Management utility. This program gives you access to many Windows XP management components, including Event Viewer, Local Users And Groups, Device Manager, Disk Management, and all the Windows XP services. To start Computer Management, select Start, Run, enter **compmgmt.msc**, and click OK.

Enhancing Your System with the Windows XP PowerToys

Some of the Windows XP developers weren't satisfied with having worked on just the Windows XP code. In their off-hours (we presume), they cobbled together a number of small program "extras" designed to make your Windows life a bit easier and more fun. The result was Microsoft PowerToys for Windows XP. (Don't be fooled by the "Microsoft" part of the name. These programs are not supported by Microsoft, so if you have any problems with them, you're on your own!) The following is the link to download these free PowerToys:

http://www.microsoft.com/windowsxp/pro/downloads/powertoys.asp

From that site, you can choose to download any or all of the individual PowerToys. In all cases, double-click the downloaded file to install the Power-Toy. (If you need to remove any of the PowerToys later on, click Start, Control Panel, Add Or Remove Programs. Each PowerToy has its own entry in the Cur-rently Installed Programs list.) The next few sections present quick summaries of what each PowerToy does.

Tweak UI

Tweak UI (which, more than any other PowerToy, we'll be mentioning throughout this book) acts as a front end for a large number of user interface customization options. Most of these options are controls for adding and work-ing with registry settings, so they give you an easier and safer way to tweak your system. Once you install the program, select Start, All Programs, Power-toys For Windows XP, TweakUI For Windows XP. As you can see in Figure 1-5, the left side of the Tweak UI window offers a treelike hierarchy of categories. When you select a category, its settings appear in the right side of the window.

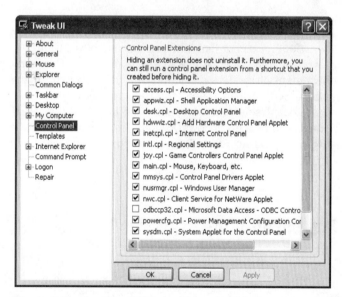

Figure 1-5   Use Tweak UI to easily and safely customize the Windows XP user interface.

Alt-Tab Replacement

Alt-Tab Replacement is a replacement for the Alt+Tab "cool switch" key com-bination that you use to switch from one running program to another. In its default incarnation, holding down Alt and tapping the Tab key cycles through a list of the icons for the running programs. When the Alt-Tab Replacement PowerToy is installed, holding down Alt and tapping Tab displays the program icons, but it also shows a preview of the program window, as shown in Figure 1-6. This is better than pressing Alt+Esc to cycle though the open application windows, because while pressing Alt+Tab you can press Esc to cancel the switch. Note that Alt+Tab Replacement runs automatically when you install it and each time you start Windows XP. The latter is controlled by the CoolSwitch setting in the following registry key (see Chapter 4, "Starting Up and Shutting Down," to learn about launching programs automatically at startup):

```
HKLM\SOFTWARE\Microsoft\Windows\CurrentVersion\Run
```

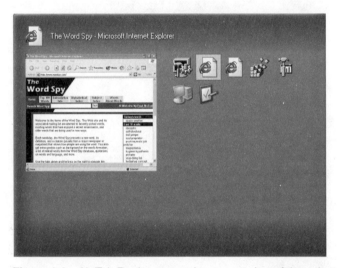

Figure 1-6   Alt-Tab Replacement shows a preview of the selected icon's program window.

Open Command Window Here

Open Command Window Here adds an Open Command Window Here item to the shortcut menu of all file folder objects. When you right-click a folder and then select Open Command Window Here, Windows XP launches a new command prompt session and changes to the folder. To accomplish this, all the PowerToy does is add a new Open Command Window Here action to the File Folder file type. (See Chapter 7, "Getting the Most Out of Files and Folders," to learn about file types.) It configures this action to run the following command:

```
cmd.exe /k "cd %L"
```

PowerToy Calculator

PowerToy Calculator is a calculator program that goes well beyond the usual addition, subtraction, multiplication, and division. It has built-in conversion functions for converting between standard and metric values; it supports all trig and log functions; it allows you to create your own functions, and it will even graph those functions for you. Once you install the program, select Start, All Programs, Powertoys For Windows XP, PowerToy Calculator. Figure 1-7 shows the PowerToy Calculator screen. You use the Input box to enter your calculations and functions, or select them using the Functions and Conversions menus.

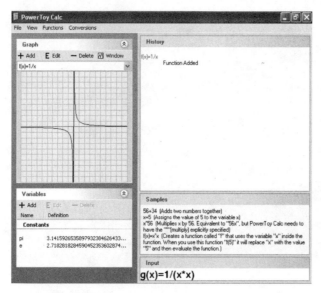

Figure 1-7   With PowerToy Calculator, you can define and graph your own functions.

Image Resizer

Image Resizer makes it easy to create a copy of an image in one of several standard sizes or in a custom size that you specify. After installing this program, select one or more image files, right-click the selection, and then select Resize Pictures to display the Resize Pictures dialog box. Click the Advanced >> button to expand the dialog box to the one shown in Figure 1-8. Select one of the standard sizes—Small, Medium, Large, or Handheld PC—or choose Custom to enter a specific width and height. You also have two options:

- **Make Pictures Smaller But Not Larger**   If you select this check box, the program will resize only those images that are larger than the selected size. For example, if you select Medium (800 × 600), the program will shrink a 1,024 × 768 image, but it won't enlarge a 640 × 480 image.

- **Resize The Original Pictures (Don't Create Copies)**   If you select this check box, the program resizes the selected images instead of making resized copies.

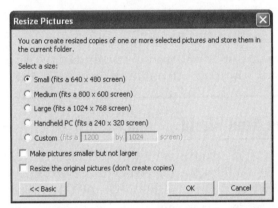

Figure 1-8   Use the Resize Pictures PowerToy to resize one or more images to the dimensions you specify in this dialog box.

CD Slide Show Generator

The CD Slide Show Generator PowerToy adds a program to your burned CDs that enables the user to view images on the CD as a slide show. After you install the CD Slide Show Generator, the CD Writing Wizard gains an extra step that asks whether you want to add the picture viewer to the CD, as shown in Figure 1-9.

If you choose the Yes, Add A Picture Viewer option, Windows XP adds an Autorun.exe file that automatically displays the CD images in a slide show when the user inserts the CD.

Figure 1-9   With the CD Slide Show Generator installed, the CD Writing Wizard asks whether you want to include the slide show viewer on the burned CD.

Notes from the Real World

Here's a simple way to make someone special in your life smile on Christmas, his or her birthday, or some other festive occasion. Every other year for the past few years I have created Christmas CDs for the two grand-mothers in our lives: one CD for my mother and one for my mother-in-law. These discs contain images of their grandchildren, taken throughout the year with my digital camera. I also have my daughter draw a nice picture that we scan to print as the cover of the CD. This has worked well, but not everyone knows how to access a CD, much less open pictures on one. This is particularly true of many of the world's grandmothers and grandfa-thers, who often are not as comfortable with technology as the younger generations. This year, I am going to ensure that our Christmas CD gift goes off without a hitch by using the CD Slide Show Generator PowerToy. Since it sets up the image slide show to run automatically when the CD is inserted, our grandmothers can view the pictures without any ado. Note, too, that the Autorun.exe program that the CD Slide Show Generator adds to the CD is backwards-compatible with Microsoft Windows 95, Windows 98, and Windows Millennium Edition (Me) machines, so it doesn't matter which version of Windows a special someone may be running.

—Scott Andersen

Virtual Desktop Manager

The Virtual Desktop Manager allows you to manage up to four different desktops. This enables you to display one set of running program on one desktop, a different set of programs on a second desktop, and so on. After you install this PowerToy, you use it by right-clicking an empty section of the taskbar and then selecting Toolbars, Desktop Manager. This displays the Virtual Desktop Manager toolbar, shown in Figure 1-10.

Figure 1-10   The Virtual Desktop Manager toolbar enables you to work with up to four different desktops.

To choose a desktop, use either of the following techniques:

■   The "Quick Switch" buttons labeled 1, 2, 3, and 4 represent the virtual desktops. Click a button to view that desktop.

■   Click the green Preview button to see a preview of all four desktops, and then click the desktop you want.

Once you've chosen a desktop, you select a program to appear on that desktop by clicking its taskbar button to restore the program to the desktop.

You can also right-click the Desktop Manager toolbar and select from the following commands:

■   **Configure Desktop Images**   Choose this command to easily choose background images for each desktop.

■   **Configure Shortcut Keys**   Choose this command to create keyboard shortcuts for selecting the preview window and the four desktops.

■   **MSVDM Help**   Choose this command to load the Virtual Desktop Manager Help window.

■   **Use Animations**   When this command is selected, Virtual Desktop Manager displays a transition animation when you switch from normal to preview mode. Clear this command to disable the animation.

■   **Shared Desktops**   When this command is selected, Virtual Desktop Manager allows you to switch a running program from one virtual desktop to another, as described in MSVDM Help. If you clear this command, programs can be displayed only on one desktop.

■   **Show Quick Switch Buttons**   If you clear this command, Virtual Desktop Manager hides the four Quick Switch buttons in the toolbar, leaving only the Preview button and the MSVDM title.

Taskbar Magnifier

The Taskbar Magnifier PowerToy is another taskbar toolbar. In this case, the toolbar contains a small window that displays a magnified view of whatever screen area the mouse pointer is positioned over, as shown in Figure 1-11. You display the Taskbar Magnifier by right-clicking an empty section of the taskbar and then selecting Toolbars, Taskbar Magnifier.

Figure 1-11   The Taskbar Magnifier displays a magnified view of the screen area under the mouse pointer.

HTML Slide Show Wizard

The HTML Slide Show Wizard PowerToy takes you step by step through the creation of a slide show suitable for posting to your Web site. Here's how it works:

1.   Select Start, All Programs, Powertoys For Windows XP, Slide Show Wizard.

2.   In the initial Slide Show Wizard dialog box, click Next.

3.   To add images to the slide show, you have two choices:

     ❑   For individual images, click Add Image, select the image (or images) in the Open dialog box, and then click Open.

     ❑   For an entire folder of images, click Add Folder, select the folder in the Browse For Folder dialog box, and then click OK. (If you make a mistake, or simply want to delete an image, select the image and click Remove, or click Remove All to clear the image list.)

4.   Click Next.

5.   Use the next wizard dialog box to enter a slide show name, select a file location, specify the size of the images, and choose the slide show type. Click Next.

6.   If the location you entered doesn't exist, the wizard asks if you want to create it. Click Yes. The wizard creates the slide show HTML files.

7. To load the slide show into the Web browser (see Figure 1-12), click View The Slide Show Now.

8. Click Finish to complete the wizard.

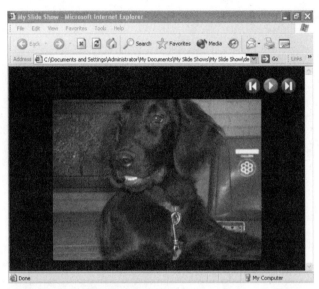

Figure 1-12 The HTML Slide Show Wizard PowerToy created this example slide show page.

Webcam Timershot

The Timershot PowerToy enables you to take a picture at a specified interval from a Webcam or other desktop camera and save the image to your hard disk. To start the program, select Start, All Programs, Powertoys For Windows XP, Timershot. When the Timershot program loads, click the >> button to expand the window to the one shown in Figure 1-13. Use the window controls to choose the device (if you have more than one), select the interval and resizing options, and specify a name and location for the image. Note, too, that you can click the camera icon to take a picture at any time.

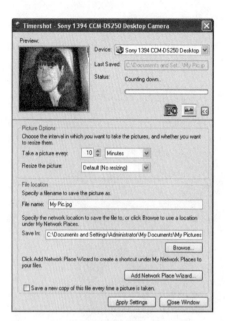

Figure 1-13   Use this window to set up the Webcam Timershot PowerToy.

If you want to use your Webcam to monitor an area while you're away, select Save A New Copy Of This File Every Time A Picture Is Taken, and set the Take A Picture Every values to ensure you capture the events you are monitoring. However, ensure that you have sufficient space on your selected storage device to hold all these pictures! Hint: After gathering this data, use Windows Explorer to select the folder in which these pictures have been saved, and then select View, Filmstrip for a quick review of the monitored area.

To end the Timershot operation, right-click the Timershot icon in the desktop's notification area and select Exit.

2

Getting the Most Out of the Registry

In this chapter, you'll learn how to:

■ Handle the registry's structure and content.

■ Keep registry data safe and sound.

■ Edit, create, rename, and delete registry keys and settings.

■ Create, export, edit, and import registration files.

All the chapters in this book are sprinkled liberally with references to the Microsoft Windows XP registry and with registry examples that enable you to modify the Windows XP environment in powerful ways. To use these examples—and, indeed, to get the most from not only this book but from Windows XP itself—you need to know what the registry is and how to use it efficiently and safely. This chapter helps you do that by telling you everything you need to know to become comfortable working with this most important of Windows XP's configuration tools.

Understanding the Registry

Say you've changed the desktop wallpaper using Control Panel's Display icon. The next time you start your computer, how does Windows XP know which wallpaper you selected? Or, if you change your video display driver, how does Windows XP know to use that driver at startup and not the original driver loaded during Setup? In other words, how does Windows XP "remember" the various settings and options either that you've selected yourself or that are appropriate for your system?

The secret to Windows XP's prodigious memory is the registry. The registry is a central database that Windows XP uses to store anything and everything that applies to the configuration of your system. This includes all of the following:

- Information about all the hardware installed on your computer.

- The resources used by those devices.

- A list of the device drivers that get loaded at startup.

- Settings used internally by Windows XP.

- File type data that associates a particular type of file with a specific application.

- Wallpaper, color schemes, and other interface customization settings.

- Other customization settings for items such as the Start menu and the taskbar.

- Settings for accessories such as Windows Explorer and Microsoft Internet Explorer.

- Internet and network connections and passwords.

- Settings and customization options for many applications.

Even better, thanks to a handy tool called the Registry Editor (discussed later in this chapter), it's yours to play with (carefully!) as you see fit.

Taking a Tour of the Registry

To launch the Registry Editor, open the Run dialog box, type **regedit**, and click OK. Figure 2-1 shows the Registry Editor window that appears.

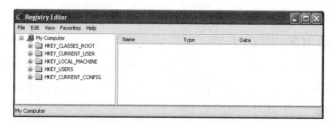

Figure 2-1   Running the REGEDIT command launches the Registry Editor, a front end that enables you to work with the registry's data.

The Registry Editor is reminiscent of Windows Explorer, and it displays information in basically the same way. The left side of the Registry Editor window is similar to Windows Explorer's Folders pane, except that rather than folders, you see *keys*. For lack of a better phrase, we'll call the left pane the *Keys pane*.

Navigating the Keys Pane

The Keys pane, like Windows Explorer's Folders pane, is organized in a treelike hierarchy. The five keys that are visible when you first open the Registry Editor are special keys called *handles* (which is why their names all begin with HKEY). These keys are referred to collectively as the registry's *root keys*. We'll tell you what to expect from each of these keys later (see the section called "Getting to Know the Registry's Root Keys," later in this chapter).

These keys all contain subkeys, which you can display by clicking the plus sign (+) to the left of each key, or by selecting a key and pressing the plus-sign key on your keyboard's numeric keypad. When you open a key, the plus sign changes to a minus sign (–). To close a key, click the minus sign or select the key and press the minus-sign key on the numeric keypad. (Again, this is just like navigating folders in Windows Explorer.)

You often have to drill down several levels to get to the key you want. For example, Figure 2-2 shows the Registry Editor after you've opened the HKEY_ CURRENT_USER key, then the Control Panel subkey, and then clicked the Mouse subkey. Notice how the status bar tells you the exact path to the current key, and that this path is structured just like a folder path.

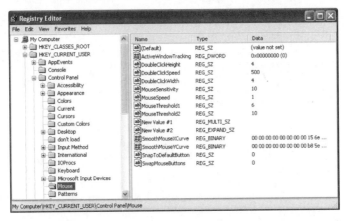

Figure 2-2   Open the registry's keys and subkeys to find the settings you want to work with.

> **Note** To see all the keys properly, you likely will have to increase the size of the Keys pane. To do this, use your mouse to drag the split bar to the right. Alternatively, select View, Split, use the Right arrow key to adjust the split bar position, and then press Enter.

Understanding Registry Settings

If the left side of the Registry Editor window is analogous to Windows Explorer's Folder pane, the right side is analogous to Windows Explorer's Contents pane. In this case, the right side of the Registry Editor window displays the settings contained in each key (so we'll call it the *Settings pane*). The Settings pane is divided into three columns:

- **Name** This column tells you the name of each setting in the currently selected key (analogous to a file name in Windows Explorer).

- **Type** This column tells you the data type of the setting. There are five common data types:

    - ❏ **REG_SZ** This is a string value.

    - ❏ **REG_MULTI_SZ** This is a series of strings.

    - ❏ **REG_EXPAND_SZ** This is a string value that contains an environment variable name that gets "expanded" into the value of that variable. For example, the %SystemRoot% environment variable holds the name of the folder in which Windows XP was installed. So if you see a registry setting with the value %SystemRoot%\System32\, and Windows XP is installed in C:\Windows, then the setting's expanded value is C:\Windows\System32\.

    - ❏ **REG_DWORD** This is a double word value: a 32-bit binary value arranged as eight hexadecimal digits. For example, 11 hex is 17 decimal, so this number would be represented in DWORD form as 0x00000011 (17). (Why "double word"? A 32-bit value represents four bytes of data, and because a word in personal-computer programming circles is defined as two bytes, a four-byte value is a double word.)

    - ❏ **REG_BINARY** This value is a series of hexadecimal digits.

- **Data** This column displays the value of each setting.

Getting to Know the Registry's Root Keys

The root keys are your registry starting points, so you need to become familiar with what kinds of data each key holds. The next few sections summarize the contents of each key.

HKEY_CLASSES_ROOT (HKCR)

HKEY_CLASSES_ROOT—usually abbreviated as HKCR—contains data related to file extensions and their associated programs, the objects that exist in the Windows XP system, as well as applications and their Automation information. HKCR also contains keys related to shortcuts and other interface features.

The top part of this key contains subkeys for various file extensions. You see .bmp for BMP (Paint) files, .doc for DOC (WordPad) files, and so on. In each of these subkeys, the Default setting tells you the name of the registered file type associated with the extension. (We discuss file types in Chapter 7, "Getting the Most Out of Files and Folders.") For example, the .txt extension is associated with the txtfile file type.

These registered file types appear as subkeys later in the HKEY_CLASSES_ROOT branch, and the registry keeps track of various settings for each registered file type. In particular, the shell subkey tells you the actions associated with this file type. For example, in the shell\open\command subkey, the Default setting shows the path for the executable file that opens. Figure 2-3 shows this subkey for the txtfile file type.

Figure 2-3 The registered file type subkeys specify various settings associated with each file type, including its defined actions.

HKEY_CLASSES_ROOT is actually a copy (or an *alias*, as these copied keys are called) of the following HKEY_LOCAL_MACHINE key:

```
HKEY_LOCAL_MACHINE\Software\Classes
```

The registry creates an alias in HKEY_CLASSES_ROOT to make these keys easier for applications to access and to improve compatibility with legacy programs.

HKEY_CURRENT_USER (HKCU)

HKEY_CURRENT_USER (usually abbreviated as HKCU) contains data that applies to the user that's currently logged on. It contains user-specific settings for Control Panel options, network connections, applications, and more. Note that if a user has group policies set on his or her account, those settings are stored in the HKEY_USERS*sid* subkey (where *sid* is the user's security ID). When that user logs on, these settings are copied to HKEY_CURRENT_USER. For all other users, HKEY_CURRENT_USER is built from the user's profile file, Ntuser.dat.

Note　How do you find out each user's SID? First, open the following registry key:

```
HKEY_LOCAL_MACHINE\SOFTWARE\Microsoft\Windows NT
\CurrentVersion\ProfileList\
```

Here you'll find a list of SIDs. The ones that begin S-1-5-21 are the user SIDs. Select one of these SIDs and then examine the ProfileImagePath setting, which will be of the form %SystemDrive% \Documents and Settings*user*, where *user* is the user name associated with the SID.

Here's a summary of the most important HKEY_CURRENT_USER subkeys:

- **AppEvents**　Contains sound files that play when particular system events occur (such as maximizing of a window).

- **Control Panel**　Contains settings related to certain Control Panel icons.

- **Identities**　Contains settings related to Microsoft Outlook Express, including mail and news options and message rules.

- **Keyboard Layout**　Contains the keyboard layout as selected via Control Panel's Keyboard icon.

- **Network**　Contains settings related to mapped network drives.

- **Software**　Contains user-specific settings related to installed applications and Windows XP.

HKEY_LOCAL_MACHINE (HKLM)

HKEY_LOCAL_MACHINE (HKLM) contains non–user-specific configuration data for your system's hardware and applications. HKLM contains three subkeys that you'll use most often:

- **Hardware**   Contains subkeys related to serial ports and modems, as well as the floating-point processor.

- **Software**   Contains computer-specific settings related to installed applications. The Classes subkey is aliased by HKEY_CLASSES_ROOT. The Microsoft subkey contains settings related to Windows XP (as well as any other Microsoft products you have installed on your computer).

- **System**   Contains subkeys and settings related to Windows XP startup.

HKEY_USERS (HKU)

HKEY_USERS (HKU) contains settings that are similar to those in HKEY_ CURRENT_USER. HKEY_USERS is used to store the settings for users with group policies defined, as well as the default settings (in the .DEFAULT subkey) that get mapped to a new user's profile.

HKEY_CURRENT_CONFIG (HKCC)

HKEY_CURRENT_CONFIG (HKCC) contains settings for the current hardware profile. If your machine uses only one hardware profile, HKEY_ CURRENT_ CONFIG is an alias for HKEY_LOCAL_MACHINE\SYSTEM\ControlSet001. If your machine uses multiple hardware profiles, HKEY_CURRENT_CONFIG is an alias for HKEY_LOCAL_MACHINE \SYSTEM\ControlSet*nnn*, where *nnn* is the numeric identifier of the current hardware profile. This identifier is given by the CurrentConfig setting in the following key:

```
HKEY_LOCAL_MACHINE\SYSTEM\CurrentControlSet\Control\IDConfigDB
```

Understanding Hives and Registry Files

The registry database actually consists of a number of files containing a subset of the registry. This subset, called a *hive,* consists of one or more registry keys, subkeys, and settings. Each hive is supported by several files that use the extensions listed in Table 2-1. Be aware, though, that other programs use the same file name extensions, but for other purposes.

Table 2-1   Extensions used by hive-supporting files

Extension	File Contains
None	A complete copy of the hive data.
.alt	A backup copy of the hive data.
.log	A log of the changes made to the hive data.
.sav	A copy of the hive data as of the end of the text mode portion of the Windows XP setup.

Table 2-2 shows the supporting files for each of the major system-default hives. (Note that not all of these files may appear on your system.)

Table 2-2 Supporting files used by each of the major system-default hives

Hive	Files
HKLM\SAM	%SystemRoot%\System32\config\Sam %SystemRoot%\System32\config\Sam.log %SystemRoot%\System32\config\Sam.sav
HKLM\Security	%SystemRoot%\System32\config\Security %SystemRoot%\System32\config\Security.log %SystemRoot%\System32\config\Security.sav
HKLM\Software	%SystemRoot%\System32\config\Software %SystemRoot%\System32\config\Software.log %SystemRoot%\System32\config\Software.sav
HKLM\System	%SystemRoot%\System32\config\System %SystemRoot%\System32\config\System.alt %SystemRoot%\System32\config\System.log %SystemRoot%\System32\config\System.sav
HKU\.DEFAULT	%SystemRoot%\System32\config\Default %SystemRoot%\System32\config\Default.log %SystemRoot%\System32\config\Default.sav

Also, users each have their own hives, which are mapped to HKEY_CURRENT_ USER during logon. The supporting files for each user hive are usually stored in \Documents and Settings*user*, where *user* is the user name. In each case, the Ntuser.dat file contains the hive data, and the Ntuser.log file tracks the hive changes. (As we mentioned earlier, if a user has group policies set on his or her account, the user data is stored in an HKEY_USERS subkey.)

> **Tip** You can also work with a registry on a remote computer over a network. See Chapter 16, "Setting Up and Administering a Small Network," for details.

Keeping the Registry Safe

The sheer wealth of data stored in one place makes the registry convenient, but it also makes it very precious. If your registry went missing somehow, or if it got corrupted, Windows XP simply would not work. With that scary thought in mind, let's take a moment to run through several protective measures. The techniques in this section should ensure that Windows XP never goes down for the count because you made a mistake while editing the registry.

> **Insider Secret**   If you share your computer with other people, you may not want to give them access to the Registry Editor. You can prevent any user from using this tool by running the Group Policy editor. Open User Configuration, Administrative Templates, System, and then enable the Prevent Access To Registry Editing Tools policy. Note that *you* won't be able to use the Registry Editor, either. However, you can overcome that by temporarily disabling this policy prior to running the Registry Editor.

Backing Up the Registry

Windows XP maintains what is known as the *system state*: the crucial system files that Windows XP requires to operate properly. Included in the system state are the files used during system startup, the Windows XP protected system files, and, naturally, the registry files. The Backup utility has a feature that enables you to easily back up the current system state, so it's probably the most straightforward way to create a backup copy of the registry should anything go wrong. Note that you must be logged on as a member of the Administrators group or the Backup Operators group in order to back up the system-state files and folders. Here are the steps to follow to back up the system state:

1. Select Start, All Programs, Accessories, System Tools, Backup. (Note that if you're using Windows XP Home Edition, you might need to install Backup from the Windows XP CD. We explain how this is done in Chapter 12, "Maintaining Your System in 10 Easy Steps.")

2. When the Backup Or Restore Wizard appears, click the Advanced Mode link.

3. Select the Backup tab.

4. In the folder tree, open the Desktop branch and then the My Computer branch, if they're not open already.

5. Select the System State check box.

6. Choose your other backup options, click Start Backup, and then follow the usual backup procedure (as discussed in Chapter 12).

> **Caution** Depending on the configuration of your computer, the system state can be quite large—up to 350 MB. Therefore, make sure the destination you choose for the backup has enough free space to handle such a large file.

Saving the Current Registry State with System Restore

Another easy way to save the current registry configuration is to use Windows XP's System Restore utility. This program takes a snapshot of your system's current state, including the registry. Then, if anything should go wrong with your system, the program enables you to restore a previous configuration. It's a good idea to set a system restore point before doing any work on the registry. We show you how to work with System Restore in Chapter 12.

> **Insider Secret** Another way to protect the registry from inappropriate editing is to ensure that its keys have the appropriate permissions. By default, Windows XP gives members of the Administrators group full control over the registry, and it gives individual users control over the HKCU key when that user is logged on. (See Chapter 5, "Managing Logons and Users," for more information on users, groups, and permissions.) To adjust the permissions, right-click the key in the Registry Editor, and then select Permissions. Make sure that only administrators have the Full Control check box selected.

Protecting Keys by Exporting Them to Disk

If you're making just a small change to the registry, backing up all of its files may seem like overkill. Another approach is to back up only the part of the registry that you're working on. For example, if you're about to make changes within the HKEY_CURRENT_USER key, you could back up just that key, or even a subkey within HKCU. You do that by exporting the key's data to a registration file, which is a text file that uses the .reg extension. That way, if the change causes a problem, you can import the .reg file back into the registry to restore things to the way they were.

Exporting a Key to a .reg File

Here are the steps to follow to export a key to a registration file:

1. Open the Registry Editor and select the key you want to export.

2. Select File, Export to display the Export Registry File dialog box.

3. Select a location for the file.

4. Use the File Name text box to enter a name for the file.

5. If you want to export only the currently highlighted key, make sure the Selected Branch option is selected. If you'd prefer to export the entire registry, select the All option.

6. If you'll be importing this file into a system running Windows 9x (Windows 95, Windows 98, or Windows 98 Second Edition), Windows Millennium Edition (Me), or Windows NT, use the Save As Type list to choose the Win9x/NT 4 Registration Files (*.reg) item.

7. Click Save.

Insider Secret   One common registry scenario is to make a change to Windows XP using a tool such as the Group Policy Editor or Tweak UI, and then try to find which registry setting (if any) was affected by the change. However, because of the sheer size of the registry, this is usually a needle-in-a-haystack exercise that ends in frustration. One way around this is to export some or all of the registry before making the change and then export the same key or keys after making the change. You can then use the FC (file compare) utility at the command prompt to find out where the two files differ. Here's the FC syntax to use for this:

```
FC /U pre_edit.reg post-edit.reg > reg_changes.txt
```

Here, change *pre_edit.reg* to the name of the registration file you exported before editing the registry; change *post_edit.reg* to the name of the registration file you exported after editing the registry; and change *reg_changes.txt* to the name of a text file to which the FC output is redirected. Note that the /U switch is required because registration files use the Unicode character set.

Importing a .reg File

If you need to restore the key that you backed up to a registration file, follow these steps:

1. Open the Registry Editor.

2. Select File, Import to display the Import Registry File dialog box.

3. Find and select the file you want to import.

4. Click Open.

5. When Windows XP tells you the information has been entered into the registry, click OK.

> **Note**   You also can import a .reg file by locating it in Windows Explorer and then double-clicking the file.

> **Caution**   Many applications ship with their own .reg files for updating the registry. Unless you're sure that you want to import these files, avoid double-clicking them. They might end up overwriting existing settings and causing problems with your system.

Working with Registry Keys and Settings

Now that you've had a look around, you're ready to start working with the registry's keys and settings. In this section, we'll give you the general procedures for basic tasks, such as modifying, adding, renaming, deleting, and searching for entries, and more. These techniques will serve you well throughout the rest of the book when we take you through some specific registry modifications.

Changing the Value of a Registry Entry

Changing the value of a registry entry is a matter of finding the appropriate key, choosing the setting you want to change, and editing the setting's value. Unfortunately, finding the key you need isn't always a simple matter. Knowing the root keys and their main subkeys, as described earlier, will certainly help, and the Registry Editor also has a Find feature that's invaluable. (We'll show you how to use it later.)

To illustrate how this process works, let's work through an example: changing your registered owner name and company name. During the Windows XP installation process, Setup may have asked you to enter your name and, optionally, your company name. (If you upgraded to Windows XP, this data was brought over from your previous version of Windows.) These "registered names" appear in several places as you work with Windows XP:

■   If you launch Control Panel's System icon, your registered names appear on the General tab of the System Properties dialog box.

■   If you select Help, About in most Windows XP programs, your registered names appear in the About dialog box.

■   If you install a 32-bit application, the installation program uses your registered names for its own records (although you usually get a chance to make changes).

With these names appearing in so many places, it's good to know that you can change either or both names (for example, if you give the computer to another person). The secret lies in the following key:

`HKLM\SOFTWARE\Microsoft\Windows NT\CurrentVersion`

To get to this key, you open the branches in the Registry Editors tree pane: `HKEY_LOCAL_MACHINE`, then `SOFTWARE`, then `Microsoft`, and then `Windows NT`. Finally, click the `CurrentVersion` subkey to highlight it. Here you'll see a number of settings, but two are of interest to us:

Tip   If you have keys that you visit often, you can save them as "favorites" to avoid trudging through endless branches in the keys pane. To do this, navigate to the key and then select Favorites, Add To Favorites. In the Add To Favorites dialog box, edit the name in the Favorite Name text box, if necessary, and then click OK. To navigate to a favorite key, open the Favorites menu and select the key name from the list that appears at the bottom of the menu.

- **RegisteredOrganization**   This setting contains the registered company name.

- **RegisteredOwner**   This setting contains your registered name.

Now you open the setting for editing by using any of the following techniques:

- Select the setting name and select Edit, Modify (or press Enter).

- Double-click the setting name.

- Right-click the setting name and select Modify from the shortcut menu.

The dialog box that appears depends on the value type you're dealing with, as discussed in the next few sections. Note that edited settings are written to the registry right away, but the changes might not go into effect immediately. In many cases, you need to exit the Registry Editor and then either log off or restart Windows XP.

Editing a String Value

If the setting is a REG_SZ value (as it is in our example), a REG_MULTI_SZ value, or a REG_EXPAND_SZ value, you see the Edit String dialog box, shown in Figure 2-4. Use the Value Data text box to enter a new string or modify the existing string, and then click OK. (For a REG_MULTI_SZ multi-string value, Value Data is a multi-line text box. Type each string value on its own line. That is, after each string, press Enter to start a new line.)

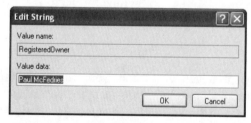

Figure 2-4   You see the Edit String dialog box if you're modifying a string value.

Editing a DWORD Value

If the setting is a REG_DWORD value, you see the Edit DWORD Value dialog box shown in Figure 2-5. In the Base section of the dialog box, select either Hexadecimal or Decimal, and then use the Value Data text box to enter the new value of the setting. (If you chose the Hexadecimal option, enter a hexadecimal value; if you chose Decimal, enter a decimal value.)

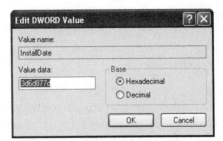

Figure 2-5   You see the Edit DWORD Value dialog box if you're modifying a string value.

Editing a Binary Value

If the setting is a REG_BINARY value, you see an Edit Binary Value dialog box like the one shown in Figure 2-6.

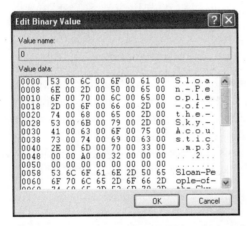

Figure 2-6   You see the Edit Binary Value dialog box if you're modifying a binary value.

For binary values, the Value Data box is divided into three vertical sections:

■   **Starting byte number**   The four-digit hexadecimal values on the left of the Value Data box tell you the sequence number of the first byte in each row of hexadecimal numbers. This sequence always begins at 0, so the sequence number of the first byte in the first row is 0000. There are 8 bytes in each row, so the sequence number of the first byte in the second row is 0008, and so on. These values can't be edited.

- **Hexadecimal data** The eight columns of two-digit numbers in the middle section display the setting's value, expressed in hexadecimal numbers, where each two-digit number represents a single byte of information. These values are editable.

- **ASCII equivalents** The third section on the right side of the Value Data box shows the ASCII equivalents of the hexadecimal numbers in the middle section. For example, in Figure 2-6 the first byte of the first row is the hexadecimal value 53, which represents the capital letter S. The values in this column are also editable.

Editing a .reg File

If you exported a key to a registration file, you can edit that file and then import it back into the registry. To make changes to a registration file, find the file in Windows Explorer, right-click the file, and then select Edit. By default, Windows XP will open the file in Notepad. Be aware that not all files having .reg for their file name extension are registration files.

Tip If you need to make global changes to the registry, export the entire registry and then load the resulting registration file into WordPad or some other word processor or text editor. Use the application's Replace feature (carefully!) to make changes throughout the file. If you use a word processor, be sure to save the file as a text file. You can then import the changed file back into the registry.

Creating a .reg File

You can create registration files from scratch and then import them into the registry. This is a handy technique if you have some customizations that you want to apply to multiple systems. To demonstrate the basic structure of a registration file and its entries, Figure 2-7 shows two windows. The top window is the Registry Editor with an example key named Test selected. The settings pane contains six example settings: the (Default) value and one each of the five common types of settings (binary, DWORD, expandable string, multistring, and string). The bottom window shows the Test key in Notepad as an exported registration file (Test.reg).

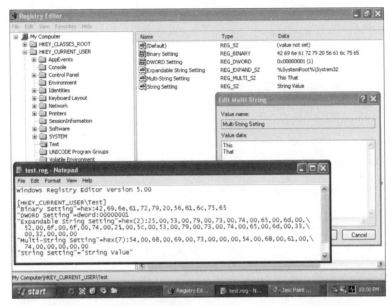

Figure 2-7   The settings in the Test key shown in the Registry Editor correspond to the data shown in Test.reg file shown in Notepad.

Windows XP registration files always start with the following header:

```
Windows Registry Editor Version 5.00
```

Tip   If you're building a registration file for a Windows 9x, Windows Me, or Windows NT 4 system, change the header to the following:

```
REGEDIT4
```

Next is an empty line followed by the full path of the registry key that will hold the settings you're adding, surrounded by square brackets:

```
[HKEY_CURRENT_USER\Test]
```

Below the key are the setting names and values, which use the following general form:

Tip If you want to add a comment to a .reg file, start a new line and begin the line with a semicolon (;).

`"SettingName"=identifier:SettingValue`

SettingName	This is the name of the setting. Note that the @ symbol used to represent the key's (Default) value.
identifier	This is a code that identifies the type of data. REG_SZ values don't use an identifier, but the other four common data types do:

dword	Use this identifier for a DWORD value.
hex	Use this identifier for a binary value.
hex(2)	Use this identifier for an expandable string value.
hex(7)	Use this identifier for a multi-string value.

SettingValue	This is the value of the setting, which you enter as follows:

String	Surround the value with quotation marks.
DWORD	Enter an eight-digit DWORD value.
Binary	Enter the binary value as a series of two-digit hexadecimal numbers, separating each number with a comma.

Expandable string	Convert each character to its hexadecimal equivalent and then enter the value as a series of two-digit hexadecimal numbers, separating each number with a comma, and separating each character with 00.
Multi-string	Convert each character to its hexadecimal equivalent and then enter the value as a series of two-digit hexadecimal numbers, separating each number with a comma, and separating each character with 00, and separating each string with space (00 hex).

Insider Secret   To delete a setting using a .reg file, set its value to a hyphen (-), as in this example:

```
Windows Registry Editor Version 5.00

[HKEY_CURRENT_USER\Test]
"BinarySetting"=-
```

To delete a key, add a hyphen to the start of the key name, as in this example:

```
Windows Registry Editor Version 5.00

[-HKEY_CURRENT_USER\Test]
```

Renaming a Key or Setting

You won't often need to rename existing keys or settings. Just in case, though, here are the steps to follow:

1.   In the Registry Editor, find the key or setting you want to work with and select it.

2.   Select Edit, Rename (or press F2).

3.   Edit the name and then press Enter.

> **Caution**   Rename only those keys or settings that you cre-
> ated yourself. If you rename any other key or setting,
> Windows XP might not work properly.

Creating a New Key or Setting

Many registry-based customizations don't involve editing an existing setting or key. Instead, you have to create a new setting or key. Here's how you do it:

1. In the Registry Editor, select the key in which you want to create the new subkey or setting.

2. Select Edit, New. (Alternatively, right-click an empty section of the Settings pane and then select New.) A submenu appears.

3. If you're creating a new key, select the Key command. Otherwise, select the command that corresponds to the type of setting you want: String Value, Binary Value, DWORD Value, Multi-String Value, or Expandable String Value.

4. Type a name for the new key or setting.

5. Press Enter.

Deleting a Key or Setting

Here are the steps to follow to delete a key or setting:

1. In the Registry Editor, select the key or setting that you want to delete.

2. Select Edit, Delete (or press Delete). The Registry Editor asks if you're sure.

3. Click Yes.

> **Caution**   Again, to avoid problems, you should delete only
> those keys or settings that you created yourself. If you're not
> sure about deleting a setting, try renaming that setting instead.
> If a problem arises, you can then return the setting back to its
> original name.

Finding Registry Entries

The registry contains only five root keys, but these root keys contain hundreds of subkeys. And the fact that some root keys are aliases for subkeys in a different branch only adds to the confusion. If you know exactly where you're going, the Registry Editor's treelike hierarchy is a reasonable way to get there. If you're not sure where a particular subkey or setting resides, however, you could spend all day poking around in the registry's labyrinthine nooks and crannies.

To help you get where you want to go, the Registry Editor has a Find feature that lets you search for keys, settings, or values. Here's how it works:

1. In the Keys pane, select My Computer at the top of the pane (unless you're certain which root key contains the value you want to find; in this case, you can select the appropriate root key instead).

2. Select Edit, Find (or press Ctrl+F). The Registry Editor displays the Find dialog box.

3. Use the Find What text box to enter your search string. You can enter partial words or phrases to increase your chances of finding a match.

4. In the Look At group, select the check boxes for the elements you want to search. For most searches, you want to leave all three check boxes selected.

5. If you want to find only those entries that exactly match your search text, select the Match Whole String Only check box.

6. Click the Find Next button. The Registry Editor selects the first match.

7. If this isn't the item you want, select Edit, Find Next (or press F3) until you find the setting or key you want.

When the Registry Editor finds a match, it displays the appropriate key or setting. Note that if the matched value is a setting name or data value, Find doesn't select the current key. This is a bit confusing, but just remember that the current key always appears at the bottom of the Keys pane, as long as you have View, Status Bar active.

3

Programming Windows XP with Scripts

In this chapter, you'll learn how to:

- Create and execute scripts.
- Program objects and use their properties and methods.
- Display text to the user.
- Run applications.
- Read, add, and delete registry keys and values.
- Control Internet Explorer via scripting.

Microsoft Windows XP comes with the welcome ability to run *scripts* that can deal with many aspects of the system, including drives, folders, files, and the registry; scripts can also interact with Windows programs via Automation. Scripts enable you to automate many routine tasks that would otherwise require tedious effort on your part. For example, you can enhance your system privacy by creating a script to automatically delete the items in your Recent Documents list when you shut down your computer. The power of these scripts lies in the Windows Script Host (WSH), an administration tool that allows you to use virtually any scripting language to exercise extensive control of most Windows components and many Windows-based applications. This chapter introduces you to the Windows Script Host, shows you how to execute scripts, and runs through the most useful elements in the Windows Script Host object model. This will help you understand and use the WSH scripts that appear throughout the rest of the book.

Understanding Scripts and Script Execution

Scripts are simple text files that you create using Notepad or some other text editor. You can use a word processor such as WordPad to create scripts, but you must make sure that you save these files using the program's "text only" document type.

When you first save the file, be sure to use the .vbs extension, which specifies the document as a VBScript script file. (We're assuming you'll be programming in VBScript, but WSH also supports other languages. If you program in a different language, you must name your files accordingly. For example, JavaScript script files must use the .js extension.)

As described in the next three sections, you have three ways to run your scripts: by launching the script files directly, by using Wscript.exe, or by using Cscript.exe.

> **Note**   We can only scratch the scripting surface in a single chapter. Fortunately, Microsoft has an extensive set of scripting tutorials and references on its MSDN Web site:
>
> *http://msdn.microsoft.com/nhp/default.asp?contentid=28001169*

Running Script Files Directly

The easiest way to run a script from within Windows XP is to launch the .vbs file directly using any of the following techniques:

- Double-click the file in Windows Explorer.

- Enter the file's path and name in the Run dialog box.

- Enter the file's path and name at the command prompt.

Using WScript for Windows-Based Scripts

The .vbs file type has an "open" action that's associated with WScript (Wscript.exe), which is the Windows-based front end for the Windows Script Host. In other words, launching a script file named, say, Myscript.vbs, is equivalent to entering the following command in the Run dialog box:

```
wscript myscript.vbs
```

The WScript host also defines several parameters that you can use to control how the script executes. Note that these parameters all start with a double-slash so as to ensure the command interpreter can distinguish these parameters from any command arguments that might start with a single slash. Here's the full syntax:

```
WSCRIPT filename arguments //B //D //E:engine //H:host //I
//Job:xxxx //S //T:ss //X
```

`filename`	Specifies the name, including the path, if necessary, of the script file.
`arguments`	Specifies optional arguments required by the script. An *argument* is a data value that the script uses as part of its procedures or calculations.
`//B`	Runs the script in batch mode, which means script errors and Echo method output lines are suppressed (the Echo method is discussed later in this chapter).
`//D`	Enables Active Debugging. If an error occurs, the script is loaded into the Microsoft Script Debugger (if it's installed) and the offending statement is highlighted.
`//E:engine`	Executes the script using the specified scripting *engine*, which is the scripting language to be used to run the script. VBScript is a popular scripting engine, and the one we use in this chapter. If you have a file that contains VBScript code but does not use the .vbs extension, you can execute the file by specifying **//E:vbscript** as part of the WScript command.
`//H:host`	Specifies the default scripting host. For *host*, use either CScript or WScript.
`//I`	Runs the script in interactive mode, which displays script errors and Echo method output lines.
`//Job:xxxx`	In a script file that contains multiple jobs, executes only the job with ID equal to *xxxx*.
`//S`	Saves the specified WSCRIPT arguments as the default for the current user. The following registry key is used to save these settings: `HKCU\Software\Microsoft\Windows Script Host\Settings`
`//T:ss`	Specifies the maximum time in seconds (*ss*) that the script can run before it is shut down automatically.
`//X`	Executes the entire script in the Microsoft Script Debugger (if it's installed).

Insider Secret A script *job* is a section of code that performs a specific task or set of tasks. Most script files contain a single job. However, it's possible to create a script file with multiple jobs. To do this, first surround the code for each job with the <script> and </script> tags, and then surround those with the <job> and </job> tags. In the <job> tag, include the id attribute and set it to a unique value that identifies the job. Finally, surround all the jobs with the <package> and </package> tags. Here's an example:

```
<package>
<job id="A">
<script language="VBScript">
    WScript.Echo "This is Job A."
</script>
</job>

<job id="B">
<script language="VBScript">
WScript.Echo "This is Job B."
</script>
</job>
</package>
```

Save the file using the .wsf (Windows Script File) extension.

For example, the following command runs Myscript.vbs in batch mode with a 60-second maximum execution time.

```
wscript myscript.vbs //B //T:60
```

Note If you plan on writing a lot of scripts, the Microsoft Script Debugger is an excellent programming tool. If there's a problem with a script, the debugger can help you pinpoint its location. For example, the debugger enables you to step through a script's execution one line at a time. If you don't have the Microsoft Script Debugger, you can download a copy from the following Microsoft site:

http://msdn.microsoft.com/scripting/

Using CScript for Command-Line Scripts

The Windows Script Host has a second host front-end application called CScript (Cscript.exe), which enables you to run scripts from the command line. At its simplest, you launch CScript and use the name of the script file (and its path, if required) as a parameter, as in this example:

```
cscript myscript.vbs
```

The Windows Script Host displays the following banner and then executes the script:

```
Microsoft (R) Windows Script Host Version 5.6
Copyright (C) Microsoft Corporation 1996-2001. All rights reserved.
```

As with WScript, the CScript host has an extensive set of parameters you can specify:

```
CSCRIPT filename arguments //B //D //E:engine //H:host //I
//Job:xxxx //S //T:ss //X //U //LOGO //NOLOGO
```

This syntax is identical to that of WScript, but adds the following three parameters:

//LOGO	Displays the Windows Script Host banner at startup.
//NOLOGO	Hides the Windows Script Host banner at startup.
//U	Uses Unicode for redirected input/output from the console.

Tip   It's also possible to set some of these options by using the properties that are associated with each script file. To see these properties, right-click a script file and then select Properties. In the property sheet that appears, select the Script tab. Note that when you make changes to these properties, the Windows Script Host saves your settings in a new file that has the same name as the script file, except with the .wsh extension. (For example, if the script file is Myscript.vbs, the settings are stored in Myscript.wsh.) To use these settings when running the script, use either WScript or CScript and specify the name of the .wsh file:

```
wscript myscript.wsh
```

Programming Objects

Although this chapter isn't a programming primer per se, we'd like to take some time now to run through a few quick notes about programming objects. This will serve you well throughout the rest of the chapter as we take you on a tour of a few Windows Script Host objects.

Note   If you're new to VBScript, see the following MSDN site for some language tutorials:

http://msdn.microsoft.com/library/en-us/script56/html/vbstutor.asp

The following MSDN site has a VBScript language reference:

http://msdn.microsoft.com/library/en-us/script56/html/vbscripttoc.asp

---

The dictionary definition of an object is "anything perceptible by one or more of the senses, especially something that can be seen and felt." In scripting, an object is an application element that exposes an "interface" to the programmer, who can then perform the programming equivalent of seeing and feeling:

- You can make changes to the object's properties (this is the seeing part).

- You can make the object perform a task by activating a method associated with the object (this is the feeling part).

Working with Object Properties

Every programmable object has a defining set of characteristics. These characteristics are called the object's properties, and they control the appearance and position of the object. For example, the WScript object (the top-level Windows Script Host object) has an Interactive property that determines whether the script runs in interactive mode or batch mode.

When you refer to a property, you use the following syntax:

`Object.Property`

`Object`	This is the name of the object.
`Property`	This is the name of the property you want to work with.

For example, the following expression refers to the Interactive property of the WScript object:

`WScript.Interactive`

Setting the Value of a Property

To set a property to a certain value, you use the following syntax:

```
Object.Property = value
```

Here, *value* is an expression that specifies the value to which you want to set the property. As such, it can be any of the scripting language's recognized data types, which usually include the following:

- A numeric value.

- A string value, enclosed in double-quotation marks (such as "My Script Application").

- A logical value: True or False.

For example, the following VBScript statement tells the Windows Script Host to run the script using interactive mode:

```
WScript.Interactive = True
```

Returning the Value of a Property

Sometimes you need to know the current setting of a property before changing the property or performing some other action. You can find out the current value of a property by using the following syntax:

```
variable = Object.Property.
```

Here, *variable* is a variable name or another property. For example, the following statement stores the current script mode in a variable named currentMode:

```
currentMode = WScript.Interactive
```

Working with Object Methods

An object's properties describe what the object is, whereas its methods describe what the object does. For example, the WScript object has a Quit method that enables you to stop the execution of a script.

How you refer to a method depends on whether or not the method requires any arguments. If it doesn't, the syntax is similar to that of properties:

```
Object.Method
```

`Object`	This is the name of the object.
`Method`	This is the name of the method you want to work with.

For example, the following statement shuts down a script:

```
WScript.Quit
```

If the method requires arguments, you use the following syntax:

```
Object.Method (Argument1, Argument2, ...)
```

For example, the WshShell object has a RegWrite method that you use to write a key or setting to the registry. (We discuss this object and method in detail later in this chapter; see "Working with Registry Entries.") Here's the syntax:

```
WshShell.RegWrite strName, anyValue, [strType]
```

`strName`	The name of the registry key or setting.
`anyValue`	The value to write. If *strName* is a key, enter the null string (""); if *strName* is a registry setting, enter the value of the setting.
`strType`	The data type of *anyValue*.

Our Naming Conventions

When presenting method arguments in this chapter, we'll follow Microsoft's naming conventions, including the use of the following prefixes for the argument names:

Prefix	Data type
any	Any type
b	Boolean
int	Integer
n	Natural number
obj	Object
str	String

For many object methods, not all the arguments are required. In the RegWrite method, for example, the *strName* and *anyValue* arguments are required, but the *strType* argument is not. Throughout this chapter, we differentiate between required and optional arguments by surrounding any optional arguments with square brackets—for example, [*strType*].

For example, the following statement creates a new registry value named Test and sets it equal to Foo:

```
WshShell.RegWrite "HKCU\Software\Microsoft\Windows Script Host\" & _
"Test\", "Foo", "REG_SZ"
```

> **Tip**   In VBScript, parentheses around the argument list are necessary only if you'll be storing the result of the method in a variable or object property. For example, later in this chapter you'll learn how to use the WshShell object's Popup method to display a dialog box to the user. This method returns an integer value that tells you which button the user clicked to close the dialog box. One way to capture that result is to store it in a variable, as in this example:
>
> ```
> intResult = objWshShell.Popup("Test Dialog Box")
> ```

Assigning an Object to a Variable

In VBScript, you assign an object to a variable by using a Set statement. Set has the following syntax:

```
Set variableName = ObjectName
```

variableName	The name of the variable.
ObjectName	The name of the object you want to assign to the variable.

You may find that you must often use a programming technology called Automation to access external objects (see "Scripting and Automation," later in this chapter, for details). For example, if you want to work with files and folders in your script, you must access the scripting engine object named FileSystemObject (see "Programming the VBScript FileSystemObject," later in this chapter). To get this access, you use the CreateObject method and store the resulting object in a variable, like so:

```
Set fs = CreateObject("Scripting.FileSystemObject")
```

Working with Object Collections

A collection is a set of similar objects. For example, WScript.Arguments is the set of all the arguments specified on the script's command line. Collections are objects, too, so they have their own properties and methods, and you can use the properties and methods to manipulate one or more objects in the collection.

The members of a collection are called the *elements* of the collection. You can refer to individual elements by using an index. For example, the following statement refers to the first command line argument (collection indexes always begin at 0):

```
WScript.Arguments(0)
```

If you don't specify an element, the Windows Script Host assumes you want to work with the entire collection.

VBScript provides the For...Next loop to enable you to cycle through a chunk of code a specified number of times. For example, the following code loops 10 times:

```
For counter = 1 To 10
    'Code entered here is repeated 10 times
Next counter
```

A useful variation on this theme is the For Each...Next loop, which operates on a collection of objects. You don't need a loop counter because VBScript just loops through the individual elements in the collection and performs—on each element—whatever operations are inside the loop. Here's the structure of the basic For Each...Next loop:

```
For Each element In collection
    [statements]
Next
```

element	A variable used to temporarily hold the name of each element in the collection.
collection	The name of the collection.
statements	The statements to be executed for each element in the collection.

The following code loops through all the arguments specified on the script's command line and displays each argument:

```
For Each arg In WScript.Arguments
    WScript.Echo arg
Next
```

Displaying Text Using the WScript Object

The WScript object represents the Windows Script Host applications (Wscript.exe and Cscript.exe). This object contains a number of properties and methods, but the one you'll use most often is the Echo method, which displays text to the user. Here's the syntax:

```
WScript.Echo [Argument1, Argument2,...]
```

Here, *Argument1*, *Argument2*, and so on, are any number of text or numeric values that represent the information you want to display to the user. In the Windows-based host (Wscript.exe), the information is displayed in a dialog box; in the command-line host (Cscript.exe), the information is displayed at the command prompt (much like the command-line ECHO utility).

Note   For a complete reference to the Windows Script Host objects, see the following MSDN page:

http://msdn.microsoft.com/library/en-us/script56/html /wsoriwshlanguagereference.asp

---

Scripting and Automation

Applications such as Microsoft Internet Explorer and Microsoft Word come with (*expose*, in the jargon) a set of objects that define various aspects of the program. For example, Internet Explorer has an Application object that represents the program as a whole. Similarly, Word has a Document object that represents a Word document. By using the properties and methods that come with these objects, it's possible to programmatically query and manipulate the applications. With Internet Explorer, for example, you can use the Application object's Navigate method to send the browser to a specified Web page. With Word, you can read a Document object's Saved property to see whether the document has unsaved changes.

This is powerful stuff, but how do you get at the objects that are exposed by these applications? You do that by using a technology called Automation. Applications that support Automation implement object libraries that expose the application's native objects to Automation-aware programming languages. Such applications are called *Automation servers*, and the applications that manipulate the server's objects are called *Automation controllers*. The Windows Script Host is an Automation controller that enables you to write script code to control any server's objects.

This means that you can use an application's exposed objects more or less as you use the Windows Script Host objects. With just a minimum of preparation, your script code can refer to and work with the Internet Explorer Application object or the Microsoft Word Document object, or any of the hundreds of other objects exposed by the applications on your system. (Note, however, that not all applications expose objects. Outlook Express and most of the built-in Windows XP programs—such as WordPad and Paint—do not expose objects.)

The WScript object's CreateObject method creates an Automation object (specifically, what programmers call an *instance* of the object). Here's the syntax used with this method:

```
WScript.CreateObject(strProgID)
```

> strProgID   A string that specifies the Automation server application and the type of object to create. This string is called a *programmatic identifier*, which is a label that uniquely specifies an application and one of its objects. The programmatic identifier always takes the following form:
>
> AppName.ObjectType
>
> Here, *AppName* is the Automation name of the application, and *ObjectType* is the object class type (as defined in the registry's HKEY_CLASSES_ROOT key). For example, here's the programmatic ID for Internet Explorer:
>
> InternetExplorer.Application

Note that you normally use CreateObject within a Set statement, and that the function serves to create a new instance of the specified Automation object. For example, you could use the following statement to create a new instance of Internet Explorer's Application object:

```
Set objIE = CreateObject("InternetExplorer.Application")
```

There's nothing else you need to do to use the Automation object. With your variable declared and an instance of the object created, you can use that object's properties and methods directly.

Programming the VBScript FileSystemObject

One of the most powerful uses for scripted Automation is accessing the object models exposed by the VBScript engine, particularly the FileSystemObject that gives you access to the local file system. This enables you to create scripts that work with files, folders, and disk drives; read and write text files; and more. You use the following syntax to refer to this object:

```
Scripting.FileSystemObject
```

For all your file system scripts, you begin by creating a new instance of FileSystemObject:

```
Set objFS = WScript.CreateObject("Scripting.FileSystemObject")
```

Here's a summary of the file system objects you can access via this Automation object:

- **Drive**   This object enables you to access the properties of a specified disk drive or network path. To reference a Drive object, use either the Drives collection (discussed next) or the FileSystemObject object's GetDrive method. For example, the following VBScript statements reference drive C:

```
Set objFS = WScript.CreateObject("Scripting.FileSystemObject")
Set objDrive = objFS.GetDrive("C:")
```

- **Drives**   This object is the collection of all available drives. To create this collection, use the FileSystemObject object's Drives property:

```
Set objFS = WScript.CreateObject("Scripting.FileSystemObject")
Set objDrives = objFS.Drives
```

- **Folder**   This object enables you to access the properties of a specified folder. To reference a Folder object, use either the Folders collection (discussed next) or the FileSystemObject object's GetFolder method:

```
Set objFS = WScript.CreateObject("Scripting.FileSystemObject")
Set objFolder = objFS.GetFolder("C:\My Documents")
```

- **Folders**   This object is the collection of subfolders within a specified folder. To create this collection, use the Folder object's Subfolders property:

```
Set objFS = WScript.CreateObject("Scripting.FileSystemObject")
Set objFolder = objFS.GetFolder("C:\Windows")
Set objSubfolders = objFolder.Subfolders
```

- **File**   This object enables you to access the properties of a specified file. To reference a File object, use either the Files collection (discussed next) or the FileSystemObject object's GetFile method:

```
Set objFS = WScript.CreateObject("Scripting.FileSystemObject")
Set objFile = objFS.GetFile("c:\boot.ini")
```

- **Files**   This object is the collection of files within a specified folder. To create this collection, use the Folder object's Files property:

```
Set objFS = WScript.CreateObject("Scripting.FileSystemObject")
Set objFolder = objFS.GetFolder("C:\Windows")
Set objFiles = objFolder.Files
```

- **TextStream**   This object enables you to use sequential access to work with a text file. To open a text file, use the FileSystemObject object's OpenTextFile method:

```
Set objFS = WScript.CreateObject("Scripting.FileSystemObject")
Set objTS = objFS.OpenTextFile("C:\Autoexec.bat")
```

Alternatively, you can create a new text file by using the FileSystemObject object's CreateTextFile method:

```
Set objFS = WScript.CreateObject("Scripting.FileSystemObject")
Set objTS = objFS.CreateTextFile("C:\test.txt")
```

Either way, you end up with a TextStream object, which has various methods for reading data from the file and writing data to the file. For example, the following script reads and displays the text from C:\Boot.ini:

```
Set objFS = WScript.CreateObject("Scripting.FileSystemObject")
Set objTS = objFS.OpenTextFile("c:\boot.ini")
strContents = objTS.ReadAll
WScript.Echo strContents
objTS.Close
```

Displaying More Detailed Information to the User

You saw earlier that the WScript object's Echo method is useful for displaying simple text messages to the user. You can gain more control over the displayed message by using the WshShell object's Popup method. WshShell refers to the Shell object that is exposed via the Automation interface of WScript. So before you can run the Popup method, you need to use CreateObject to create an instance of the WshShell object:

```
Set objWshShell = WScript.CreateObject("WScript.Shell")
```

If you're familiar with Microsoft Visual Basic, the Popup method is similar to the MsgBox function in that it enables you to control both the dialog box title and the buttons that are displayed, as well as to determine which of those buttons the user pressed. Here's the syntax:

```
Popup strText, [nSecondsToWait], [strTitle], [nType]
```

strText	The message you want to display in the dialog box. (You can enter a string up to 1,024 characters long.)
nSecondsToWait	The maximum number of seconds the dialog box will be displayed.
strTitle	The text that appears in the dialog box title bar. If you omit this value, the string "Windows Script Host" appears in the title bar.
nType	A number or constant that specifies, among other things, the command buttons that appear in the dialog box (see "Setting the Style of the Message," next). The default value is 0.

For example, the following statements display the dialog box shown in Figure 3-1:

```
Set objWshShell = WScript.CreateObject("WScript.Shell")
objWshShell.Popup "Couldn't find MEMO.DOC!", , "Warning"
```

Figure 3-1   This is a simple message dialog box produced by the Popup method.

> **Tip**   For long messages, VBScript wraps the text inside the dialog box. If you prefer to create your own line breaks, use VBScript's vbCrLf constant to add a carriage-return and line-feed after a line:
>
> ```
> objWshShell.Popup "First line" & vbCrLf & "Second line"
> ```

Setting the Style of the Message

The default Popup dialog box displays only an OK button. You can include other buttons and icons in the dialog box by using different values for the *nType* parameter. Table 3-1 lists the available options.

Table 3-1   The Popup method's *nType* parameter options

VBScript Constant	Value	Description
Buttons		
vbOKOnly	0	Displays only an OK button. (This is the default.)
vbOKCancel	1	Displays the OK and Cancel buttons.
vbAbortRetryIgnore	2	Displays the Abort, Retry, and Ignore buttons.
vbYesNoCancel	3	Displays the Yes, No, and Cancel buttons.
vbYesNo	4	Displays the Yes and No buttons.
vbRetryCancel	5	Displays the Retry and Cancel buttons.
Icons		
vbCritical	16	Displays the Critical Message icon.
vbQuestion	32	Displays the Warning Query icon.
vbExclamation	48	Displays the Warning Message icon.
vbInformation	64	Displays the Information Message icon.
Default Button		
vbDefaultButton1	0	The first button displayed is the default (that is, the button selected when the user presses Enter).
vbDefaultButton2	256	The second button displayed is the default.
vbDefaultButton3	512	The third button displayed is the default.

You derive the *nType* argument in one of two ways:

■ By adding up the values for each option.

■ By using the VBScript constants separated by plus signs (+).

The script below shows an example:

```
' First, set up the message
strText = "Are you sure you want to copy" & vbCrLf & _
        "the selected files to drive A?"
strTitle = "Copy Files"
nType = vbYesNoCancel + vbQuestion + vbDefaultButton2

' Now display it
Set objWshShell = WScript.CreateObject("WScript.Shell")
intResult = objWshShell.Popup(strText, ,strTitle, nType)
```

Figure 3-2 shows the resulting dialog box. Here, three variables—*strText*, *strTitle*, and *nType*—store the values for the Popup method's arguments. In particular, the following statement derives the *nType* argument:

```
nType = vbYesNoCancel + vbQuestion + vbDefaultButton2
```

You also could derive the *nType* argument by adding up the values that these constants represent (3, 32, and 256, respectively), but the script becomes less readable that way.

Figure 3-2   This is the dialog box that's displayed when you run the script.

Getting Return Values from the Message Dialog Box

A dialog box that displays only an OK button is straightforward. The user either clicks OK or presses Enter to remove the dialog from the screen. The multibutton styles are a little different, however; the user has a choice of buttons to select, and your script needs a way to find out which button the user chose.

You do this by storing the Popup method's return value in a variable. Table 3-2 lists the seven possible return values.

Table 3-2   The Popup method's return values

VBScript Constant	Value	Button Selected
vbOK	1	OK
vbCancel	2	Cancel
vbAbort	3	Abort
vbRetry	4	Retry
vbIgnore	5	Ignore
vbYes	6	Yes
vbNo	7	No

To process the return value, you can use an If...Then...Else or Select Case structure to test for the appropriate values. For example, the script shown earlier used a variable called intResult to store the return value of the Popup method. The following script shows a revised version of the script that uses a VBScript Select Case statement to test for the three possible return values, based on using vbYesNoCancel.

```
' First, set up the message
strText = "Are you sure you want to copy" & vbCrLf & _
          "the selected files to drive A?"
strTitle = "Copy Files"
nType = vbYesNoCancel + vbQuestion + vbDefaultButton2

' Now display it
Set objWshShell = WScript.CreateObject("WScript.Shell")
intResult = objWshShell.Popup(strText, ,strTitle, nType)

' Process the result
Select Case intResult
    Case vbYes
        WScript.Echo "You clicked ""Yes""!"
    Case vbNo
        WScript.Echo "You clicked ""No""!"
    Case vbCancel
        WScript.Echo "You clicked ""Cancel""!"
End Select
```

Running Applications

When you need your script to launch another application, use WshShell's Run method:

Run *strCommand*, [*intWindowStyle*], [*bWaitOnReturn*]

strCommand	The name of the file that starts the application. Unless the file is in the Windows folder, you should include the drive and path to make sure that the script can find the file.
intWindowStyle	A constant or number that specifies how the application window will appear. These are some of the more useful values:

intWindowStyle	**Window Appearance**
0	Hidden
1	Normal size with focus
2	Minimized with focus (this is the default)
3	Maximized with focus

intWindowStyle	**Window Appearance**
4	Normal without focus
6	Minimized without focus
bWaitOnReturn	A Boolean value that determines whether the application is run asynchronously. If this value is True, the script halts execution until the user exits the launched application; if this value is False, the script continues running once it has launched the application.

Here's an example:

```
Set objWshShell = WScript.CreateObject("WScript.Shell")
objWshShell.Run "CONTROL.EXE INETCPL.CPL", 1, True
```

This Run method launches Control Panel's Internet Properties dialog box in a normal-sized window, gives control to the dialog box, and waits for the user to close the dialog box before control returns to the script, which immediately exits.

> **Note** To learn more about launching individual Control Panel icons using Control.exe, please see Chapter 1, "Mastering Control Panel, Policies, and PowerToys."

Working with Registry Entries

Chapter 2, "Getting the Most Out of the Registry," illustrates that the registry is one of Windows XP's most crucial data structures. However, the registry isn't a tool wielded only by Windows XP. Most 32-bit applications make use of the registry as a place to store setup options, customization values selected by the user, and much more. Interestingly, your scripts can get in on the act as well. Not only can your scripts read the current value of any registry setting, but they can also use the registry as a storage area. This lets you keep track of user settings, recently used files, and any other configuration data that you'd like to save between sessions. This section shows you how to use the WshShell object to manipulate the registry from within your scripts.

Reading Registry Keys or Values

To read any value from the registry, use WshShell's RegRead method:

`RegRead(strName)`

> strName   The name of the registry value or key that you want to read.

If *strName* ends with a backslash (\), RegRead returns the default value for the key; otherwise, RegRead returns the data stored in the value. Note, too, that *strName* must begin with one of the following root key names:

Short Name	Long Name
HKCR	HKEY_CLASSES_ROOT
HKCU	HKEY_CURRENT_USER
HKLM	HKEY_LOCAL_MACHINE
N/A	HKEY_USERS
N/A	HKEY_CURRENT_CONFIG

The following example displays the name of the registered owner of this copy of Windows XP:

```
Set objWshShell = WScript.CreateObject("WScript.Shell")
strSetting = "HKLM\SOFTWARE\Microsoft" & _
"\Windows NT\CurrentVersion\RegisteredOwner"
strRegisteredUser = objWshShell.RegRead(strSetting)
WScript.Echo strRegisteredUser
```

Storing Registry Keys or Values

To store a setting in the registry, use WshShell's RegWrite method:

`RegWrite strName, anyValue [, strType]`

> strName   The name of the registry value or key that you want to set. If *strName* ends with a backslash (\), RegWrite sets the default value for the key; otherwise, RegWrite sets the data for the value. *strName* must begin with one of the root key names detailed in the RegRead method.
>
> anyValue   The value to be stored.
>
> strType   The data type of the value, which must be one of the following: REG_SZ (the default), REG_EXPAND_SZ, REG_DWORD, or REG_BINARY.

The following statements create a new key named ScriptSettings in the HKEY_CURRENT_USER root:

```
Set objWshShell = WScript.CreateObject("WScript.Shell")
objWshShell.RegWrite "HKCU\ScriptSettings\", ""
```

The following statements create a new value named NumberOfReboots in the HKCU\ScriptSettings key, and set this value to 1:

```
Set objWshShell = WScript.CreateObject("WScript.Shell")
objWshShell.RegWrite "HKCU\ScriptSettings\NumberOfReboots", 1, _
"REG_DWORD"
```

Deleting Registry Keys or Values

If you no longer need to track a particular key or value setting, use the RegDelete method to remove the setting from the registry:

```
RegDelete (strName)
```

strName   The name of the registry value or key that you want to delete. If *strName* ends with a backslash (\), RegDelete deletes the key; otherwise, RegDelete deletes the value. *strName* must begin with one of the root key names detailed in the RegRead method.

To delete the NumberOfReboots value used in the previous example, you would use the following statements:

```
Set objWshShell = WScript.CreateObject("WScript.Shell")
objWshShell.RegDelete "HKCU\ScriptSettings\NumberOfReboots"
```

Scripting Example: Programming Internet Explorer

To give you a taste of the power and flexibility of Automation programming, this section shows you how to program a specific Automation server: Internet Explorer. You'll see that your scripts can control just about everything associated with Internet Explorer:

- The position and dimensions of the window.
- Whether or not the menu bar, toolbar, and status bar are displayed.
- The current URL.
- Sending the browser backward and forward between navigated URLs.

Displaying a Web Page

To get started, we'll show you how to use the InternetExplorer object to display a specified URL. You use the Navigate method to do this, and this method uses the following syntax:

```
InternetExplorer.Navigate URL, [Flags,] [TargetFrameName,] [PostData,]
[Headers]
```

InternetExplorer	A reference to the InternetExplorer object with which you're working.
URL	The address of the Web page you want to display.
Flags	One of (or the sum of two or more of) the following integers that control various aspects of the navigation:
	1 Opens the URL in a new window.
	2 Prevents the URL from being added to the history list.
	4 Prevents the browser from reading the page from the disk cache.
	8 Prevents the URL from being added to the disk cache.
TargetFrameName	The name of the frame in which to display the URL. (You won't ever need to use this parameter when scripting Internet Explorer.)
PostData	Specifies additional POST information that HTTP requires to resolve the hyperlink. The most common uses for this argument are to send a Web server the contents of a form, the coordinates of an image map, or a search parameter for an ASP file. If you leave this argument blank, this method issues a GET call.
Headers	Specifies header data for the HTTP header.

Here's an example:

```
Set objIE = CreateObject("InternetExplorer.Application")
objIE.Navigate "http://www.microsoft.com/"
```

Navigating Pages

Displaying a specified Web page isn't the only thing the InternetExplorer object can do. It also has quite a few methods that give you the ability to navigate backwards and forwards through visited Web pages, refresh the current page, stop the current download, and more. Here's a summary of these methods:

- **GoBack**   Navigates backward to a previously visited page.

- **GoForward**   Navigates forward to a previously visited page.

- **GoHome**   Navigates to Internet Explorer's default Home page.

- **GoSearch**   Navigates to Internet Explorer's default Search page.

- **Refresh**   Refreshes the current page.

- **Refresh2**   Refreshes the current page using the following syntax:

  `Refresh2(Level)`

  Level   A constant that determines how the page is refreshed:
  - 0   Refreshes the page with a cached copy.
  - 1   Refreshes the page with a cached copy only if the page has expired.
  - 3   Performs a full refresh (doesn't use a cached copy).

- **Stop**   Cancels the current download or shuts down dynamic page objects, such as background sounds and animations.

Using the InternetExplorer Object's Properties

Here's a summary of many of the properties associated with the InternetExplorer object:

- **Busy**   Returns True if the InternetExplorer object is in the process of downloading text or graphics. This property returns False when the complete document has been downloaded.

- **FullScreen**   A Boolean value that toggles Internet Explorer between the normal window and a full-screen window in which the title bar, menu bar, toolbar, and status bar are hidden.

- **Height**   Returns or sets the window height.

- **Left**   Returns or sets the position of the left edge of the window.

- **LocationName**   Returns the title of the current document.

- **LocationURL**   Returns the URL of the current document.

- **MenuBar**   A Boolean value that toggles the menu bar on and off.

- **StatusBar**   A Boolean value that toggles the status bar on and off.

- **StatusText**   Returns or sets the status bar text.

- **ToolBar**   A Boolean value that toggles the toolbar on and off.

- **Top**   Returns or sets the position of the top edge of the window.

- **Type**   Returns the type of document currently loaded in the browser.

- **Visible**   A Boolean value that toggles the object between hidden and visible.

- **Width**   Returns or sets the window width.

Running Through an Example Script

To put some of the properties and methods into practice, here's an example script:

```
Option Explicit
Dim objIE, objWshShell, strMessage, intResult

' Set up the Automation objects
Set objIE = WScript.CreateObject("InternetExplorer.Application")
Set objWshShell = WScript.CreateObject("WScript.Shell")

' Navigate to a page and customize the browser window
objIE.Navigate "http://www.wordspy.com/"
objIE.Toolbar = False
objIE.StatusBar = False
objIE.MenuBar = False

' Twiddle thumbs while the page loads
Do While objIE.Busy
Loop

' Get the page info
strMessage = "Current URL:  " & objIE.LocationURL & vbCrLf & _
    "Current Title: " & objIE.LocationName & vbCrLf & _
    "Document Type: " & objIE.Type & vbCrLf & vbCrLf & _
    "Would you like to view this document?"

' Display the info
intResult = objWshShell.Popup(strMessage, , _
"Scripting IE", vbYesNo + vbQuestion)

' Check the result
If intResult = vbYes Then

    ' If Yes, make browser visible
    objIE.Visible = True
```

```
Else

    ' If no, bail out
    objIE.Quit
End If
Set objIE = Nothing
Set objWshShell = Nothing
```

The script begins by creating instances of the InternetExplorer and WScript Shell objects. The Navigate method displays a page, and then the toolbar, status bar, and menu bar are turned off. A Do...Loop checks the Busy property and loops while it's True. In other words, this loop won't exit until the page is fully loaded. Then a string variable is used to store the URL, title, and type of the page, and this string is then displayed in a Popup box, which also asks if the user wants to see the page. If the user clicks Yes, the browser is made visible; if the user clicks No, the Quit method shuts down the browser.

II

Getting the Most Out of Your Everyday Tasks

In Part II, you'll learn insider techniques to help you:

4

Starting Up and Shutting Down

In this chapter, you'll learn how to:

■   Launch applications and scripts automatically at startup.

■   Synchronize your system time with an external time server.

■   Control the startup using the System Configuration Utility.

■   Control the startup using Boot.ini.

■   Customize the shutdown process using batch files and scripts.

In times past, launching Microsoft Windows was the perfect opportunity to catch up on your voice mail or grab another cup of coffee. That's because the Windows startup used to be a glacially paced affair that often took minutes to complete (and few minutes are as long as those spent waiting for a computer to boot). Windows XP changed all that by being, if not exactly zippy, at least pleasingly faster than previous incarnations. Note, however, that we're talking here about out-of-the-box startup performance. Drivers, network logons and scripts, and program launches can still slow the startup process to a crawl. To ensure the best startup performance, and to ensure that Windows XP is set up the way you want it each time you boot your machine, you need to take charge of all phases of the startup process. This chapter will show you how to do just that by taking you through some little known but very useful tools. Tools and techniques such as launching programs and scripts, editing Boot.ini, and using the Windows Advanced Options Menu will expedite startup, and using the SHUTDOWN command and deleting files while shutting down will expedite shutdown.

Launching Applications and Scripts at Startup

If you have one or more programs that you start as soon as Windows XP fires up, you can save yourself the hassle of launching these programs manually by getting Windows XP to do it for you automatically at startup. Similarly, you can direct Windows XP to automatically launch scripts or batch files at startup. To get these applications or scripts started automatically when Windows XP starts up, you can use the Startup folder, the registry, or the Group Policy snap-in.

Using the Startup Folder

The Startup folder is a regular file folder, but Windows XP treats the contents of this folder uniquely: You can enjoy automatic startup for your desired program or script simply by adding a shortcut for that item to the Startup folder. (Adding shortcuts to the Startup folder is one of the Start menu customizations that is discussed in more detail in Chapter 10, "Customizing the Interface.") Note that the Startup folder appears twice in the Windows XP interface:

- Via the Start menu (click Start, select All Programs, Startup; or left-click Start, select Open).

- Via Windows Explorer as a subfolder in *d*:\Documents and Settings (where *d* is the drive on which Windows XP is installed). Actually, three different subfolders are available here:

    - ***user*\Start Menu\Programs\Startup** Here, *user* is the name of a user defined on the system (see Chapter 5, "Managing Logons and Users"). A shortcut placed in this folder will run automatically when this user logs on to the system.

    - **\All Users\Start Menu\Programs\Startup** A shortcut placed in this folder will run automatically when any user logs on to the system.

    - **\Default User\Start Menu\Programs\Startup** A shortcut placed in this folder will be copied automatically to a user's Startup folder whenever you create a new user account. (Note that the Default User subfolder is hidden by default. To display it, select Tools, Folder Options in Windows Explorer, select the View tab, and then select the Show Hidden Files And Folders option.)

Note that only users with administrator-level rights can access all three of these subfolders. Users with lesser privileges can work only with their own Startup folders. (They can see the All Users version of the Startup folder, but Windows XP prevents them from adding files to it.)

Later in this chapter, we'll show you how to use the System Configuration Utility to control the launching of individual Startup folder items. For now, though, let's mention that you can prevent *all* of the Startup items from running by holding down the Shift key while Windows XP loads user-specific files (hold down Shift after logging on).

Using the Registry

The Startup folder method has two drawbacks: Users can easily delete shortcuts from their own Startup folders, and users can bypass Startup items by holding down the Shift key while Windows XP loads. You can avoid both issues by using the Registry Editor (regedit.exe) instead. (We cover the Registry Editor in Chapter 2, "Getting the Most Out of the Registry.") Assuming you're logged on as the user you want to work with, the registry offers two keys:

- **HKCU\Software\Microsoft\Windows\CurrentVersion\Run**
  The values in this key run automatically each time the user logs on.

- **HKCU\Software\Microsoft\Windows\CurrentVersion\RunOnce**
  The values in this key run only the next time the user logs on, and are then deleted from the key. (Note that this key may not be present in your registry. In that case, you need to add this key yourself.)

If you want an item to run at startup no matter who logs on, use the following keys:

- **HKLM\SOFTWARE\Microsoft\Windows\CurrentVersion\Run**
  The values in this key run automatically each time any user logs on.

- **HKLM\SOFTWARE\Microsoft\Windows\CurrentVersion\RunOnce**   The values in this key run only the next time any user logs on, and are then deleted from the key. (Don't confuse this key with the RunOnceEx key. This is an "extended" version of RunOnce that's used by developers to create more robust startup items that include features such as error handling and improved performance.)

To create a startup item, add a string value to the appropriate key, give it whatever name you like, and then set its value to the full path of the executable file or script file that you want to launch at startup.

Caution   Placing the same startup item in both the HKCU and the HKLM hives will result in that item being started twice, once at initial boot and again at logon.

Insider Secret   If the program is in the %SystemRoot% folder, you can get away with entering only the name of the executable file. Also, if the program you want to run at startup is capable of running in the background, you can load it in this mode by appending **/background** after the path.

Using Group Policies

If you prefer not to edit the registry directly, or if you prefer to place a graphical user interface (GUI) between you and the registry, the Group Policy snap-in can help. (See Chapter 1, "Mastering Control Panel, Policies, and PowerToys," for details on using this snap-in.) Note, however, that Group Policy doesn't work directly with the Run keys in the HKLM and HKCU hives. Instead, those Run keys are considered to be *legacy keys*, meaning that they're used mainly by older programs. The new keys (new as of Windows 2000, that is) are the following:

- HKLM\SOFTWARE\Microsoft\Windows\CurrentVersion\policies \Explorer\Run

- HKCU\Software\Microsoft\Windows\CurrentVersion \Policies\Explorer\Run

Note that these keys do not appear in Windows XP by default. You see them only after you specify startup programs in the Group Policy Editor, as discussed in the next section. (Alternatively, you can add these keys yourself using the Registry Editor.)

Insider Secret   The startup items run in the following order:
HKLM\SOFTWARE\Microsoft\Windows\CurrentVersion\RunOnce
HKLM\SOFTWARE\Microsoft\Windows\CurrentVersion\policies\Explorer\Run
HKLM\SOFTWARE\Microsoft\Windows\CurrentVersion\Run
HKCU\Software\Microsoft\Windows\CurrentVersion\Run
HKCU\Software\Microsoft\Windows\CurrentVersion\Policies\Explorer\Run
HKCU\Software\Microsoft\Windows\CurrentVersion\RunOnce
Startup folder (all users)
Startup folder (current user)

Adding Programs to the Run Keys

As mentioned, you can add values to these keys either via the Registry Editor or via the Group Policy snap-in. In the Group Policy Editor, you have two choices:

■   To work with startup programs for all users, select Computer Config-uration, Administrative Templates, System, Logon. The items here will affect the registry keys in the HKLM (all users) registry hive.

■   To work with startup programs for the current user, select User Con-figuration, Administrative Templates, System, Logon. The items here will affect the registry keys in the HKCU (current user) hive.

Either way you'll see at least the following three items:

■   **Run These Programs At User Logon**   Use this item to add or remove startup programs using the \Policies\Explorer\Run keys in the registry. To add a program, double-click the item, select the Enabled option, and then click Show. In the Show Contents dialog box, click Add, enter the full path of the program or script you want to run at startup, and then click OK.

■   **Do Not Process The Run Once List**   Use this item to toggle whether Windows XP processes the RunOnce registry keys (which we discussed in the previous section). Double-click this item and then select the Enabled option to put this policy into effect (that is, programs listed in the RunOnce key are not launched at startup).

■   **Do Not Process The Legacy Run List**   Use this item to toggle whether Windows XP processes the legacy Run key. Double-click this item and then select the Enabled option to put this policy into effect (that is, programs listed in the legacy Run key are not launched at startup).

Specifying Startup and Logon Scripts

You also can use the Group Policy snap-in to specify script files to run at startup or at logon. You can specify script files at two places:

- **Computer Configuration, Windows Settings, Scripts (Startup/ Shutdown)** Use the Startup item to specify one or more script files to run each time the computer starts (and before the user logs on). Note that by default, if you specify two or more scripts, Windows XP runs them synchronously. That is, Windows XP runs the first script, waits for it to finish, runs the second script, waits for it to finish, and so on.

- **User Configuration, Windows Settings, Scripts (Logon/Logoff)** Use the Logon item to specify one or more script files to run each time any user logs on. By default, logon scripts are run asynchronously.

Finally, note that Windows XP has policies that dictate how these scripts run. For example, you can see the startup script policies by selecting Computer Configuration, Administrative Templates, System, Scripts. Three items reside there that affect logon and startup scripts:

- **Run Logon Scripts Synchronously** If you select this item, Windows XP runs the logon scripts at the same time that it loads the user interface.

- **Run Startup Scripts Asynchronously** If you select this item, Windows XP runs the startup scripts at the same time.

- **Run Startup Scripts Visible** If you select this item, Windows XP makes the startup script commands visible to the user in a command window.

> **Caution** Logon scripts are supposed to execute before the Windows XP interface is displayed to the user. However, Windows XP's new Fast Logon Optimization can interfere with that by displaying the interface before all the scripts are done. (The Fast Logon Optimization feature runs both the computer logon scripts and the user logon scripts asynchronously, which greatly reduces the logon time since no script has to wait for another to finish.) To prevent this interference, select Computer Configuration, Administrative Templates, System, Logon and choose the Always Wait For The Network At Computer Startup And Logon setting.

Note that for logon scripts, a similar set of policies appears in the User Configuration, Administrative Templates, System, Scripts section. However, any setting for Run Logon Script Synchronously in Computer Configuration takes precedence over the value for that policy in User Configuration.

Note Yet another way to set up a program or script to run at startup is to use the Scheduled Tasks folder (select Start, All Programs, Accessories, System Tools, Scheduled Tasks; select Scheduled Tasks from Control Panel; or use Windows Explorer to display the %SystemRoot%\Tasks folder). When you create a new task, two of the options you'll see are:

- **When My Computer Starts** Choose this option to run the program when your computer boots, no matter which user logs on. Note that only someone logged on under the Administrator account can select this option. (The tasks will run otherwise, but they won't be displayed.)

- **When I Log On** Choose this option to run the program only when the user logs on. This is the option to use for accounts other than Administrator.

Tip Note that a bug in Windows XP prevents it from running a scheduled task if your user account doesn't have a password. You need to assign a password to your account and then add the password to the scheduled task.

Some Startup Scripts

In this section, we'll take you through a few sample scripts that you can implement to improve your Windows XP startups.

Adding a Network Printer

One of the hassles faced by mobile users is the need to access resources when they return to the office and connect to the network. For example, the user may have to connect to a network printer. If you face this or a similar chore, you can take some of the drudgery out of it by using a script that automates the process.

Here's some VBScript code that asks the user whether he or she wants to connect to the network printer. (We discuss scripting in Chapter 3, "Programming Windows XP with Scripts.") If the user clicks Yes in the popup, the script connects the printer and sets it as the default.

```
Option Explicit
Dim wshShell, wshNetwork, strPrinterName, strDriverName

' First ask the user if he or she wants to connect the printer
Set wshShell=CreateObject("WScript.Shell")
If wshShell.Popup("Do you want to connect to the network printer?", ,
"Logon", vbYesNo + vbQuestion) = vbYes Then

    ' If so, use the Network object to connect to the network printer
    Set wshNetwork = CreateObject("WScript.Network")

    ' Store the UNC path and driver
    strPrinterName = "\\ComputerName\PrinterName"
    strDriverName = "DriverName"

    ' Connect the printer and set it to the default
    wshNetwork.AddWindowsPrinterConnection strPrinterName, strDriverName
    wshNetwork.SetDefaultPrinter strPrinterName
End If
```

Note that when you're setting the strPrinterName value, you need to change *ComputerName* to the name of the network computer that hosts the printer, and you need to change *PrinterName* to the shared named of the printer. Similarly, for the strDriverName value, change *DriverName* to the name of the printer driver.

Synchronizing the System Time

Computer clocks are often unreliable beasts, sometimes gaining or losing minutes in a day. To keep your system time accurate, create a startup item that synchronizes your machine's time with the time on a server.

If your computer is part of an Active Directory (AD) domain, the Windows Time Service will automatically synchronize your system time with the time of the domain controller. If your computer is part of a non-AD domain or a workgroup, and the network has a computer that keeps accurate time, include the following line in a startup batch file and replace *ComputerName* with the name of the network computer that keeps the accurate time:

```
NET TIME //ComputerName /SET
```

The NET TIME command used with the /SET switch synchronizes your system time with the system time on the computer specified by *ComputerName*.

How do you ensure your network has a computer that holds accurate time? The best way is to synchronize the computer with an external source, such as an Internet host that offers public access to a time server. Windows XP should already be set up to do this. (To check, open Control Panel's Date And Time icon, select the Internet Time tab, and make sure the Automatically Synchronize With An Internet Time Server check box is selected.) To sync up with another external time server, open the Windows XP command prompt and enter the following two commands:

```
W32TM /CONFIG /MANUALPEERLIST:peerlist /SYNCFROMFLAGS:MANUAL
W32TM /CONFIG /UPDATE
```

W32TM	This is the command-line version of the Windows Time service, which synchronizes the system date and time.
/CONFIG	This switch specifies that the time service is being reconfigured.
/MANUALPEERLIST:*peerlist*	This switch specifies the location of a time server. Replace *peerlist* with the Domain Name System (DNS) name of the time server. You can also use the Internet Protocol (IP) address, but these addresses often change, so the DNS name is better.
SYNCFROMFLAGS:MANUAL	This switch tells the time service to synchronize the time, based on the server named in the *peerlist*.
UPDATE	This switch tells the time service to put the new configuration into effect.

For example, you can synchronize with the National Institute of Standards and Technology time server—*time.nist.gov*—by running the following commands:

```
W32TM /CONFIG /MANUALPEERLIST:time.nist.gov /SYNCFROMFLAGS:MANUAL
W32TM /CONFIG /UPDATE
```

You can place these commands in a startup batch file to ensure your computer is always synchronized with the external server. The addresses of other time servers can be found at the following sites:

http://www.boulder.nist.gov/timefreq/service/time-servers.html
http://www.ntp.org/

Configuring Services to Display an Alert When They Fail to Start

Most Windows XP services will display an alert if they fail to start, but not all do. Here's a script that uses Windows Management Instrumentation (WMI) to get a list of the services that don't display failure alerts and reconfigures them so that they will display an alert:

```
Option Explicit
Dim objWMIService, objService, colServiceList
Dim strServices, errReturn
Const NORMAL_ERROR_CONTROL = 2

' Connect to WMI on the local computer
Set objWMIService=GetObject("winmgmts:{impersonationLevel=impersonate}_
    " & "!\\.\root\cimv2")

' Query WMI to get the collection of services
' that don't issue alerts when they fail to start
Set colServiceList = objWMIService.ExecQuery _
    ("Select * from Win32_Service where ErrorControl = 'Ignore'")

' Run through the collection of services
strServices = ""
For Each objService in colServiceList

    ' Configure the service to issue an alert if it fails to start
    errReturn = objService.Change( , , , NORMAL_ERROR_CONTROL)
    strServices = strServices & objService.DisplayName & vbCrLf
Next

' Display the list of services that were changed
WScript.Echo "Alerts activated for the following services:" & _
vbCrLf & vbCrLf & strServices
```

Controlling Startup Using the System Configuration Utility

As you saw earlier in this chapter, Windows XP offers many different ways to handle startup programs and scripts, and working with all of these methods can be confusing. You can simplify things a great deal by using the System Configuration Utility, which gives you a graphical front end that offers precise control over how Windows XP starts.

To launch the System Configuration Utility, select Start, Run, type **msconfig**, and click OK. The System Configuration Utility window appears, as shown in Figure 4-1.

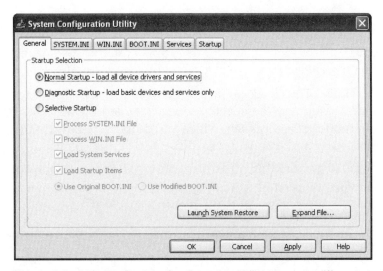

Figure 4-1   Use the System Configuration Utility to create different startup configurations.

The General tab has three startup options:

- **Normal Startup**   This option loads Windows XP normally.

- **Diagnostic Startup**   This option loads Windows XP with a minimal set of drivers. If Windows XP won't start normally, diagnostic startup is useful because it should enable you to load a basic version of Windows XP and then troubleshoot the problem.

- **Selective Startup**   When you select this option, the check boxes below it become available. You use these check boxes to select which of the startup options should be processed.

For a selective startup, you control how Windows XP processes items in five categories, represented in the utility by the other five tabs:

- **SYSTEM.INI**   The file associated with this tab contains system-specific information about your computer's hardware and device drivers. Most such hardware data is stored in the registry, but the System.ini file retains a few settings that are needed for backward compatibility with older programs.

- **WIN.INI**   The file associated with this tab contains some configuration settings relating to Windows XP and to installed Windows applications. Again, the bulk of such data is stored in the registry, but Win.ini is kept around for compatibility.

- **BOOT.INI** The file associated with this tab controls how Windows XP boots and governs the layout of the OS (operating system) Choices menu that appears at system startup. See the next section for details.

- **Services** This category refers to the system services that Windows XP loads at startup. The specific services loaded by Windows XP are listed on the Services tab, which you'll notice has an Essential column. Only those services that have Yes in this column are loaded when you choose the Diagnostic Startup option.

- **Startup** This refers to items in your Windows XP Startup menu and the Run items specified in the registry.

To control these startup items, the System Configuration Utility gives you two choices:

- To prevent Windows XP from loading every item in a particular category, choose Selective Startup on the General tab and then clear the check box for the category you want. For example, to disable all items in Win.ini, clear the Process WIN.INI File check box.

- To prevent Windows XP from loading only specific items in a category, select the category's tab and then clear the check box beside the items you want to bypass at startup.

Note that making changes on any of the System Configuration Utility tabs, other than the General tab, will cause the Selective Startup option to be set on the General tab. After completing your problem diagnosis and correction, you will need to return to the General tab in the System Configuration Utility and reselect the Normal Startup option.

Here's a basic procedure to follow for using the System Configuration Utility to troubleshoot a startup problem:

1. In the System Configuration Utility, select the Diagnostic Startup option and then reboot the computer. If the problem did not occur during the restart, then you know the cause lies in System.ini, Win.ini, the system services, or the startup items.

2. Choose the Selective Startup option.

3. Select one of the four check boxes and then reboot the computer.

4.   Repeat step 3 for each of the other check boxes until the problem reoccurs. When this happens, you know that the source of the problem is in whatever item you selected just before rebooting.

5.   Select the tab of the item that is causing the problem. For example, if the problem reoccurred after you selected the Load Startup Items check box, select the Startup tab.

6.   Select Disable All to clear all the check boxes.

7.   Select one of the check boxes to enable an item and then reboot the computer.

8.   Repeat step 7 for each of the other check boxes until the problem reoccurs. When this happens, you know that the source of the problem is in whatever item you selected just before rebooting.

Insider Secret   If you have a large number of check boxes to test (such as on the Services tab), selecting one check box at a time and rebooting can be tedious, to say the least. A faster method—called "troubleshooting by halves"—is to begin by selecting the first half of the check boxes and rebooting. One of two things will happen:

■   The problem doesn't reoccur. This means that one of the items represented by the cleared check boxes is the culprit. Clear all the check boxes, select the other half of the check boxes, and then reboot.

■   The problem reoccurs. This means that one of the selected check boxes is the problem. Select only half of those check boxes and reboot.

Keep halving the number of selected check boxes until you isolate the offending item.

---

9.   On the System Configuration Utility's General tab, select the Normal Startup option.

10.   Fix or work around the problem:

❑   If the problem is an item in System.ini or Win.ini, select the appropriate tab, select the problem item, and then click Disable.

> **Tip**   Another way to edit System.ini or Win.ini is by using the System Configuration Editor. To load this program, select Start, Run, type **sysedit** in the Run dialog box, and then click OK. Note that you disable a line in these files by preceding it with a semicolon (;).

❑   If the problem is a system service, you can either disable the service or expand a new copy of the service executable file from the Windows XP installation files (use the Expand File button on the System Configuration Utility's General tab).

❑   If the problem is caused by a Startup item, either delete the program from the Startup menu or delete the item from the appropriate Run key in the registry. (If the item is a program, consider uninstalling or reinstalling the program.)

Controlling Startup Using Boot.ini

If your system can boot to one or more operating systems other than Windows XP, you'll see the OS Choices menu at startup, which will be similar to the following:

```
Please select the operating system to start:

    Microsoft Windows XP Professional
    Microsoft Windows

Use the up and down arrow keys to move the highlight to your choice.
Press ENTER to choose.
Seconds until highlighted choice will be started automatically: 30
```

If you do nothing at this point, Windows XP will boot automatically after 30 seconds. Otherwise, you select the operating system you want and then press Enter to boot it.

The specifics of the OS Choices menu are determined by a hidden text file named Boot.ini, which resides in the root folder of your system's bootable partition (usually drive C). To work with this file, you have two choices:

- In Windows Explorer, double-click the file to open it in Notepad.
- Select the BOOT.INI tab in the System Configuration Utility.

> **Tip** To open the System Configuration Utility with the BOOT.INI tab already displayed, run the command **msconfig -4**. Note, too, that you can also modify Boot.ini from the command line using the BOOTCFG utility. Run the command **bootcfg /?** at the command prompt to see a list of switches you can use with this utility.

Either way, you see text similar to the following:

```
[boot loader]
timeout=30
default=multi(0)disk(0)rdisk(0)partition(1)\WINDOWS
[operating systems]
multi(0)disk(0)rdisk(0)partition(1)\WINDOWS="Microsoft Windows XP
    Professional" /fastdetect
C:\="Microsoft Windows"
```

There are two sections in the Boot.ini file: [boot loader] and [operating systems]. The [boot loader] section always has two values:

- **timeout** This value determines the number of seconds after which NTLDR will boot the operating system that's selected on the menu by default. (Changing this value to 0 will prevent the OS Choices menu from appearing at startup.)
- **default** This value determines which item listed in the [operating systems] section is selected on the menu by default at startup.

The [operating systems] section lists the operating systems to which the system can boot. The first line is almost always a reference to Windows XP, and subsequent lines reference the other bootable operating systems. The Windows XP line has a strange configuration. The part up to the equal sign (=) is called an Advanced Risc Computer (ARC) path. Let's run through all the various parts of this line so you understand what you're seeing.

- **multi(*n*)** This is a reference to the drive controller that's used to access the Windows XP installation. The value *n* is 0 for the first controller, 1 for the second, and so on. On systems that use a SCSI controller, you may see scsi(*n*) instead of multi(*n*) (the exception is on systems that have the SCSI BIOS disabled).

- **disk(*n*)** This is a reference to the SCSI ID of the device on which Windows XP is installed. (For multi devices, the value of *n* is always 0.)

- **rdisk(*n*)** This is a reference to the hard disk on which Windows XP is installed. This disk is attached to the controller specified by multi(*n*). The value of *n* is 0 for the first hard disk, 1 for the second hard disk, and so on.

- **partition(*n*)** This is a reference to the partition on which Windows XP is installed. This partition is part of the disk specified by rdisk(*n*).

- **WINDOWS** This is the name of the folder into which Windows XP was installed.

- **Microsoft Windows XP Professional** This is the text that appears on the OS Choices menu.

- **/fastdetect** The entry closes with one or more switches that determine how the operating system boots. In this example, the /fastdetect switch tells Windows XP to not enumerate the system's serial and parallel ports during startup. These ports aren't needed during the boot process, so this reduces the system startup time. See "Using the Boot.ini Switches," on the following page.

Changing the Default Startup OS

To change which operating system is chosen by default at startup, you need to modify the default value in the [boot loader] section:

- If you're working in Notepad, find the OS in the [operating systems] section, copy all the text to the left of the equal sign, and then paste it as the new default value.

- If you're working with the BOOT.INI tab of the System Configuration Utility, select the operating system you want to use and then click the Set As Default button.

Using the Boot.ini Switches

The ARC path syntax supports more than 30 different switches that enable you to control various aspects of the Windows XP startup (or another operating system, as long as it's Windows XP, Windows 2000, or Windows NT 4). You can either enter these switches by hand when editing Boot.ini in Notepad, or use the check boxes on the BOOT.INI tab of the System Configuration Utility. Here's a summary of the switches that are most useful:

- **/safeboot:minimal**   Boots Windows XP in safe mode, which uses only a minimal set of device drivers. Use this switch if Windows XP won't start, if a device or program is causing Windows XP to crash, or if you can't uninstall a program while Windows XP is running normally.

- **/safeboot:minimal(alternateshell)**   Boots Windows XP in safe mode but also bypasses the Windows XP GUI and boots to the command prompt instead. Use this switch if the programs you need in order to repair a problem can be run from the command prompt or if you can't load the Windows XP GUI.

- **/safeboot:network**   Boots Windows XP in safe mode but also includes networking drivers. Use this switch if the drivers or programs you need to repair a problem exist on a shared network resource, if you need access to e-mail or other network-based communications for technical support, or if your computer is running a shared Windows XP installation.

- **/safeboot:dsrepair**   Boots Windows XP in safe mode and also restores a backup of the Active Directory directory service (this option applies only to domain controllers).

- **/noguiboot**   Tells Windows XP not to load the display driver that normally is used to display the progress bar during startup. Use this switch if Windows XP hangs while switching video modes for the progress bar, or if the display of the progress bar is garbled.

- **/bootlog**   Boots Windows XP and logs the boot process to a text file named Ntbtlog.txt that resides in the %SystemRoot% folder. Open Ntbtlog.txt. in Notepad, move to the end of the file, and you may see a message telling you which device driver failed. You probably need to reinstall or roll back the driver. Use this switch if the Windows XP startup hangs, if you need a detailed record of the startup process, or if you suspect (after using one of the other Startup menu options) that a driver is causing Windows XP startup to fail.

■ **/basevideo** Boots Windows XP using the standard VGA mode: 640 × 480 with 256 colors. This is useful for troubleshooting video display driver problems. Use this switch if Windows XP fails to start using any of the safe mode options, if you recently installed a new video card device driver and the screen is garbled or the driver is balking at a resolution or color depth setting that's too high, or if you can't load the Windows XP GUI. Once Windows XP loads, you can either reinstall or roll back the driver, or you can adjust the display settings to values that the driver can handle.

■ **/sos** Displays the path and location of each device driver (using the ARC path syntax) as it is loaded, as well as the operating system version and build number and the number of processors.

■ **/maxmem=*MB*** Specifies the maximum amount of memory, in megabytes, that Windows XP can use. Use this value when you suspect a faulty memory chip might be causing problems.

■ **/numproc=*n*** In a multiprocessor system, specifies the maximum of processors that Windows XP can use. Use this switch if you suspect that using multiple processors is causing a program to hang.

■ **/pcilock** Tells Windows XP not to dynamically assign hardware resources for PCI devices during startup. The resources assigned by the BIOS during the POST are "locked" in place. Use this switch if installing a PCI device causes the system to hang during startup.

■ **/debug** Enables remote debugging of the Windows XP kernel. This sends debugging information to a remote computer via one of your computer's serial ports. You can also add any of the following switches:

❑ **/debugport=*port*** Specifies the serial port, where *port* is one of com1, com2, com3, com4, or 1394. Specifying 1394 will require that you also use the /channel switch.

❑ **/baudrate=*speed*** If you use a COM port, use this switch to specify the transmission speed of the debugging information, where *speed* is one of the following: 300, 1200, 2400, 4800, 9600, 19200, 38400, 57600, or 115200.

❑ **/channel=*number*** If you use an IEEE 1394 (FireWire) connection, use this switch to specify the channel, where *number* is a value between 1 and 64.

Controlling Startup with the Advanced Options Menu

When the OS Choices menu appears at startup, you see the following message at the bottom of the screen:

```
For troubleshooting and advanced startup options for Windows, press F8.
```

> **Tip**   If you have only one operating system installed on your computer, the OS Choices menu won't appear. To display the Advanced Options menu in this case, press F8 after your computer completes its Power-On Self Test (usually indicated by a single beep) but before the Windows XP logo is displayed.

This message remains on the screen while the progress bar that tracks the loading of startup devices is displayed. If you press F8, you get to the Advanced Options menu, which looks like this:

```
Windows Advanced Options Menu
Please select an option:

    Safe Mode
    Safe Mode with Networking
    Safe Mode with Command Prompt

    Enable Boot Logging
    Enable VGA Mode
    Last Known Good Configuration (your most recent settings
       that worked)
    Directory Services Restore Mode (Windows domain controllers only)
    Debugging Mode

    Start Windows Normally
    Reboot
    Return to OS Choices Menu
```

The Start Windows Normally option loads Windows XP in the usual fashion. You use the other options to control the rest of the startup procedure. Table 4-1 lists each advanced option and shows the corresponding Boot.ini switches.

Table 4-1 Advanced Options menu choices and their corresponding Boot.ini switches

Advanced Option	Boot.ini Switch (If Any)
Safe Mode	/safeboot:minimal /bootlog /noguiboot /sos
Safe Mode With Networking	/safeboot:network /bootlog /noguiboot /sos
Safe Mode With Command Prompt	/safeboot:minimal(alternateshell) /bootlog /noguiboot /sos
Enable Boot Logging	/bootlog
Enable VGA Mode	/basevideo
Last Known Good Configuration	This option boots Windows XP using the last hardware configuration that produced a successful boot. Choose this option if you suspect the problem is hardware-related, but you can't figure out the driver that's causing the problem, or if you don't have time to try out the other more detailed inspections. See Chapter 13, "Troubleshooting and Recovering from Problems," for more information on this option.
Directory Services Restore Mode	/safeboot:dsrepair
Debugging Mode	/debug
Reboot	This option reboots the computer.
Return To OS Choices Menu	This option displays the OS Choices menu.

Insider Secret For those Advanced Options that have equivalent Boot.ini switches, you can use those switches to place individual Advanced Options choices on the OS Choices menu. You do this by adding an item to Boot.ini's [operating systems] section that starts Windows XP with the appropriate switches. For example, to add an option to the OS Choices menu to start Windows XP in safe mode, you'd add the following to Boot.ini's [operating systems] section:

```
multi(0)disk(0)rdisk(0)partition(1)\WINDOWS="Safe Mode"
/safeboot:minimal /bootlog /noguiboot /sos
```

Getting the Most Out of the Shutdown Procedure

Shutdown is usually a relatively uneventful procedure, and most people simply initiate it and then leave their computer to handle the details. (This is particularly true on most newer systems that shut themselves off automatically after Windows XP closes up shop.) But few people know that, similar to the startup, you can also run programs and scripts as part of the shutdown routine. And since performance isn't as much of an issue as it is with startup, shutdown is a great place to run scripts that perform time-consuming tasks such as deleting files you no longer need. We'll close this chapter with a look at a few useful techniques that help you take advantage of the Windows XP shutdown procedure.

Using the SHUTDOWN Command

You normally log off, restart, or shut down your computer using the Start, Shut Down command (if logon was through the Classic logon screen) or the Start, Turn Computer Off command (if logon was through the Welcome screen). However, you can get one-click or shortcut-key access to any of these operations by using the SHUTDOWN command-line utility:

```
SHUTDOWN [-I | -L | -S | -R | -A] [-F] [-M \\computername] [-T xx]
[-C "comment"] [-D [U] [P]:xx:yy]
```

I	Displays the Remote Shutdown Dialog, which enables you to set the SHUTDOWN parameters using a GUI interface. If you use this, it must be the first switch after the command.
L	Logs off (note that you can't use this with the *M* switch).
S	Shuts down the computer.
R	Restarts the computer.
A	Aborts a pending shutdown.
M \\computername	Shuts down, restarts, or aborts the remote computer given by *computername*.
T xx	Sets timeout for the shutdown to *xx* seconds. The default is 30 seconds when the parameter is part of the SHUTDOWN command. When the *–I* parameter is used in the SHUTDOWN command to open the System Shutdown dialog box, the timeout default is 20 seconds.
C "comment"	Specifies the shutdown comment that appears while the shutdown is pending (you can enter a maximum of 127 characters).
F	Forces all running applications to close without warning.

D [U][P]:*xx:yy*   Specifies the reason code for the shutdown, where *U* is an unplanned shutdown and *P* is a planned shutdown code. For either case, *xx* is the major reason code (a positive integer less than 256, and *yy* is the minor reason code (a positive integer less than 65536).

For example, to restart the computer in 60 seconds, you can create a shortcut or batch file that runs the following command:

```
SHUTDOWN -R -T 60 -C "The system is about to reboot."
```

When you run the SHUTDOWN command, the System Shutdown dialog box appears with a warning that the system is about to shut down. If you include a comment, it appears in the Message box, as shown in Figure 4-2.

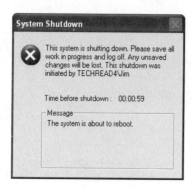

Figure 4-2   The System Shutdown dialog box appears when you run the SHUTDOWN command.

Deleting Files at Shutdown

If you work with sensitive or private data on your computer, it's a good idea to delete the telltale traces of your work that Windows XP leaves lying around when you shut down the system for the day.

For example, Windows XP uses a paging file to store data in virtual memory as you work. To keep that data secure and private, you should have Windows XP delete the paging file at shutdown. You can do this via the Group Policy snap-in by opening the Computer Configuration, Windows Settings, Security Settings, Local Policies, Security Options branch. In the Policy list, choose the Shutdown: Clear Virtual Memory Pagefile item. Note that this is equivalent to changing the value of the following registry setting to 1:

```
HKLM\SYSTEM\CurrentControlSet\Control\Session Manager\Memory Management
\ClearPageFileAtShutdown
```

You can also automatically clear the Start menu's My Recent Documents list at shutdown. To do this, open the Group Policy snap-in, and display the User Configuration, Administrative Templates, Start Menu And Taskbar branch. There are two policies to work with here:

- **Clear History Of Recently Opened Documents On Exit**   Enable this policy to clear the My Recent Documents list at shutdown. This is equivalent to setting the following registry value to 1:

```
HKCU\Software\Microsoft\Windows\CurrentVersion
\Group Policy Objects\LocalUser\Software\Microsoft\Windows
\CurrentVersion\Policies\Explorer\ClearRecentDocsOnExit
```

- **Do Not Keep History Of Recently Opened Documents**   Enable this policy to prevent Windows XP from tracking recently used documents altogether. This is equivalent to setting the following registry value to 1:

```
HKCU\Software\Microsoft\Windows\CurrentVersion
\Group Policy Objects\LocalUser\Software\Microsoft\Windows
\CurrentVersion\Policies\Explorer\NoRecentDocsHistory
```

Running Scripts at Logoff or Shutdown

In the same way that you can run scripts when you start the computer or log on, you can also run scripts when you log off or shut down the computer. The Group Policy snap-in enables you to perform this task at two places:

- **Computer Configuration, Windows Settings, Scripts (Startup/Shutdown)**   Use the Shutdown item to specify one or more script files to run each time the computer shuts down. Note that if you specify two or more scripts, Windows XP runs them synchronously. That is, Windows XP runs the first script, waits for it to finish, runs the second script, waits for it to finish, and so on.

- **User Configuration, Windows Settings, Scripts (Logon/Logoff)**   Use the Logoff item to specify one or more script files to run each time any user logs off. Logoff scripts are run asynchronously.

5

Managing Logons and Users

In this chapter, you'll learn how to:

- Customize your logon in various ways.

- Set up an automatic logon.

- Implement logon policies.

- Handle the rights and privileges of built-in account types.

- Use advanced methods for working with user accounts.

- Create and enforce strong passwords.

- Share your computer securely with other users.

If you have Microsoft Windows XP set up in the simplest configuration—a standalone computer with you as the sole user—you might be excused for not knowing that Windows XP even has a logon process or user accounts. That's because, in the simplest-configuration scenario, Windows XP "hides" its logon and user features because they don't need to be conspicuous. But what if you're prudent (or even, let's say it, a bit paranoid) and don't want other people to use your computer when you're not around? What if you're concerned that a virus or Trojan horse program might gain control of your machine? What if you share your computer with other people and you want to keep your (and everyone else's) files and settings secure and private? For these situations, you need to understand Windows XP's logon and user features, and set them up to ensure peace of mind. This chapter shows you how to do that.

Useful Windows XP Logon Strategies

When you install Windows XP, the setup program asks you to enter a user name for each of the people who will be accessing the computer. How you initially log on to Windows XP depends on what you did at that point of the installation:

- If you entered only a single user name and your computer is not part of a network domain, Windows XP logs on that user name automatically.

- If you entered multiple user names and your computer is not part of a domain, Windows XP displays the Welcome screen, which lists the users (Figure 5-1 shows an example). Click the user name that you want to log on.

Figure 5-1 You see the Windows XP Welcome screen if your workgroup or standalone computer is set up with multiple users.

- If your computer is part of a domain, Windows XP first displays the Welcome To Windows dialog box, which prompts you to press Ctrl+Alt+Delete. When you do that, you see the Log On To Windows dialog box, shown in Figure 5-2. (Windows XP refers to this process as the "Classic" logon.) Change the User Name, if necessary, enter the Password, and click OK.

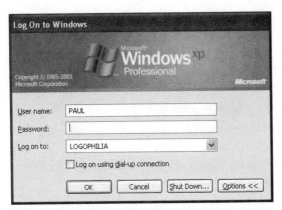

Figure 5-2   You see the Log On To Windows dialog box if your computer is part of a network domain.

Customizing the Logon

The default logon is fine for most users, but there are many ways to change Windows XP's logon behavior. The rest of this section looks at a few tips and techniques for altering your Windows XP logon method.

Switching Between the Welcome Screen and the Classic Logon

Many people prefer the Classic Windows XP logon because the initial step of pressing Ctrl+Alt+Delete adds an extra level of security. (It prevents automatic logons and thwarts any malicious programs—such as a password-stealing program—that might have been activated at startup.) If your computer uses the Welcome screen logon, you switch to the Classic logon by using any of the following techniques:

- Launch Control Panel's User Accounts icon, click Change The Way Users Log On Or Off, and then clear the Use Welcome Screen check box.

- In the registry (see Chapter 2, "Getting the Most Out of the Registry"), set the following DWORD value to 0 (reset it to 1 to revert to the Welcome screen):

  ```
  HKLM\SOFTWARE\Microsoft\Windows NT\CurrentVersion\Winlogon
  \LogonType
  ```

- In the Group Policy editor, open Computer Configuration, Administrative Templates, System, Logon, and then enable the Always Use Classic Logon policy. (Note that setting this policy takes precedence over the User Accounts option or the registry setting.)

> **Note** If your computer is part of a domain, you can't change the logon from the Classic method to the Welcome screen.

Toggling Fast User Switching On and Off

Windows XP's *fast user switching* feature enables another user to log on to the system without logging off the current user. (Note, however, that fast user switching is available only if you use the Windows XP Welcome screen.) You use the feature by following these steps:

1. Select Start, Log Off. The Log Off Windows dialog box appears.

2. Click Switch User. The Welcome screen appears.

3. Click the name of the user who wants to log on.

If your computer doesn't have much memory, fast user switching can be a problem because the programs and windows of other users remain open, which can slow down overall computer performance. If you have this problem, you can turn off fast user switching by launching Control Panel's User Accounts icon, clicking Change The Way Users Log On Or Off, and then clearing the Use Fast User Switching check box.

Accessing the Administrator Account

Another chore you performed during the Windows XP setup routine was to specify an Administrator password. One of the confusing aspects about Windows XP is that after the setup is complete, the Administrator account seems to disappear. The secret is that Administrator actually is a hidden account that appears only in a limited set of circumstances, such as when you boot Windows XP in Safe Mode or when no other administrative-level accounts are defined on your system. Outside of these scenarios, there are several ways to log on to Windows XP using the Administrator account:

- If you're using the Welcome screen, press Ctrl+Alt+Delete twice.

- If you're using the Classic logon, enter **Administrator** in the User Name text box.

- Set up an automatic logon using the Administrator (see the next section).

■   Tweak Windows XP to make the Administrator account visible in the
    Welcome screen. To do this, open the Registry Editor and navigate to
    the following key:

```
HKLM\SOFTWARE\Microsoft\Windows NT\CurrentVersion\Winlogon
\SpecialAccounts\UserList
```

Add a new DWORD value named **Administrator** and set its value
to **1**. (To hide Administrator in the Welcome screen, set this value
to **0**.)

> **Insider Secret**   The UserList registry key is also useful for
> hiding accounts. If you have a user account defined but you
> don't want other users to see that name in the Welcome
> screen, add a DWORD value to the UserList key, give it the
> same name as the user, and set its value to **0**. You can access
> this account using the same methods that we outlined in this
> section for the Administrator account.

Setting Up an Automatic Logon

If you're using a standalone computer that no one else has access to (or that
will be used by people you trust), you can save some time at startup by not
having to type a user name and password. In this scenario, the easiest way to
do this is to set up Windows XP with just a single user account, which means
Windows XP will log on that user automatically at startup. If you have multiple user accounts (for testing purposes, for example), or if you want the Administrator account to be logged on automatically, then you need to set up
Windows XP for automatic logons.

Previous versions of Windows required you to edit the registry to set up
an automatic logon, but this capability is built into Windows XP. Here are the
steps to follow:

1.   In the Run dialog box, enter **control userpasswords2** and press
     Enter. Windows XP displays the User Accounts dialog box, which
     we'll discuss in more detail later in this chapter (see "The User
     Accounts Dialog Box").

2.   On the Users tab, clear the Users Must Enter A User Name And Pass-
     word To Use This Computer check box.

3. Click OK. Windows XP prompts you to specify the account you want to log on automatically.

4. Fill in the User Name, Password, and Confirm Password text boxes and then click OK.

If you have Tweak UI (described in Chapter 1, "Mastering Control Panel, Policies, and PowerToys"), open the Logon, Autologon setting and select the Log On Automatically At System Startup check box. Enter the user name, the domain (your computer name), and click Set Password to enter the account password. When you click OK, Tweak UI makes some changes in the following registry key:

`HKLM\SOFTWARE\Microsoft\Windows NT\CurrentVersion\Winlogon\`

The AutoAdminLogon value is set to 1; your user name appears in the DefaultUserName setting; your computer name appears in the DefaultDomainName setting. Note that previous versions of Tweak UI stored your password in the DefaultPassword setting. Your password appeared as plain text, so anyone could have read it or even changed it. Tweak UI for Windows XP is more secure because it stores your password in the Local Security Authority database, which is the Windows XP component that manages and validates local security credentials.

> **Tip** You can temporarily suspend the automatic logon by holding down the Shift key while Windows XP starts up.

If you want the automatic logon to occur a set number of times only, open the following registry key:

`HKLM\SOFTWARE\Microsoft\Windows NT\CurrentVersion\Winlogon\`

Create a new string setting named AutoLogonCount and set its value to the number of times you want the automatic logon to occur. With each logon, Windows XP decrements this setting until it reaches zero, at which point Windows XP sets AutoAdminLogon to 0 to disable the automatic logon.

Setting Logon Policies

Windows XP Professional defines a number of security policies related to the logon process. (See Chapter 1 to learn how to use Windows XP's policy editors.) You can get to these policies in two ways:

- In the Group Policy editor, select Computer Configuration, Windows Settings, Security Settings, Local Policies, Security Options.

- In the Local Security Settings editor, select Security Settings, Local Policies, Security Options.

Most of the logon options are listed in the Interactive Logon group of policies. Here's a list of the most useful options (note that all of these options apply to the Classic logon):

- **Do Not Display Last User Name**   Enable this option to clear the User Name text box each time the Log On To Windows dialog box appears. Although it adds a bit of inconvenience to the logon, this is a good security feature because it denies an intruder an important piece of information: a legitimate system user name. (This is particularly true if you rename the Administrator account, as we'll describe later in this chapter in the "Setting Account Policies" section.) This policy modifies the following registry key (0 = disable; 1 = enable):

```
HKLM\SOFTWARE\Microsoft\Windows\CurrentVersion\policies
\system\dontdisplaylastusername
```

- **Do Not Require CTRL+ALT+DEL**   Enable this policy to bypass the initial Welcome To Windows dialog box (the one that prompts you to press Ctrl+Alt+Delete) and go directly to the Log On To Windows dialog box. This can save you a startup step, but it decreases the security of the logon. The main concern here is that your system might get infected with a virus or Trojan horse program that displays a fake Log On To Windows dialog box as a ruse to capture your user name and password. If you decide to enable this policy, make sure you have a good anti-virus program and that you use it often. This policy modifies the following registry key (0 = disable; 1 = enable):

```
HKLM\SOFTWARE\Microsoft\Windows\CurrentVersion\policies
\system\DisableCAD
```

- **Message Text For User Attempting To Log On**   Use this option to specify a text message that appears in a dialog box after any user presses Ctrl+Alt+Delete (but before the Log On To Windows dialog box appears). This policy modifies the following registry setting:

  ```
  HKLM\SOFTWARE\Microsoft\Windows\CurrentVersion\policies
  \system\legalnoticetext
  ```

- **Message Title For Users Attempting To Log On**   Use this option to set the title of the dialog box that contains the message to the user that you specified in the previous setting. This policy modifies the following registry setting:

  ```
  HKLM\SOFTWARE\Microsoft\Windows\CurrentVersion\policies
  \system\legalnoticecaption
  ```

- **Number of Previous Logons To Cache (In Case Domain Controller Is Not Available)**   Use this option to set the number of previous domain logons (user name, password, and domain) that Windows XP will retain. By retaining a logon, Windows XP enables that user to log on to Windows XP even if a domain controller isn't present (for example, on a notebook that isn't always connected to the network at startup). This policy modifies the following registry setting:

  ```
  HKLM\SOFTWARE\Microsoft\Windows NT\CurrentVersion\Winlogon
  \cachedlogonscount
  ```

- **Prompt User To Change Password Before Expiration**   Use this option to set the number of days prior to password expiration that a message forewarning the expiration will be displayed. (We'll show you how to set an expiration date for a password later in this chapter.) This policy modifies the following registry setting:

  ```
  HKLM\SOFTWARE\Microsoft\Windows NT\CurrentVersion\Winlogon
  \passwordexpirywarning
  ```

More Logon Registry Tweaks

As you saw in the previous section, the logon security policies are stored in the registry. Windows XP has a number of other registry-related logon settings that we'll explore in this section:

- **Controlling the Shift key override of an automatic logon**   Create the following string value and use it to determine whether the user can override an automatic logon by holding down the Shift key during startup (0 = enable Shift override; 1 = disable Shift override):

  ```
  HKLM\SOFTWARE\Microsoft\Windows NT\CurrentVersion\Winlogon
  \IgnoreShiftOverride
  ```

- **Forcing an automatic logon**   This is similar to overriding the Shift key at startup. That is, the following string setting (you need to add it by hand) determines whether the user can bypass an automatic logon (0 = bypass possible; 1 = bypass not possible):

  ```
  HKLM\SOFTWARE\Microsoft\Windows NT\CurrentVersion\Winlogon
  \ForceAutoLogon
  ```

- **Disabling logon options**   The Log On To Windows dialog box (Classic logon) has an Options button that toggles on and off the Log On To list, the Log On Using Dial-Up Connection check box, and the Shut Down button. Use the following DWORD value to control whether these options appear (0 = disable; 1 = enable):

  ```
  HKLM\SOFTWARE\Microsoft\Windows NT\CurrentVersion\Winlogon
  \ShowLogonOptions
  ```

- **Adding text to the logon dialog box**   Specify text in the following string setting (you need to create the setting by hand) to display a message in the Log On To Windows dialog box above the User Name text box:

  ```
  HKLM\SOFTWARE\Microsoft\Windows NT\CurrentVersion\Winlogon
  \LogonPrompt
  ```

- **Disabling the dial-up logon**   If you don't want users to attempt to use a dial-up connection to log on, create the following string setting and use it to disable the Log On Using Dial-Up Connection check box in the Log On To Windows dialog box (0 = disable; 1 = enable):

  ```
  HKLM\SOFTWARE\Microsoft\Windows NT\CurrentVersion\Winlogon
  \RASDisable
  ```

Getting the Most Out of User Accounts

In Windows XP, a *user account* is a user name (and an optional password) that uniquely identifies a person who uses the system. The user account enables Windows XP to control the user's *privileges*; that is, the user's access to system resources (*permissions*) and the user's ability to run system tasks (*rights*). Stand-alone and workgroup machines use *local* user accounts that are maintained on the computer, while domain machines use *global* user accounts that are maintained on the domain controller. This section looks at local user accounts.

Security for Windows XP user accounts is handled most often (and most easily) by assigning each user to a particular *security group*. For example, the default Administrator account and all the user accounts you created during the Windows XP setup process are part of the Administrators group. Each security group is defined with a specific set of permissions and rights, and any user added to a group is automatically granted that group's permissions and rights. There are two main security groups:

- **Administrators**   Members of this group have complete control over the computer, meaning they can access all folders and files; install or uninstall programs (including legacy programs) and devices; create, modify, and remove user accounts; install Windows updates, service packs, and fixes; use Safe Mode; repair Windows; take ownership of objects; and more.

- **Users (also known as Limited Users or Restricted Users)** Members of this group can access files only in their own folders and in the computer's shared folders; change their own account passwords and associated pictures; add .NET Passport support; and install and run programs that don't require administrative-level rights.

Besides these two groups, Windows XP also defines seven others that you'll use less often:

- **Backup Operators**   Members of this group can access the Backup program and use it to back up and restore folders and files, no matter what permissions are set on those objects.

- **Guests**   Members of this group have the same privileges as those of the Users group. The exception is the default Guest account, which is not allowed to change its account password.

- **HelpServicesGroup**   Members of this group (generally, Microsoft personnel and the manufacturers of your computer) can connect to your computer to resolve technical issues using the Remote Assistance feature.

- **Network Configuration Operators**   Members of this group have a subset of the Administrator-level rights that enables them to install and configure networking features.

- **Power Users (also known as Standard Users)**   Members of this group have a subset of the Administrator group privileges. Power Users can't back up or restore files, replace system files, take ownership of files, or install or remove device drivers. Also, Power Users can't install applications that explicitly require the user to be a member of the Administrators group.

- **Remote Desktop Users**   Members of this group can log on to the computer from a remote location using the Remote Desktop feature.

- **Replicator**   Members of this group can replicate files across a domain.

Each user is also assigned a *user profile*, which contains all the user's folders and files, as well as the user's Windows settings. The folders and files are stored in %SystemRoot%\Documents and Settings*user*, where *user* is the user name. This location contains a number of subfolders that hold the user's home folder (My Documents), Internet Explorer cookies (Cookies), desktop icons and subfolders (Desktop), Internet Explorer favorites (Favorites), Start menu items (Start Menu), and more. If a logged-on user has been assigned any group policies, the user's settings are stored in the HKU*sid*\\ registry key, where *sid* is a unique *security identifier* (SID) typically in the form *S-1-5-nn*, and *nn* is a variable-length string of numbers interspersed with hyphens. To determine which currently logged-on user is associated with a particular SID, see the following registry setting:

```
HKU\sid\Software\Microsoft\Windows\CurrentVersion\Explorer
\Logon User Name
```

The rest of this section shows you the various methods Windows XP offers to create, modify, and remove local user accounts.

Control Panel's User Accounts Icon

Windows XP has a number of methods for working with user accounts. The most direct route is to launch Control Panel's User Accounts icon. If you're using a standalone or workgroup computer, you'll see the User Accounts window, which we'll discuss in this section. (Domain-based computers display the User Accounts dialog box, which we discuss in the next section.)

If you're a member of the Administrators or Power Users group, you create a new user account by clicking the Create A New Account link, entering a name for the account (don't use spaces), and then clicking Next. Windows XP then asks you to choose the account type. Note that you have only two choices here: Computer Administrator (Administrators group) or Limited (Users group). Make your choice and click Create Account.

To modify an existing account, click the account in the User Accounts window to see a list of tasks for changing the account. (If you're a member of the Users or Guests group, launching Control Panel's User Accounts icon takes you directly to the task list.) Depending on your account's privileges, you can then change the account name, create or change the account password, change the picture associated with the account, change the account type, apply a .NET Passport to the account, or delete the account.

The User Accounts Dialog Box

Control Panel's User Accounts window has one major limitation: It offers only the Administrator and Limited (Users) account types. If you want to assign a user to one of the other groups, you need to use the User Accounts dialog box, shown in Figure 5-3. You get there by entering the command **control userpasswords2** in the Run dialog box.

Figure 5-3   The User Accounts dialog box enables you to assign users to any Windows XP security group.

To enable the list of users, make sure the Users Must Enter A User Name And Password To Use This Computer check box is selected. You can now perform the following tasks:

- **Add a new user**   Click Add to launch the Add New User Wizard. You use the first two dialog boxes to specify the user's name and password. You use the third and final dialog box to specify the user's security group: Standard User (Power Users group), Restricted User (Users group), or Other. Select Other to assign the user to any of the nine default Windows XP groups.

- **Delete a user**   Select the user and click Remove.

- **Change the user's name or group**   Select the user's name and click Properties. The resulting property sheet enables you to change the user's name and assign the user to a different group.

- **Change the user's password**   Select the user's name and click Reset Password. (Note that this option is not enabled for the Administrator account.)

> **Tip**   How do you change the Administrator password? If you have the Welcome screen disabled (as described earlier) and have logged on as Administrator, press Ctrl+Alt+Delete to display the Windows Security dialog box, and then click Change Password. If the Welcome screen is enabled, use the NET USER command (described later in this chapter). You can also use the Local Users And Groups snap-in, discussed next.

On the Advanced tab, click the Advanced button to select the Local Users And Groups snap-in (discussed in the next section). Also, you can force users to press Ctrl+Alt+Delete before logging on by selecting the Require Users To Press Ctrl+Alt+Delete check box. (Note that this check box will be cleared if you applied the Do Not Require CTRL+ALT+DEL policy discussed earlier in this chapter.)

The Local Users And Groups Snap-In

The most powerful of the Windows XP tools for working with users is the Local Users And Groups snap-in. To load this snap-in, open Computer Management and select System Tools, Local Users And Groups. Alternatively, either click the Advanced button on the Advanced tab of the User Accounts dialog box (see the previous section), or use the Run dialog box to launch **lusrmgr.msc**. Select the Users branch to see a list of the users on your system, as shown in Figure 5-4.

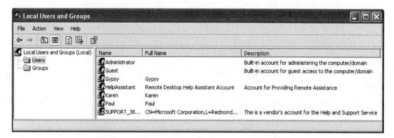

Figure 5-4 The Users branch lists all the system's users and enables you to add, modify, and delete users.

From here, you can perform the following tasks:

- **Add a new user** Make sure no user is selected and then select Action, New User. In the New User dialog box, specify the user name and password (we discuss the password-related check boxes later in this chapter), and click Create.

- **Change the user's name** Right-click the user and then select Rename.

- **Change the user's group** Right-click the user and then select Properties. On the Member Of tab, click Add, use the Enter The Object Names To Select box to enter the group name, and then click OK.

- **Change the user's profile** Right-click the user and then select Properties. Use the Profile tab to change the profile path, logon script, and home folder (select the Local Path option to specify a local folder, or select Connect to specify a shared network folder).

- **Disable an account** Right-click the user and then select Properties. On the General tab, select the Account Is Disabled check box.

- **Delete a user**   Right-click the user's name and then select Delete.

- **Change the user's password**   Right-click the user's name and then select Set Password.

> **Note**   Another way to change a user's group is to select the Groups branch, right-click the group you want to work with, and then select Add To Group. Now click Add, type the user name in the Enter The Object Names To Select box, and then click OK.

Setting Account Policies

Windows XP offers several sets of policies that affect user accounts. There are three kinds of account policies: security options, user rights, and lockout policies. The next three sections take you through these policies.

Account Security Options

To see these policies, open the Group Policy editor and select Computer Configuration, Windows Settings, Security Settings, Local Policies, Security Options. (You can also launch the Local Security Policy snap-in and select Security Settings, Local Policies, Security Options.) The Accounts group of policies has five options:

- **Administrator Account Status**   Use this option to enable or disable the Administrator account. This is useful if you think someone else might be logging on as the Administrator. (A less drastic solution would be to change the Administrator password or rename the Administrator account.) Note that only a different member of the Administrators group can enable a disabled Administrator account.

> **Note**   The Administrator account is always used during a Safe Mode boot, even if you disable the account.

- **Guest Account Status**   Use this option to enable or disable the Guest account.

- **Limit Local Account Use Of Blank Passwords To Console Logon Only**   When this option is enabled, Windows XP allows users with blank passwords only to log on to the system directly by using either the Welcome screen or the Log On To Windows dialog box. Such users can't log on via the RunAs command or remotely over a network.

   This policy modifies the following registry setting:

   `HKLM\SYSTEM\CurrentControlSet\Control\Lsa\limitblankpassworduse`

- **Rename Administrator Account**   Use this option to change the name of the Administrator account.

- **Rename Guest Account**   Use this option to change the name of the Guest account.

Setting User Rights Policies

Windows XP also has a long list of policies associated with user rights. To view these policies in the Group Policy editor, select Computer Configuration, Windows Settings, Security Settings, Local Policies, User Rights Assignment. (You can also launch the Local Security Policy snap-in and select Security Settings, Local Policies, User Rights Assignment.) Each policy here is a specific task or action, such as Back Up Files And Directories, Deny Logon Locally, and Shut Down The System. For each task or action, the Security Setting column shows the users and groups who can perform the task or to whom the action applies. To change the setting, double-click the policy. In the policy's Properties window, click Add User Or Group to add an object to the policy; delete an object from the policy by selecting it and clicking Remove.

Setting Account Lockout Policies

Lastly, Windows XP has a few policies that determine when an account gets locked out, which means the user is unable to log on. A lockout occurs when the user fails to log on after a specified number of attempts. This is a good security feature because it prevents an unauthorized user from trying a number of different passwords. These policies are in the Group Policy editor under Computer Configuration, Windows Settings, Security Settings, Account Policies, Account Lockout Policy. (You can also launch the Local Security Policy snap-in and select Security Settings, Account Policies, Account Lockout Policy.) There are three policies:

- **Account Lockout Duration**   This policy sets the amount of time, in minutes, that the user is locked out. Note that to change this policy, you must set the Account Lockout Threshold (described next) to a non-zero number.

- **Account Lockout Threshold**   This policy sets the maximum number of logons the user can attempt before being locked out. Note that after you change this to a non-zero value, Windows XP offers to set the other two policies to 30 minutes.

- **Reset Account Lockout Counter After**   This policy sets the amount of time, in minutes, after which the counter that tracks the number of invalid logons is reset to 0.

Working with Users and Groups from the Command Line

You can script your user and group chores by taking advantage of the NET USER and NET LOCALGROUP command-line utilities. These commands enable you to add users, change passwords, modify accounts, add users to groups, and remove users from groups.

For local users, the NET USER command has the following syntax:

```
NET USER [username [password | * | /RANDOM] [/ADD] [/DELETE] [options]]
```

`username`	The name of the user you want to add or work with. If you run NET USER with only the name of an existing user, the command displays the user's account data.
`password`	The password you want to assign to the user. If you use * instead, Windows XP prompts you for the password; if you use the /RANDOM switch instead, Windows XP assigns a random password (containing eight characters, consisting of a random mix of letters, numbers, and symbols), and then displays that password on the console.
`/ADD`	Creates a new user account.
`/DELETE`	Deletes the specified user account.
`options`	These are optional switches you can append to the command:
`/ACTIVE:{YES	NO}`	Specifies whether the account is active or disabled.

/EXPIRES:{date | NEVER}	The date (expressed in the system's Short Date format) on which the account expires. This parameter cannot be set nor viewed by other Windows XP tools.
/HOMEDIR:path	The home folder for the user (make sure the folder exists).
/PASSWORDCHG:{YES | NO}	Specifies whether the user is allowed to change his or her password.
/PASSWORDREQ:{YES | NO}	Specifies whether the user is required to have a password. This parameter cannot be set nor viewed by other Windows XP tools.
/PROFILEPATH:path	The folder that contains the user's profile.
/SCRIPTPATH:path	The folder that contains the user's logon script.

/TIMES:{times | ALL}	Specifies the times that the user is allowed to log on to the system. Use single days or day ranges (for example, Sa or M-F). For times, use 12-hour notation with *am* or *pm*, or 24-hour notation. Separate the day and time with a comma; separate day/time combinations with semicolons. Here are some examples:
	  M-F,9am-5pm
	  M,W,F,08:00-13:00
	  Sa,12pm-6pm;Su,1pm-5pm
	Note that the abbreviated form of Thursday, Saturday, or Sunday requires the use of the first two characters of the day's name. This parameter cannot be set or viewed by other Windows XP tools.

Caution   If you use the /RANDOM switch to create a random password, be sure to make a note of the new password so that you can communicate it to the new user.

Note that if you run NET USER without any parameters, it displays a list of the local user accounts.

> **Tip**   If you want to force a user to log off when his or her logon hours expire, open the Group Policy editor and select Computer Configuration, Windows Settings, Security Settings, Local Policies, Security Options. In the Network Security group of policies, enable the Force Logoff When Logon Hours Expire policy.

The NET LOCALGROUP has the following syntax for adding users to, or removing users from, a group:

```
NET LOCALGROUP [group name1 [name2 ...] {/ADD | /DELETE}
```

group	This is the name of the local group with which you want to work. If the *name1* [*name2*...] parameters are not provided, then the /ADD or /DELETE switch applies to the named group.
name1 [*name2* ...]	One or more user names that you want to add or delete, separated by spaces.
/ADD	Adds the user or users to the named group or, if no users are named, the named group is added to the system.
/DELETE	Removes the user or users from the named group or, if no users are named, the named group is deleted from the system.

Creating and Enforcing Bulletproof Passwords

Windows XP sometimes gives the impression that passwords aren't all that important. After all, each user account you specify during Setup is supplied with both administrative-level privileges *and* a blank password. That's a dangerous setup, but it's one that's easily remedied by supplying *all* local users a password. This section gives you some pointers for creating strong passwords and runs through Windows XP's password-related options and policies.

Creating a Strong Password

Ideally, when you're creating a password for a user, you want to pick one that provides maximum protection without sacrificing convenience. Keeping in mind that the whole point of a password is to select one that nobody can guess, here are some guidelines you can follow when choosing a password.

■ **Don't be too obvious.** Because forgetting a password is inconvenient, many people use meaningful words or numbers so that their password will be easier to remember. This means that they often use extremely obvious things such as their name, the name of a family member or colleague, their birth date or Social Security number, or even their system user name. Being this obvious is just asking for trouble.

■ **Don't use single words.** Many crackers break into accounts by using "dictionary programs" that just try every word in the dictionary. So, yes, *xiphoid* is an obscure word that no person would ever guess, but a good dictionary program will figure it out in seconds flat. Using two or more words in your password (or *pass phrase*, as multiword passwords are called) is still easy to remember, and would take much longer to crack by a brute force program.

■ **Use a misspelled word.** Misspelling a word is an easy way to fool a dictionary program. (Make sure, of course, that the resulting arrangement of letters doesn't spell some other word.)

■ **Use passwords that are at least eight characters long.** Shorter passwords are susceptible to programs that just try every letter combination. You can combine the 26 letters of the alphabet into about 12 million different five-letter word combinations, which is no big deal for a fast program. If you bump things up to eight-letter passwords, however, the total number of combos rises to 200 *billion*, which would take even the fastest computer quite a while. If you use 12-letter passwords, as many experts recommend, the number of combinations goes beyond mind-boggling: 90 *quadrillion*, or 90,000 trillion!

■ **Mix uppercase and lowercase letters.** Windows XP passwords are case-sensitive, which means that if your password is, say, *YUMMY ZIMA*, trying *yummy zima* won't work. Now the 26 letters of the alphabet become 52 unique characters. So you can really throw snoops for a loop by mixing the case. Something like *yuMmY zIMa* would be almost impossible to figure out.

■ **Add numbers to your password.** You can throw more permutations and combinations into the mix by adding a few numbers to your password.

- **For extra variety, toss in one or more punctuation marks or special symbols, such as % or #.**

- **Try using acronyms.**   One of the best ways to get a password that appears random but is easy to remember is to create an acronym out of a favorite quotation, saying, or book title. For example, if you've just read *The Seven Habits of Highly Effective People,* you could use the password T7HoHEP.

- **Don't write down your password.**   After going to all this trouble to create an indestructible password, don't blow it by writing it on a sticky note and then attaching it to your keyboard or monitor! Even writing it on a piece of paper and then throwing the paper away is dangerous. Determined crackers have been known to go through a company's trash looking for passwords (this is known in the trade as *Dumpster diving*). Certainly, don't place your password in the password hint.

- **Don't tell your password to anyone.**   If you've thought of a particularly clever password, don't suddenly become unclever and tell someone. Your password should be stored in your head alongside all those "wasted youth" things you don't want anyone to know about.

- **Change your password regularly.**   If you change your password often (say, once a month or so), even if some skulker does get access to your account, at least he or she will have it for only a relatively short period.

User Account Password Options

Each user account has a number of options related to passwords. To view these options, open the Local Users And Groups snap-in (as described earlier in this chapter), right-click the user you want to work with, and then select Properties. There are three password-related check boxes in the property sheet that appears:

- **User Must Change Password At Next Logon**   If you select this check box (the Password Never Expires option must not be active), the next time the user logs on, the user will see a dialog box with the message that the user is required to change his or her password. When the user clicks OK, the Change Password dialog box appears and the user enters his or her new password.

- **User Cannot Change Password**   Select this check box to prevent a user from changing his or her password.

- **Password Never Expires**   If you clear this check box, the user's password will expire. The expiration date is determined by the Maximum Password Age policy, discussed in the next section.

Taking Advantage of Windows XP's Password Policies

Windows XP maintains a small set of useful password-related policies that govern settings such as when passwords expire and the minimum length of a password. In the Group Policy editor, select Computer Configuration, Windows Settings, Security Settings, Account Policies, Password Policy. (In the Local Security Policy snap-in, select Security Settings, Account Policies, Password Policy.) There are six policies:

- **Enforce Password History**   This policy determines the number of old passwords that Windows XP stores for each user. This is to prevent a user from reusing an old password. For example, if you set this value to 10, the user can't reuse a password until he or she has used at least 10 other passwords. Enter a number between 0 and 24.

- **Maximum Password Age**   This policy sets the number of days after which passwords expire. This only applies to user accounts where the Password Never Expires property has been disabled (see the previous section). Enter a number between 1 and 999.

- **Minimum Password Age**   This policy sets the numbers of days that a password must be in effect before the user can change it. Enter a number between 1 and 998 (but less than the Maximum Password Age value).

- **Minimum Password Length**   This policy sets the minimum number of characters for the password. Enter a number between 0 and 14 (where 0 means no password is required).

- **Password Must Meet Complexity Requirements**   If you enable this policy, Windows XP examines each new password and accepts it only if it meets the following criteria: it doesn't contain all or part of the user name; it's at least six characters long; and it contains characters from three of the following four categories: uppercase letters, lowercase letters, digits (0-9), and non-alphanumeric characters (such as $ and #).

■ **Store Password Using Reversible Encryption For All Users In The Domain**   Enabling this policy tells Windows XP to store user passwords using reversible encryption. Some applications require this, but they're rare and you should never need to enable this policy.

Recovering a Forgotten Password

Few things in life are as frustrating as a forgotten password. To avoid this headache, Windows XP offers a couple of precautions that you can take now just in case you forget your password sometime in the future.

The first precaution is called a *password hint*, which is a word, phrase, or other mnemonic device that can help you remember your password. To see the hint, click the question mark (?) button that appears beside the password box in the Welcome screen (hints are not available in Classic logon mode). To set up a password hint, follow these steps:

1.   Launch Control Panel's User Accounts icon.

2.   If you have administrative-level privileges, select the user you want to work with.

3.   From here, you have two choices:

    ❑   If the user doesn't have a password, click Create A Password, enter the password (twice) and enter the password hint in the Type A Word Or Phrase To Use As A Password Hint text box.

    ❑   If the user already has a password, click Change My Password, enter the existing password in all three text boxes, and then enter the password hint in the Type A Word Or Phrase To Use As A Password Hint text box. Note that if Enforce Password History has been set to a non-zero value, you wil have to provide a new password in the second and third text boxes.

The second precaution you can take is the Password Reset Disk. This is a floppy disk that enables you to reset the password on your account without knowing the old password. The account's password is required to prepare the disk, so don't wait until you've forgotten the password to try and create the disk.

To create a Password Reset Disk, follow these steps:

1.   Log on as the user for whom you want to create the disk.

2.   Launch Control Panel's User Accounts icon.

3.   Click your account name, if necessary.

4. In the Related Tasks list, click Prevent A Forgotten Password. This runs the Forgotten Password Wizard.

5. Run through the wizard's dialog boxes. (Note that you'll need a blank, formatted disk.)

The password reset disk contains a single file named Userkey.psw, which is an encrypted backup version of your password. If you need to use this disk down the road, follow these steps:

1. Start Windows XP normally.

2. When you get to the logon screen, leave your password blank and press Enter. Windows XP will then ask if you want to use your password reset disk.

3. If you're using the Welcome screen, click the Use Your Password Reset Disk link; if you're using the Classic logon, click Reset. Windows XP launches the Password Reset Wizard. Click Next.

4. Insert the password reset disk and click Next.

5. Enter a new password (twice), enter a password hint, and click Next.

6. Click Finish.

Sharing Your Computer Securely

If you're the only person who uses your computer, you don't have to worry all that much about "profile security," a phrase we use to describe the security of your user profile—that is, your files and Windows XP settings. However, if you share your computer with other people, either at home or at the office, then you'll need to set up some kind of security to ensure that users each have their "own" Windows and can't mess with anyone else's (either purposely or accidentally). Here's a list of security precautions to set up when sharing your computer:

■ **Create an account for each user.** Everyone who uses the computer, even if they use it only occasionally, should have their own user account. (If a user needs to access the computer rarely, or only once, activate the Guest account and let him or her use that. You should disable the Guest account after the user has finished his or her session.)

- **Remove unused accounts.**   If you have accounts set up for users who no longer require access to the computer, you should delete those accounts.

- **Limit the number of Administrators.**   Members of the Administrators group can do just about *anything* in Windows XP, including granting themselves privileges that they might not have by default. These all-powerful accounts should be kept to a minimum. Ideally, your system should have just one: the Administrator account.

- **Rename the Administrator account.**   Renaming the Administrator account ensures that no other user can be certain of the name of the computer's top-level user.

- **Don't display the last logged-on user.**   Use the Classic logon, and tell Windows XP not to display the name of the user who last logged on to the system.

- **Put all other accounts in the Users (Limited) group.**   Most users can perform almost all of their everyday chores with the permissions and rights assigned to the Users group, so that's the group you should use for all other accounts.

- **Use strong passwords on all accounts.**   Supply each account with a strong password so that no user can access another's account by logging on with a blank or simple password.

- **Set up each account with a screen saver and be sure the screen saver resumes to the Unlock Computer screen.**   To do this, launch Control Panel's Display icon, select the Screen Saver tab, choose a screen saver, and then select the On Resume, Password Protect check box.

- **Use disk quotas.**   To prevent users from taking up an inordinate amount of hard disk space (think: MP3 downloads), set up disk quotas for each user. To enable quotas, right-click a hard disk in Windows Explorer, and then select Properties. On the Quota tab, select the Enable Quota Management check box. Select and set options in this dialog box consistent with your needs.

Notes from the Real World

When Windows XP was first released, I upgraded my children's computer to ensure there would be fewer crashes and fewer support headaches for the home IT staff (often just called DAD — Desktop Application Debugger). I then had to leave town for a week, expecting to hear grumblings and complaints from the kids about the changes I had made to their computer. When I got home Friday night the kids were all in bed, so I went to clean up their computer and check for updates. To my surprise, while booting, the computer now played a unique sound that my daughter had installed, and the desktop had been changed to a picture of her dog. Then the screen saver kicked in, but I couldn't get back to the desktop because the screen saver was locked with a new password that I didn't know. Windows XP: Ease of use, ease of software management, and so simple a 9-year-old can do it!

—Scott Andersen

6

Installing and Running Programs

In this chapter, you'll learn how to:

- Install software safely.

- Launch programs easily using a variety of methods.

- Run an application as a different user.

- Operate older programs with success by understanding application compatibility.

Almost all users purchase and learn how to use their computers for one reason: to run applications. This means that we who spend a not-insignificant chunk of our computing lives installing software and launching programs also expend our fair share of time trying to recover from problems created by recent software installations, or when other users run programs they weren't supposed to. It makes sense, therefore, to learn the right ways to add software to our computers and run those new programs so that we minimize the amount of time we exhaust on software installation and on troubleshooting. This chapter will help free up some fresh hours by discussing various techniques for safely installing and uninstalling applications, running applications, and solving program incompatibility issues.

Tips and Techniques for Installing Applications

User accounts, and their inherent permissions and rights, absolutely affect the installation process. Not only that, but there are many other factors to take into account before installing any program. Unfortunately, it's all too easy to simply launch the software's installation program and see what happens. Our goal in this section is to make you think twice before installing applications on your system. We show you the relationship between user accounts and installing applications, and we take you through a checklist of actions and precautions to take in order to make installing programs a relatively painless process.

User Accounts and Installing Programs

If you're coming to Microsoft Windows XP from Windows 9x or Windows Me, you'll find that something as straightforward as installing software isn't necessarily what you've come to expect. More specifically, the Windows XP security model won't let just anyone install just any program. If you're logged on with administrative-level privileges, you'll have no problem with installation. If, however, you're logged on as a member of the Users group (a Limited account with more limited privileges than Administrators), then Windows XP will run into problems for any installation program that attempts to either:

■ Install files anywhere other than within the %USERPROFILE% folder (the folder that contains the files of the currently logged-on user).

■ Add or edit registry keys and settings anywhere other than within the HKEY_CURRENT_USER key (or its corresponding subkey in HKEY_USERS).

If you're having trouble installing an application as a Limited user, you can usually work around the problem by upgrading the software to be Windows XP–compatible, which means that Limited users then are able to install programs safely for their own use.

A related problem occurs when you're logged on as a member of the Administrators group but you don't want an installation program to abuse those privileges. For example, you don't want an installation program to make changes to sensitive portions of the registry of the file system. Here's how to fix that:

1. In Windows Explorer, right-click the installation program's executable file and then select Run As.

2. In the Run As dialog box, make sure the Current User option is selected, and also make sure the Protect My Computer And Data From Unauthorized Program Activity check box is selected.

3. Click OK.

When you launch the installation program, Windows XP will run it as though you were a Limited user.

Working Through a Preinstallation Checklist

For those who enjoy working with computers, few things are as tempting as a new software package. The tendency is to just tear into the box, liberate the source disks, and let the installation program rip without further ado. This approach often loses its luster when, after a willy-nilly installation, the system starts to behave erratically. This will happen usually because the application's setup program has made adjustments to one or more important configuration files and has given one's system a case of indigestion in the process. That's the hard way to learn the hazards of a haphazard installation.

To avoid such a fate, you should always look before you leap. That is, you should follow a few simple safety measures before double-clicking that Setup.exe file. Here's a list of things to check into before you install any program:

■   **Verify whether the program is compatible with Windows XP.** The easiest and safest setups occur with programs certified to work with Windows XP. See "Understanding Application Compatibility," later in this chapter, to learn how to tell whether a program is Windows XP–compatible.

■   **Set a restore point.** The quickest way to recover from a bad installation is to restore your system to the way it was before you ran the setup program. The only way to do that is to set a system restore point just before you run the setup program. See Chapter 13, "Troubleshooting and Recovering from Problems."

■   **Read the Readme.txt and other setup files.**   Although it's the easiest thing in the world to skip, you really should peruse whatever documentation the program provides that pertains to the setup. This includes the appropriate installation material in the manual, Readme files found on the disk, and whatever else looks promising. By spending a few minutes perusing these resources, you can glean the following information:

❑   Any advance preparation you need to perform on your system.

❑   What to expect during the installation.

❑   Information you need to have on hand in order to complete the setup (such as a product's serial number).

❑   Changes the installation program will make to your system or to your data files (if you're upgrading).

❑   Changes to the program and/or the documentation that were put into effect after the manual was printed.

■   **Check downloaded files for viruses.**   If you downloaded the application you're installing from the Internet, or if a friend or colleague sent you the installation file as an e-mail attachment, you should scan the file using a good (and up-to-date) virus checker.

■   **Understand the effect on your data files.**   Few software developers want to alienate their installed user base, so they usually emphasize upward compatibility in their upgrades. That is, the new version of the software will almost always be able to read and work with documents created with an older version. However, in the interest of progress, you often find that the data file format used by the latest incarnation of a program is different from its predecessors, and this new format is rarely *downward-compatible*. That is, an older version of the software will usually gag on a data file that was created by the new version. So you're faced with two choices:

❑   Continue to work with your existing documents in the old format, thus possibly foregoing any benefits that come with the new format.

❑   Update your files and thus risk making them incompatible with the old version of the program, should you decide to uninstall the upgrade.

One possible solution to this dilemma is to make backup copies of all your data files before installing the upgrade. That way, you can always restore the good copies of your documents if the upgrade causes problems or destroys some of your data. If you've already used the upgrade to make changes to some documents, but you want to uninstall the upgrade, most programs have a Save As command that lets you save these documents in their old format.

■ **Use the Add Or Remove Programs feature.** Launching Control Panel's Add Or Remove Programs icon displays the dialog box shown at the top of Figure 6-1. If you're not sure which executable to run to install a program, insert the CD or floppy disk, click the Add New Programs icon, and then click CD Or Floppy to find the file using a wizard. However, most experienced Windows users don't need a wizard to install a program. Instead, Add Or Remove Programs is useful for two things:

❑ **Modifying a program's installation.** Clicking the Change Or Remove Programs icon displays a list of your computer's installed programs. When you select a program, the window shows you the size of the installation; how frequently the program has been used (rarely, occasionally, or frequently); and when the program was last used. You also get a Change button that you can click to modify the program's installation. (Some programs display a combined Change/Remove button, instead.) Depending on the program, modifying its installation may mean adding or removing program features, reinstalling files, or repairing damaged files.

❑ **Removing the program.** Click the Remove (or Change/Remove) button to uninstall the program. Note that most items in the Add Or Remove Programs list that are capable of being uninstalled have a corresponding subkey of the HKLM\SOFTWARE\Microsoft\Windows\CurrentVersion\Uninstall registry key, as shown in Figure 6-1, though some of these program subkeys are identified by those long hexadecimal strings enclosed in brackets .

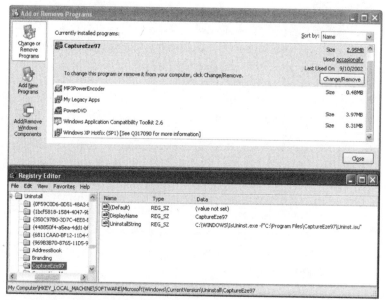

Figure 6-1 Most items that can be uninstalled via Add Or Remove Programs have corresponding registry entries.

Insider Secret After you uninstall a program, you may find that it still appears in the list of programs in the Add Or Remove Programs dialog box. To fix this, open the Registry Editor, display the Uninstall key, and look for the subkey that represents the program (if you're not sure, click a subkey and examine the DisplayName setting, the value of which is the name that appears in the Add Or Remove Programs list) and then delete that subkey.

■ **Take control of the installation.** Some setup programs give new meaning to the term "brain-dead." You slip in the source disk, run Setup.exe (or whatever name the software manufacturer provides for installation), and the program proceeds to impose itself on your hard disk without so much as a how-do-you-do. Thankfully, most installation programs are a bit more thoughtful than that. They usually give you some advance warning about what's to come, and they prompt you for information as they go along. You can use these prompts to assume a certain level of control over the installation. Here are a couple of things to watch for:

❑   **Choose your folder wisely.**   Most installation programs offer to install their files in a default folder. Rather than just accepting this without question, think about where you want the program to reside. Personally, we prefer to use the Program Files folder to house all applications. If you have multiple hard disks or partitions, you might prefer to use the one with the largest amount of free space. If the setup program lets you select data directories, you might want to use a separate folder that makes it easy to back up the data.

> **Tip**   Most installation programs offer to copy the program's files to a subfolder of %SystemDrive%\Program Files. You can change this default installation folder by editing the registry. In the registry key HKLM\SOFTWARE\Microsoft\Windows \CurrentVersion\ the setting ProgramFilesDir holds the default install path. Change this setting to the path you prefer (say, one that's on a drive with the most free disk space).

❑   **Use the custom install option.**   The best programs offer you a choice of installation options. Whenever possible, choose the Custom option, if one is available. This will give you maximum control over the components that are installed, including where they're installed and how they're installed.

Launching Applications

Launching programs is one of the most fundamental operating system tasks, so it isn't surprising that Windows XP offers an impressive number of ways to go about doing this:

■   **Click the Start button to open the Start menu.**   If you've run a program repeatedly, its name should appear in the list of most frequently used applications, so click its icon. Otherwise, click All Programs and then open the menus until you see the program's icon, and then click the icon.

■   **Double-click the executable file's name.**   Use Windows Explorer to find the application's executable file, and then double-click that file name.

- **Double-click a shortcut icon on the desktop.** If a shortcut points to a program's executable file, double-clicking the shortcut will launch the program. Likewise, if the shortcut points to a data file, the associated application program (generally, the program that created the file) is launched, and then the data file is opened in that application.

- **Double-click a document name.** If you can use the application to create documents, double-clicking the name of one of those documents in Windows Explorer should launch the program and load the document automatically. (If the document was one of the last 15 that you used, select Start, My Recent Documents, and then click the document name in the submenu that appears.)

- **Use the Open With command.** If double-clicking a document name opens the file in the wrong application, right-click the file and then select Open With. One of two things will happen:

  ❑ The Open With dialog box appears, as shown in Figure 6-2.

  ❑ If the file type already has a defined "Open With" list (see Chapter 7, "Getting the Most Out of Files and Folders"), you'll see a submenu that lists the applications that can open this file type. Select the application you want. If you don't see the application, click Choose Program to display the Open With dialog box.

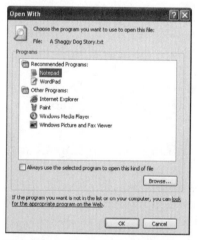

Figure 6-2   Use the Open With dialog box to choose the application you want to use to open the document.

In the Open With dialog box, either click the program you want to use, or click Browse to choose the executable file of a different program. If you want this to be the default application for this file type, select the Always Use The Selected Program To Open This Kind Of File check box.

■ **Insert a CD or DVD disc.**   Most CDs and DVDs support Windows XP's AutoPlay feature that automatically starts a default program when the disc is inserted. The program that launches is determined by the contents of the Autorun.inf file in the disc's root folder. Open the file in Notepad and look for the open value in the [AutoRun] section.

> **Insider Secret**   To disable the AutoRun feature for your CD and DVD drives, open the Registry Editor and find the HKLM \SYSTEM\CurrentControlSet\Services\CDRom key. Change the value of the AutoRun setting to 0.

■ **Use the Run dialog box.**   Select Start, Run to display the Run dialog box. Use the Open text box to specify the application (click OK when you're done):

❏   If the application resides within the %SystemRoot% or %SystemRoot%\System32 folder, within a folder listed as part of the PATH environment variable, or if it has an application-specific path in the registry (described later in this section), just type the primary name of the executable file.

❏   For all other applications, enter the full path (drive, folder, and file name) for the executable file.

❏   You can also enter the full path of a document. If you want to open the document using a program other than the one associated with the document's file type, precede the document path with the application's path (separate the two paths with a space).

> **Tip**   A quick way to open the Run dialog box is to press ⊞+R.

- **Set up the program to run automatically at startup.**   Refer to Chapter 4, "Starting Up and Shutting Down," to learn how to launch programs automatically at startup.

- **Use the Scheduled Tasks folder.**   The Scheduled Tasks folder can run programs automatically at a given date and time, or on a regular schedule.

Launching Programs from the Command Prompt

Running programs within a command prompt session or a batch file is straight-forward. At the command prompt (or in the batch file), enter the full path of the executable file. Note that you need use only the file's primary name if the application resides within the current folder, the %SystemRoot% folder, the %SystemRoot%\System32 folder, or a folder in the PATH variable. For example, the full path of the Registry Editor's executable file is %SystemRoot%\Regedit.exe, but you can launch this program using only the primary part of the file name: Regedit.

> **Caution**   To avoid errors when working at the command prompt, either use the 8.3 format for the folder and file's name, or surround the long folder or file name with quotation marks.

To gain more control over launching Windows applications from the command prompt or in a batch file, use the START command:

```
START ["title"] [/B] [/Dpath] [/I] [/MIN] [/MAX] [/SEPARATE |
/SHARED] [/LOW | /NORMAL | /HIGH | /REALTIME | /ABOVENORMAL |
/BELOWNORMAL] [/WAIT] [program] [parameters]
```

"title"	The text that is displayed in the title bar of the application's window.
/Dpath	The *path* of the folder in which the application starts.
/B	Starts the application without creating a new window. The application has Ctrl+C handling ignored. Unless the application enables Ctrl+C processing, Ctrl+Break is the only way to interrupt the application.
/I	The application's environment will be the same as the command prompt's original environment.
/MIN	Starts the application window minimized.
/MAX	Starts the application window maximized.

/SEPARATE	Loads a 16-bit Windows program into a separate memory space.
/SHARED	Loads a 16-bit Windows program into a shared memory space.
/LOW	The application's threads are given the lowest priority. This will make the program run slowly, but it will improve the performance of other running programs.
/NORMAL	The application's threads are given normal priority.
/HIGH	The application's threads are given the highest priority. This will make the program run as fast as possible, but other programs may run more slowly.
/REALTIME	The application's threads are executed with the REALTIME priority class.
/ABOVENORMAL	The application's threads are given above normal (but less than the highest) priority.
/BELOWNORMAL	The application's threads are given below normal (but more than the lowest) priority.
/WAIT	Starts the application and then waits for it to terminate before processing more commands. (This is useful in a batch file where you don't want the next batch command to run until after the program terminates.)
program	The full path and file name of the application. You need only use the file's primary name if the application resides within the current folder, the %SystemRoot% folder, the %SystemRoot% \System32 folder, or a folder in the PATH variable.
parameters	The parameters or switches that are passed to the application.

Running a Program as a Different User

As we explained earlier in this chapter, some applications—especially installation programs—may fail because the current user account may have insufficient privileges to support some program operations. Similarly, a user account may have privileges that are too high to safely run a program. For either case, you can run a program as a different user with any of the following techniques:

- **Use the Run As menu command.** Right-click the executable file and then select Run As on the shortcut menu. In the Run As dialog box, choose The Following User and then choose a user from the User Name list. Enter the user's Password and click OK. Note that only members of the Administrators group appear in the User Name list, allowing members of the Limited group to run a program as an Administrator, if they have the password, but Administrators will not be able to select the name of a member of the Limited group.

■ **Prompt for a user.**   Create a shortcut to the executable file, right-click the shortcut, and then select Properties. On the Shortcut tab, click Advanced and then select the Run With Different Credentials check box. Click OK. When you launch the shortcut, Windows XP will display the Run As dialog box so that you can choose a user. This procedure is not available to members of the Limited group.

■ **Use the RUNAS command-line tool.**   You use RUNAS at the command prompt to specify the user name, and Windows XP then prompts you to enter the user's password. Here's the basic syntax (type **RUNAS /?** for the complete list of switches):

```
RUNAS /user:domain\user program
```

`/user:domain\user`	The *user* name under which you want the program to run. Replace *domain* with either the computer name (for a standalone or workgroup machine) or the domain name.
`program`	The full path and file name of the application. You need only use the file's primary name if the application resides within the current folder, the %SystemRoot% folder, the %SystemRoot%\System32 folder, or a folder in the PATH variable.

This procedure allows members of an Administrators group as well as members of the Limited group to run a program as either an Administrator or a Limited user, assuming correct passwords are provided.

Creating Application-Specific Paths

When you install a 32-bit application, it usually stores the path to its executable file in the registry. This is called an *application-specific path*. It means that you can start almost any 32-bit application simply by entering the name of its executable file either in the Run dialog box or at the command prompt (using the START command). You don't need to spell out the complete path. For example, here's the full path for the System Configuration Utility:

```
%SystemRoot%\PCHEALTH\HELPCTR\Binaries\msconfig.exe
```

However, to launch this program you need only enter **Msconfig.exe** in the Run dialog box or enter **START Msconfig.exe** at the command prompt.

This pathless execution is handy, but it doesn't work in the following two situations:

■ **16-bit applications**   These older programs don't store the paths to their executables in the registry.

■   **Documents**   You can't load a document just by typing its file name and extension in the Run dialog box or at the command prompt (unless the document is in the current folder).

To solve both these problems, and to handle the rare case when a 32-bit application doesn't create its own application-specific path, you can edit the registry to add a path to an executable file (an application-specific path) or to a document (a document-specific path).

In the Registry Editor, open the following key:

```
HKLM\SOFTWARE\Microsoft\Windows\CurrentVersion\App Paths
```

The App Paths key has subkeys for each installed 32-bit application. Each of these subkeys has one or both of the following settings, and possibly some others that we won't explore:

■   **(Default)**   This setting spells out the path to the application's executable file. All the App Paths subkeys have this setting.

■   **Path**   This setting specifies one or more folders that contain files needed by the application. An application first looks for its files in the same folder as its executable file. If it can't find what it needs there, it checks the folder or folders listed in the Path setting. Not all App Paths subkeys use this setting.

To create an application-specific path, select the App Paths key, create a new subkey, and assign it the name of the application's executable file. For example, if the program's executable file name is Oldapp.exe, name the new subkey **Oldapp.exe**. For this new subkey, change the Default setting to the full path of the executable file.

> **Tip**   You don't have to give the new App Paths subkey the name of the executable file. You can use any name you like as long as it ends with .exe and doesn't conflict with the name of an existing subkey. Why does it have to end with .exe? Unless you specify otherwise, Windows XP assumes that anything you enter in the Run dialog box or at the command prompt (via the START command) ends with .exe. So, by ending the subkey with .exe, you need to type only the subkey's primary name. For example, if you name your new subkey *Oldapp.exe*, you can run the program by typing **oldapp** in the Open text box in the Run dialog box, or **START oldapp** at the command prompt.

You create document-specific paths the same way. (Note, however, that the document's file type must be registered with Windows XP.) In this case, though, the Default setting takes on the full path of the document. Again, if you want to load the document just by typing its primary name, make sure that the new App Paths subkey uses the .exe extension.

Restricting Program Launches for Users

Windows XP has several group policies that enable any member of the Administrators group to restrict the usage of Windows programs for each logged-on user. For example, you can prevent users from running the System Configuration Utility, a program that—in the wrong hands—can do much damage to a system. You can also prevent users from accessing the command prompt (where they could start unauthorized programs) or the Registry Editor.

In the Group Policy editor, select User Configuration, Administrative Templates, System. There are five program-restriction policies:

- **Prevent Access To The Command Prompt** Enable this policy to prevent each logged-on user from getting to the command prompt.

- **Prevent Access To Registry Editing Tools** Enable this policy to prevent each logged-on user from running the Registry Editor.

- **Run Only Allowed Windows Applications** Enable this policy to specify a list of executable file names that each logged-on user is allowed to run. Note that this policy doesn't prevent users from starting other programs at the command prompt, so you should also disable command prompt access.

- **Don't Run Specified Windows Applications** Enable this policy to specify a list of executable file names that each logged-on user is not allowed to run. Again, users can still run these programs via the command prompt, unless that access also has been denied.

- **Turn Off Autoplay** Enable this setting to disable the AutoPlay feature for inserted CD or DVD discs.

Understanding Application Compatibility

Most new software programs are certified as Windows XP–compatible, meaning that they will install and run without mishap on any Windows XP system. But what about older programs that were coded before Windows XP was released? They can be a bit more problematic. Since Windows XP is based on the code for Windows 2000—which was in turn based on Windows NT—programs that are compatible with those operating systems will probably (although not definitely) be compatible with Windows XP. But the real problems lie with programs written for Windows 9x and Windows Me. Windows XP—even Windows XP Home Edition—uses a completely different code base than the old consumer versions of Windows, so it's inevitable that some of those so-called *legacy* programs either will be unstable while running under Windows XP, or they won't run at all.

Why do such incompatibilities arise? One common reason is that the programmers of a legacy application hard-wired certain data into the program's code. For example, installation programs often poll the operating system for its version number. If an application is designed for, say, Windows 95, the programmers may have set things up so that the application installs if and only if the operating system returns the Windows 95 version number. The program may run perfectly well under any later version of Windows, but this simplistic brain-dead version check prevents it from even installing on anything but Windows 95.

Another reason incompatibilities arise is that calls to API functions return unexpected results. For example, the programmers of an old application may have assumed that the FAT file system would always be the standard, so when checking for free disk space before installing the program, they'd expect to receive a number that is 2 GB or less (the maximum size of a FAT partition). But FAT32 and NTFS partitions can be considerably larger than 2 GB, so a call to the API function that returns the amount for free space on a partition could return a number that blows out a memory buffer and crashes the installation program.

These types of problems may make it seem as though getting older programs to run under Windows XP would be a nightmare. Fortunately, that's not true, because the Windows XP programmers did something very smart: Since many of these application incompatibilities are predictable, they gave Windows XP the ability to make allowances for them and so enable many older programs to run under Windows XP without modification. In Windows XP, *application compatibility* refers to a set of concepts and technologies that enable the operating system to adjust its settings or behavior to compensate for the shortcomings of legacy programs. This section shows you how to work with Windows XP's application compatibility tools.

Determining Whether a Program Is Windows XP–Compatible

One way to determine whether an application is compatible with Windows XP is to go ahead and install it. If the program is not compatible with Windows XP, you may see a dialog box similar to the one shown in Figure 6-3.

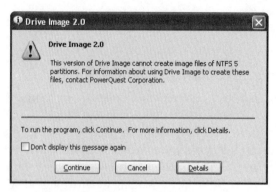

Figure 6-3 You may see a dialog box such as this if you try to install a program that isn't compatible with Windows XP.

At this point you could click Continue (in some dialog boxes, the button is instead named Run Program), but this is a risky strategy since you can't be sure how the program will interact with Windows XP. (This approach is riskiest when dealing with disk utilities, backup software, anti-virus programs, and other software that requires low-level control of the system. It's extremely unlikely that Windows XP would ever allow such programs to run. You should *always* upgrade such products to Windows XP–compatible versions, even if you are successful in forcing them to install.) A much safer route is to click Cancel to cancel the installation and then visit the vendor's Web site or the Windows Update site to see if a Windows XP–friendly update is available. (You can often get the company's Web address by clicking the Details button.)

Insider Secret Where does the information in these dialog boxes come from? In the %SystemRoot%\AppPatch folder, Windows XP has a file named Apphelp.sdb that contains messages such as the one shown in Figure 6-3 for all known applications that don't have compatibility fixes (discussed later in this section). The .sdb files are not text files, so opening them with Notepad or WordPad will not allow you to read any of those stored messages.

A better approach is to find out in advance whether the program is compatible with Windows XP. The most obvious way to do this is to look for the Designed For Windows XP logo on the box. For older programs, check the manufacturer's Web site to see if it tells you whether the program can be run under Windows XP, or if an upgrade is available. Alternatively, Microsoft has a Web page that enables you to search on the name of a program or manufacturer to find out compatibility information:

http://www.microsoft.com/windows/catalog

What if you're upgrading to Windows XP and you want to know if your installed software is compatible? The easiest way to find out is to use the Microsoft Windows Upgrade Advisor tool, which is available on the Windows XP Professional CD. (The Windows XP Home Edition CD doesn't have the Upgrade Advisor.) Insert the Windows XP Professional CD and, when the Welcome To Microsoft Windows XP screen appears, click Check System Compatibility. Run through the Upgrade Advisor's dialog boxes until you get to the report on system compatibility. This report will list any software that doesn't support Windows XP and possibly software that needs to be reinstalled after the Windows XP setup is finished.

Understanding Compatibility Mode

To help you run programs under Windows XP, especially those programs that worked properly in a previous version of Windows, Windows XP offers a new way to run applications using *compatibility layers*. This means that Windows XP runs the program by doing one or both of the following:

■ Running the program in a *compatibility mode*. This involves emulating the behavior of a previous version of Windows. Windows XP can emulate the behavior of Windows 95, Windows 98, Windows Me, Windows NT 4.0 with Service Pack 5, or Windows 2000.

■ Temporarily changing the system's visual display so that it's compatible with the program. There are three possibilities here: setting the color depth to 256 colors; changing the screen resolution to 640 × 480; and disabling Windows XP's visual themes.

> **Note**   Windows XP and Microsoft often use the terms *compatibility layer* and *compatibility mode* interchangeably, depending on which compatibility tool you're using. In some cases, the emulations of previous Windows versions are called *operating system modes*.

These are the broad compatibility layers supported by Windows XP. As you'll see a bit later, Windows XP also offers fine-tuned control over these and other compatibility settings. For now, however, you have two ways to set up a compatibility layer:

- Right-click the program's executable file (or a shortcut to the file), select Properties, and then select the Compatibility tab in the property sheet that appears (see Figure 6-4). To set the compatibility mode, select the Run This Program In Compatibility Mode For check box, and then use the list to choose the Windows version the program requires. You can also use the check boxes in the Display Settings section of the dialog box to adjust the video mode that Windows XP will switch to when you use the program.

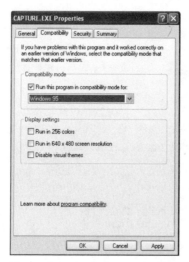

Figure 6-4   In the property sheet for an executable file, use the Compatibility tab to set the compatibility layer for the program.

■ Run the Program Compatibility Wizard by selecting Start, All Programs, Accessories, Program Compatibility Wizard. Use the wizard's windows to select the program's executable file, choose a compatibility mode, set the visual options, and then test the program.

Scripting Compatibility Layers

What do you do if you have a batch file that needs to run one or more programs within a temporary compatibility layer? You can handle this by using the following command within the batch file before you start the program. Look closely at the command: The word SET is followed by a space, then *two* underscore characters.

```
SET __COMPAT_LAYER=[!]layer1 [ layer2...]
```

Here, *layer1* and *layer2* are codes that represent the compatibility layers. Table 6.1 lists the 11 codes you can use.

Table 6-1   Codes to use when scripting compatibility layers

Code	Compatibility Layer
Win95	Windows 95
Win98	Windows 98 / Windows Me
Win2000	Windows 2000
NT4SP5	Windows NT 4.0 SP 5
256Color	256 Color
640x480	640 × 480 Screen Resolution
DisableThemes	Disable Visual Themes
International	International This layer handles incompatibilities caused by double-byte character sets.
LUA	Limited User Access This layer redirects some registry and file operations to non-restricted areas for users that don't have permission to access restricted areas (such as the HKLM key).
LUACleanup	Limited User Access Cleanup This layer removes the registry settings and files that were redirected using the LUA layer.
ProfilesSetup	Profile Setup Support This layer is used for older programs that install only for the current user; the layer ensures the program is installed for all users.

Note, too, that if you've already applied one or more layers to the program using the techniques from the previous section, you can tell Windows XP not to use one of those layers by preceding its keyword with the ! symbol. Also, to turn off the compatibility layers, run the command without any parameters, like so:

```
SET __COMPAT_LAYER=
```

For example, the following commands set the compatibility layers to Windows 95 and 256 colors, run a program, and then remove the layers:

```
SET __COMPAT_LAYER=Win95 256Color
D:\Legacy\oldapp.exe
SET __COMPAT_LAYER=
```

> **Note**   The compatibility layers created by SET __COMPAT_LAYER apply also to any processes that are spawned by the affected application. For example, if you set the Windows 95 layer for Setup.exe, the same layer will also apply to any other executable called by Setup.exe. More information regarding the SET __COMPAT_LAYER command and its parameters can be found at *http://support.microsoft.com/default.aspx?scid=kb;en-us;Q286705*.

Using the Application Compatibility Toolkit

When you execute a program using a compatibility layer, Windows XP creates an environment within which the program can function properly. For example, a program running under the Win95 layer actually believes that Windows 95 is the operating system. Windows XP accomplishes that not only by returning the Windows 95 version number when the program calls the GetVersion or GetVersionEx API functions, but also by "fixing" other incompatibilities between Windows 95 and Windows XP. For example, Windows 95 programs expect components such as Calculator and Solitaire to be in the %SystemRoot% folder, but in Windows XP these are in the %SystemRoot%\System32\ folder. The Win95 layer intercepts such file calls and reroutes them to the appropriate location.

The Win95 layer is composed of more than 50 such fixes, which are part of a large database of incompatibilities maintained by Microsoft. As of this writing, nearly 200 incompatibilities have been identified, and others may be found in the future. To get access to all these fixes and thus get fine-tuned control over the compatibility issues relating to any legacy program, you need to use the Application Compatibility Toolkit (ACT).

To install the ACT, you have two choices:

- In the Windows XP Professional CD, open the \SUPPORT\TOOLS\ folder and launch the Act20.exe file.

- Download and run the latest version of ACT from the following Microsoft Web page:

  http://www.microsoft.com/windows/WindowsXP/appexperience/

The ACT package consists of a number of programs and tools. Some of these are for programmers only, so the next two sections look at the end-user tools: QFixApp and the Compatibility Administrator.

Using QFixApp

QFixApp enables you to apply either a layer or a specific set of fixes to an executable file, and then run the file to test the fixes. If the program works properly, you can then use the Compatibility Administrator (discussed in the next section) to apply the fixes to the file. Note, however, that the latest version of the ACT doesn't require QFixApp because it enables you to choose fixes and test executables from within the Compatibility Administrator.

If you're still using the original version of the ACT, follow these steps to test an executable using QFixApp:

1. Select Start, All Programs, Application Compatibility Toolkit, QFixApp. (Newer versions of ACT still have QFixApp, but it's not available via the Start menu. Open the folder into which you installed the ACT and double-click the Qfixapp.exe file instead.)

2. In the QFixApp window, click Browse to choose the executable file you want to test. If the executable requires parameters or switches, add them to the Command Line text box.

3. If you want to apply a layer, choose it from the Layers tab.

4. If you want to apply specific fixes instead (or in addition to the fixes associated with the specified layer), display the Fixes tab and use the check boxes to select the fixes you want to test. Selecting a fix displays its description in the Fix Description box, as shown in Figure 6-5.

5. Click Run to test the file.

6. Click View Log. The top part of the log will show you the fixes that Windows XP used to run the program. In the following example, Windows XP used three fixes—EmulateHeap, Win95VersionLie, and EmulateGetDiskFreeSpace:

```
---------------------------------------------
Log  "D:\oldapp.exe"
---------------------------------------------
09/10/2002 11:55:59 EmulateHeap 3 -
[NotifyFn] Win9x heap manager initialized
09/10/2002 11:55:59 Win95VersionLie 3 -
[GetVersionExA] Return Win95
09/10/2002 11:56:15 EmulateGetDiskFreeSpace 3 -
[GetDiskFreeSpaceA] Called. Returning <=2GB free space
```

7. On the Fixes tab, clear all the fixes that the application did not require.

8. Repeat steps 5 through 7 until the fixes selected in QFixApp match the fixes required by the program.

Figure 6-5   QFixApp allows you to interactively determine parameters for application compatibility.

The fixes you've determined for your program are in effect only during the current QFixApp session. To create a permanent fix, you need to use the Compatibility Administrator, discussed next.

Using the Compatibility Administrator

To create a usable compatibility fix for an application—one that you can use on your own computer or distribute to other computers—you use the Compatibility Administrator. The Compatibility Administrator stores fixes in databases:

- **System database** This database contains three items: a list of applications for which Microsoft has applied fixes for known problems; a list of the available compatibility fixes (these are the items that QFixApp displays on its Fixes tab); and the defined compatibility modes (that is, the compatibility layers discussed earlier).

- **Installed databases** These are databases that have been installed on this computer.

- **Custom databases** These are databases that contain fixes that you applied to one or more applications.

There are two ways to start this program:

- If you're using the original version of the ACT, select Start, All Programs, Application Compatibility Toolkit, Compatibility Administration Tool.

- If you're using the latest version of the ACT, select Start, All Programs, Windows Application Compatibility Toolkit, Compatibility Administration Tool.

Here's how to create a custom fix database (note that we're using version 2.6 of the Compatibility Administrator for these instructions):

1. In the Compatibility Administrator window, a new database is created for you automatically under the Custom Databases branch. Either select this database or create a new one by selecting Custom Database and selecting File, New.

2. Right-click the new database, select Rename, and then enter a name for the database.

3. To create a new application fix, click the Fix button in the toolbar to launch the Create New Application Fix Wizard.

4. Enter the program's name, vendor, and location, and then click Next.

5. Choose an operating system mode and use the check boxes in the Select Additional Compatibility Modes section to choose additional layers to apply to the program. Click Next.

6. In the Compatibility Fixes list, use the check boxes to apply specific compatibility fixes and then click Next.

7. The Compatibility Administrator also needs to know how to identify the program. Click Auto-Generate to have the wizard set up the matching attributes for you, and then click Finish.

You'll see your program listed in the database. To try it out, select the program and click Run. Then select View, View Log to see the log that the Compatibility Administrator created. As with QFixApp, use the log to determine which fixes were required by the program. Then edit the fix to clear any fixes that aren't required by the program. (To change the fixes, right-click the program's executable file name in the right pane and then select Edit Application Fix.

Once you've added all the fixes for all your incompatible programs to the database, save the database file. To enable Windows XP to use the resulting .sdb file, you need to install the file by selecting it and selecting File, Install. To distribute the fix to another computer, copy the .sdb file to the machine, launch the Compatibility Administrator, and then click Open to open the .sdb file. You can then install the database.

7

Getting the Most
Out of Files and Folders

In this chapter, you'll learn how to:

■ View details such as image dimensions and music bit rates in Windows Explorer.

■ Customize the Send To command, the New menu, and the Open With list.

■ Run Windows Explorer from the command line.

■ Create and edit file types.

■ Move My Documents to a new location.

Besides dealing with applications, most Microsoft Windows users probably spend much of their computing time performing file maintenance chores such as copying and moving files and folders, creating new folders, renaming files, and deleting files and folders. The procedures for these basic tasks are all well known, so we won't cover them here. Instead, we'll look at quite a few techniques that you can incorporate into your file maintenance routines to take some of the drudgery out of this unglamorous side of Windows, and to help you perform these chores faster and more efficiently.

A Dozen Little-Known Windows Explorer Techniques

Since everyone has to perform file and folder maintenance chores, Windows Explorer (or its My Computer incarnation) is probably one of the most familiar of the programs that come with Windows XP. However, like any reasonably complex program, Windows Explorer has hidden nooks and crannies that few people have seen. This section presents our list of 12 of the most useful of these little-known Windows Explorer facts.

Viewing Extra Details

Windows Explorer's Details view (displayed when you select View, Details) is the preferred choice for power users because it shows you not only the name of each file but also its size, type, and the date it was last modified. These particulars are useful, to be sure, but Windows XP's version of Windows Explorer can display many more file tidbits, including the following:

- **For Music files**   Windows Explorer can show the duration, the bit rate at which the song was recorded, and sometimes even the artist and album name.

- **For Images**   Windows Explorer can show the image dimensions and, for digital camera images, the date the picture was taken and the camera model used.

- **For Microsoft Office files**   Windows Explorer can show the author name, document title, subject, comments, and number of pages.

To see these and other extra details, select View, Choose Details. The Choose Details dialog box that appears (see Figure 7-1) enables you to select the check boxes for the details you want to see, as well as rearrange the column order. Note, too, that you can also choose details by right-clicking any column header in Details view.

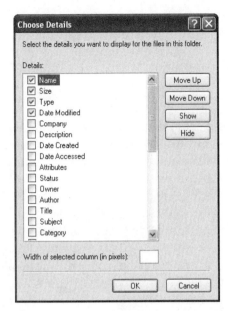

Figure 7-1   Use the Choose Details dialog box to add or remove columns in Windows Explorer's Details view.

Choosing "No To All" When Copying or Moving

When you copy or move a file and the destination folder has a file with the same name as a file in the original folder, the Confirm File Replace dialog box appears and asks whether you want to replace the file in the destination folder with the one being copied or moved. If you're moving multiple files and there are multiple potential file replacements in the destination folder, the dialog box will have a Yes To All button that you can click to avoid being prompted about each file.

That's fine if you want to replace every file, but what if you don't want to replace any files? Rather than clicking No for each prompt, hold down the Shift key and click No. This tells Windows Explorer not to replace any files, so it's the next best thing to having a No To All button.

Determining Selection Size

When you select one or more files and folders, the Windows Explorer status bar (which is turned off by default; select View, Status Bar to see it) shows you how many objects you've selected and the total size of the selected objects. However, the status bar numbers don't take into account any objects that might be inside a selected folder or subfolder. To allow for subfolders and their contents, right-click the selection and then select Properties. In the property sheet that appears, Windows Explorer shows you both the actual Size of the selected objects and the Size On Disk of the objects.

Insider Secret   What's the difference between the Size and Size On Disk values? Windows XP stores files in discrete chunks of hard disk space called *clusters*, which have a fixed size. This size depends on the file system and the size of the partition, but 4 KB is typical. The important thing to remember is that Windows XP always uses full clusters to store all or part of a file. Suppose, for example, that you have two files, one that's 2 KB and another that's 5 KB. The 2-KB file will be stored in an entire 4-KB cluster. For the 5-KB file, the first 4 KB of the file will take up a whole cluster, and the remaining 1 KB will be stored in its own 4-KB cluster. So the total size of these two files is 7 KB, but they take up 12 KB on the hard disk.

Running Windows Explorer in Full-Screen Mode

If you want the largest possible screen area for the contents of each folder, you can place Windows Explorer in *full-screen* mode by holding down Ctrl and clicking the Maximize button. (If Windows Explorer is already maximized, you first need to click the Restore button.) This mode takes over the entire screen, removes the text from the toolbar buttons, turns off the title bar, menu bar, status bar, and Address bar, and hides the Folders list. (To choose a menu command, hold down Alt and press the menu's accelerator key, such as Alt+F for the File menu; to see the Folders list, move the mouse pointer to the left edge of the screen.) To restore the window, click the Restore button.

Tip   You can customize the Windows Explorer toolbar to display a Full Screen button. Right-click the toolbar and then select Customize to display the Customize Toolbar dialog box. In the Available Toolbar Buttons list, click Full Screen and then click Add.

Making Quick Backup Copies

Before working on a file, you might want to make a backup copy just in case something goes wrong. A quick way to do this is to select the file, press Ctrl+C, and then Ctrl+V. This makes a copy of the file with *Copy of* preceding the name in the same folder as the original file. Note, too, that you can also use this trick with folders.

Dragging and Dropping via the Taskbar

This is a two-for-one tip:

- **Drag a file to a hidden window.**   If you want to drag a file from Windows Explorer and drop it on a window that you can't see (because one or more other windows are on top of it), first hover the mouse over that window's button on the taskbar. After a second or two, Windows XP will bring that window to the foreground, so you can then drop the file on the window.

- **Drag a file to the desktop.**   If you want to drag a file from Windows Explorer and drop it on the desktop (either to place it in the Recycle Bin or to create a desktop shortcut), and the desktop is covered, first hover the mouse over an empty area of the taskbar. After a second or two, Windows XP will minimize all open windows, leaving the desktop exposed. Drop the file on the desktop or on an application icon, not on the taskbar.

Customizing the Send To Command

Windows Explorer's Send To command (displayed when you select File, Send To or when you right-click a file name and then select Send To) displays a menu of locations, such as My Documents, or your floppy drive. If you select one of these menu items, Windows Explorer moves or copies the selected files or folders to that location. Interestingly, most of the Send To items are shortcuts that reside in the %UserProfile%\SendTo folder. (The exceptions are the Send To items that represent your floppy disk, writable CD drive, or other removable media.) This means that you're free to add your own shortcuts to this folder, and they'll appear on the Send To menu. For example, you could add a shortcut for a target folder, drive, or network drive that you use frequently. However, there's no reason you have to restrict the Send To commands to folders and disk drives only. Since you can create shortcuts for just about anything in Windows XP, you can populate the Send To folder with any number of

interesting destinations, including printers, the Recycle Bin, and even executable files (for sending documents to open in that program). To add such a destination, right-click and drag a resource—a printer entry from Control Panel, an
application's executable file in Windows Explorer, and the like—and then drop
the resource in the %UserProfile%\SendTo folder, selecting Create Shortcuts
Here from the shortcut menu.

Searching Faster with the Indexing Service

Windows Explorer's Search tool (accessed by selecting View, Explorer Bar,
Search, or by clicking the Search button) enables you to search for files based
on name, modification date, and size. But the most powerful Search feature is
the ability to search based on the contents of files. Enter a search term into the
A Word Or Phrase In The File text box, and Windows Explorer will match the
word or phrase with those files that contain the text. This process works well if
you're searching only a few documents, but if you have hundreds or even thou-
sands of documents, the search can be very slow. To speed things up considerably, use the Indexing Service, which indexes the files' contents so that the
search process examines just the index rather than the files themselves.

To use the Indexing Service, start the Search tool to open the Search Com-
panion in the left pane, click Change Preferences, click With Indexing Service,
and then select the Yes, Enable Indexing Service option.

Running Windows Explorer from the Command Line

For extra control over how Windows Explorer starts, you can use a few command-line options in the Run dialog box or from the command prompt. Here's
the syntax:

```
EXPLORER [/N]|[/E],[/ROOT,[folder]] [/SELECT,subfolder]
```

/N	Starts Windows Explorer without the Folders list.
/E	Starts Windows Explorer with the Folders list.
/ROOT,folder	Specifies the folder that will be the root of the new Windows Explorer view. (In other words, *folder* will appear at the top of the Folders list.) If you omit this switch, the desktop is displayed as the root.
/SELECT,subfolder	Specifies the subfolder of the root folder to display in the Folders list. If you don't also include the /ROOT switch, the subfolder is selected only in the contents pane.

> **Note**   If you run the EXPLORER command without any switches, Windows XP launches My Computer.

For example, if you want to open Windows Explorer with C:\Windows as the root and you want the C:\Windows\System32 folder displayed in the contents pane, use the following command:

```
explorer /e, /root,c:\windows /select,c:\windows\system32
```

Here's another example that opens Windows Explorer with the current user's profile folder selected:

```
explorer /e, /root, /select,%userprofile%
```

> **Tip**   A quick way to start Windows Explorer is to press ⊞+E. If you want to start Windows Explorer with the Search bar activated, press ⊞+F.

Moving the My Documents Folder

The default location of the My Documents folder is %UserProfile% \My Documents. This is not a great location because, in general, it means that your documents and Windows XP are on the same hard disk partition. If you have to wipe that partition in order to reinstall Windows XP or some other operating system, you'll need to back up your documents first. Similarly, you may have another partition on your system that has lots of free disk space, so you may prefer to store your documents there. For these and other reasons, moving the location of My Documents is a good idea. Here's how:

1. In Windows Explorer, right-click My Documents and then select Properties. The property sheet for My Documents appears.

2. On the Target tab, use the Target text box to enter the drive and folder where you want your documents stored. (Or click Move to select the folder using a dialog box.).

3. Click OK. (If Windows Explorer asks if you want to create the new folder and then to move your documents to the new location, click Yes in both cases.)

Restricting Windows Explorer's Features with Group Policies

If other people use your computer, you might want to disable certain features of Windows Explorer to prevent problems. For example, you might want to remove the Folder Options command from the Tools menu, hide certain drives, or disable Windows XP's CD burning features. You can do all of this and much more via the Group Policy editor. Select User Configuration\Administrative Templates\Windows Components\Windows Explorer, and enable the policies you want to work with (see Figure 7-2).

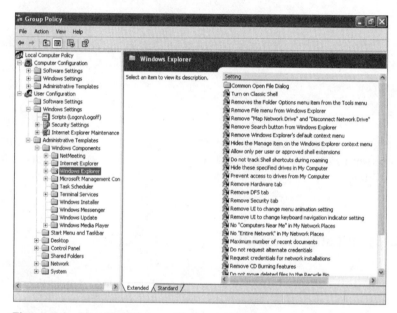

Figure 7-2   Use the Windows Explorer policies to customize Windows Explorer for the current user.

Working with Compressed Folders

When you download files from the Internet, they often arrive as ZIP files (they use the .zip extension). These are compressed archive files that contain one or more files that have been compressed for faster downloading. Windows XP offers built-in support for these files, but calls them *compressed folders*. Why a "folder"? Because a ZIP file "contains" one or more files, just like a regular folder. As you'll see, this makes it easy to deal with the files within the ZIP file, and it enables Windows XP to offer a few useful compression and decompression features.

To see what's inside a ZIP file, double-click it. Windows XP opens a new folder window that shows the name of the ZIP file in the Folders list and the files within the ZIP file in the Contents list. From here, use the following techniques to work with the archived files:

- To extract some or all of the files, select them, drag them out of the compressed folder, and then drop them on the destination folder.

- To extract all the files, select File, Extract All to launch the Extraction Wizard.

- To run a file (such as a program's setup file) from the compressed folder, double-click the file. Likewise, if the file is an object file and you double-click that file name, the program associated with the object file's extension is started and the object is opened in that application program.

Besides viewing existing ZIP files, Windows XP also enables you to create new ZIP files via either of these two methods:

- Select the objects you want to store in the ZIP file and then run the File, Send To, Compressed (Zipped) Folder command. Windows XP creates a ZIP file with the same primary name as the first selected file. For example, if the first file is Project.doc, the compressed folder is Project.zip.

- Create a new, empty ZIP file by selecting the File, New, Compressed (Zipped) Folder command. Windows XP creates a new ZIP file with an active text box for the new file name. Edit the name and press Enter. You can then drag the files you want to archive and drop them on the ZIP file.

> **Tip**   If you don't want just anyone to be able to extract files from a ZIP, Windows XP enables you to encrypt a ZIP with a password. To do this, double-click the ZIP to open it, and then select File, Add A Password. Use the Add Password dialog box to enter a password (twice) and click OK.

Getting Familiar with File Types

A document's *file type* is determined by the extension used in its file name, and it defines which actions you can perform on the document. For example, a text document—that is, a document with a name that ends with .txt—has two actions: Open, which displays the document in Notepad; and Print, which sends the document to the Windows XP default printer. (Technically, the Print action opens Notepad, loads the document, selects File, Print, and then closes Notepad. This all happens in the blink of an eye.) Each file type has a default action that runs when you double-click a document of that type. (For text files, the default action is Open.) When a file name is selected in Windows Explorer, the default action appears in bold type on the File menu and on the document's shortcut menu.

File types that have associated actions are said to be *registered* with Windows XP (because this data is stored in the registry). To see the list of Windows XP's registered file types, start Windows Explorer, select Tools, Folder Options to display the Folder Options dialog box, and then select the File Types tab. As you can see in Figure 7-3, the Registered File Types list shows the extensions for each registered file type. When you select one of these items, the Details section of the dialog box shows the application (if any) that opens the file type.

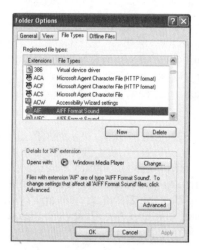

Figure 7-3 The File Types tab displays a list of Windows XP's registered file types.

Modifying Actions for an Existing File Type

If an existing file type uses an action you don't like, it's easy enough to change it. For example, if you create lots of HTML files, you might prefer them to open in Notepad instead of Microsoft Internet Explorer. The next few sections show you how to modify file type actions.

Changing the Application Associated with a File Type

Use the Open With list to display the Open With dialog box, as we discussed in Chapter 3. Remember to select the Always Use The Selected Program To Open This Kind Of File check box. Note, too, that you can also get to the Open With dialog box via the File Types tab. Use the Registered File Types list to select the file type you want, and then click the Change button.

Changing a File Type Action

Follow these steps to change a file type action:

1. Use the File Types tab to select the file type you want to work with, and then click the Advanced button. The Edit File Type dialog box appears.

2. Use the Actions list to select the action you want to change, and then click Edit. The Editing Action For Type dialog box appears.

3. Use the Action text box to change the name of the action (this is optional), and use the Application Used To Perform Action text box to enter the full path of the application you want to use for the action. Here are some notes to bear in mind:

   ❑ If the path of the executable file contains a space, be sure to enclose the path in quotation marks, like so:
   ```
   "C:\Program Files\My HTML Editor\editor.exe"
   ```

   ❑ If you'll be using documents that have spaces in their file names, add the "%1" parameter after the path:
   ```
   "C:\Program Files\My HTML Editor\editor.exe" "%1"
   ```

   The %1 part tells the application to load the specified file (such as a file name you click), and the quotation marks ensure that no problems occur with multiple-word file names.

   ❑ If you're changing the Print action, be sure to include the /P switch after the application's path, like this:
   ```
   "C:\Program Files\My HTML Editor\editor.exe" /P
   ```

Creating a New Action for a File Type

Instead of replacing an action's underlying application with a different application, you might prefer to create new actions. In our HTML file example, you could keep the default Open action as it is and create a new action—called, for example, Open For Editing—that uses Notepad (or another text editor) to open an HTML file. When you select an HTML file and open the File menu, or right-click an HTML file, the menu that appears will show both commands: Open (to invoke Internet Explorer) and Open For Editing (to invoke Notepad). To create a new action for an existing file type, follow these steps:

1. Use the File Types tab to select the file type and then click Advanced to display the Edit File Type dialog box.

2. Click New to display the New Action dialog box.

3. Use the Action text box to enter a name for the action.

> **Insider Secret**   In the Action text box, if you precede a letter with an ampersand (&), Windows XP designates that letter as the menu accelerator key. For example, entering **Open For &Editing** defines E as the accelerator key. You can then press this letter's key to select the command on either the File menu or the shortcut menu.

4. Use the Application Used To Perform Action text box to enter the full path of the application you want to use for the new action. (Follow the guidelines that we outlined in the previous section.)

5. Click OK.

Changing the Default Action

To change a file type's default action, follow these steps:

1. Use the File Types tab to select the file type and then click Advanced to display the Edit File Type dialog box.

2. Select the action in the Actions list.

3. Click Set Default; you should now be able to see the selected action displayed in bold type. (If there is but a single action listed, the Set Default button will not be active.)

4. Click OK.

Insider Secret When you're working in Windows Explorer, you occasionally may find that you need to do some work at the command prompt. For example, the current folder may contain multiple files that need to be renamed, a task that's most easily done within a command line session. Selecting Start, All Programs, Accessories, Command Prompt starts the session in the %UserProfile% folder, so you have to use one or more CD commands to get to the folder you want to work in. An easier way would be to create a new action for the Folder file type that launches the command prompt and automatically displays the current Windows Explorer folder. To do this, select Folder in the File Type column in the Registered File Types list on the File Types tab, click Advanced, and click New. Type **Command Prompt** in the Action text box, and enter the following in the Application Used To Perform Action text box

```
cmd.exe /k cd "%L"
```

The %L placeholder represents the name of the folder in which the command prompt will appear. Using %L directs Windows XP to display the folder's long path at the prompt. Note, too, that you can't edit or delete the new action in the Edit File Type dialog box. If you need to make changes to the action, use the following registry key:

```
HKCR\Folder\shell\
```

Creating a New File Type

Windows XP defines well over 200 file types, but that isn't nearly enough to cover every possible extension. For example, many applications come with text files named Read.me or Readme.1st. It would be handy to associate these text files with Notepad. That's not a problem because Windows XP lets you define new file types and create actions for them.

Tip If you use Microsoft Word, the .doc extension is associated with Word rather than WordPad. If you like to create small notes in WordPad, it's a pain to double-click these files and have them open in Word. Instead, you should create a new file type for WordPad documents (using an extension of, say, .pad or .wpd).

If all you want is to set up an association between a particular file extension and an application, use the Open With list. That is, right-click a file that uses the extension, select Open With, and then select the application you want to use. Again, remember to select the Always Use The Selected Program To Open This Kind Of File check box.

If you need to define more than just the Open action for a new file type (for example, you might also want a Print action for the file type), you need to use the File Types tab. Here are the steps to follow:

1. On the File Types tab, click the New button. The Create New Extension dialog box appears.

2. Enter the new extension in the File Extension text box.

3. If you want the new file type to have the same actions as an existing file type, click Advanced and use the Associated File Type list to select the file type you want to use.

4. Click OK.

If you didn't associate the new file type with an existing file type, use the Change and Advanced buttons on the File Types tab to modify the new file type's actions, as we discussed in the previous section. However, if you did associate the new file type with an existing file type, you should select the new entry in the Registered File Types list, click the Advanced button, and ensure that the listed actions are appropriate for this new file type, and that the correct action—if any—is selected as the default.

Notes from the Real World

As a consultant, I am obliged to carry my office around with me in the form of a laptop. This represents both an asset and, sometimes, a liability. Like many computer-using professionals, I have to back up my laptop files to limit my liability from losses in the unfortunate event that my laptop is stolen or damaged. Any number of software programs and backup devices can be configured to do this, but I have an even easier way, and it's built right into Windows XP.

The feature is called *offline files*, and what I do is set up a network-shared folder on the computer in my home and also set up my laptop to work with those files offline. After creating the original set of new files on the home computer and saving them in that network-shared folder, I can then use this feature on my laptop to store all of my documents in the "offline files" folder on the laptop, and that folder is automatically synchronized every time I connect to my home network. In this way, I always have an up-to-date version of my files on both my laptop and my home computer! The steps to accomplish this synchronization are as follows:

1. On the laptop computer, turn off Fast User Switching if it's currently selected; see Chapter 5, "Managing Logons and Users," for details. (You can't use offline files while Fast User Switching is selected.)

2. On the laptop, open Windows Explorer and select Tools, Folder Options to display the Folder Options dialog box.

3. On the Offline Files tab, select the Enable Offline Files check box, as shown in Figure 7-4.

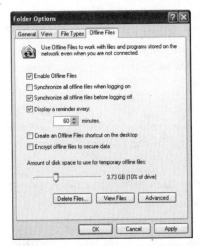

Figure 7-4   Select the Enable Offline Files check box to establish support for offline files.

(continued)

Notes from the Real World   *(continued)*

4. Select Synchronize All Offline Files Before Logging Off to get a full synchronization. A full synchronization ensures that you have the most current version of every shared network file that you work with offline. Alternatively, leave this check box cleared for a quick synchronization. A quick synchronization ensures that you have complete versions of your offline files, although they may not be the most current versions. You might select a quick synchronization if you are the only person working on a file or if you do not need the most current version of a file.

5. Set the other options, as needed, and then click OK.

Here are some notes to bear in mind when working with offline files on the laptop:

- **Making a file or folder available offline.** Open Windows Explorer, navigate to the home computer's listing of files and folders, right-click the shared folder or file you want to work with on the laptop, and then select Make Available Offline. The first time you do this, the Offline Files Wizard appears so that you can set some options for offline files. In subsequent operations, Windows XP just synchronizes the folder or file by placing it in your laptop computer's Offline Files folder.

- **Synchronizing offline files.** In Windows Explorer, select the Tools, Synchronize command, select the check boxes beside the items you want to synchronize in the Offline Files list, and then click Synchronize.

- **Viewing a list of all offline files.** In Windows Explorer, select the Tools, Folder Options command, select the Offline Files tab, and click View Files.

- **Making a network file or folder unavailable offline.** In Windows Explorer, right-click the shared network file or folder and then clear the Make Available Offline command. Note that when an entire folder is selected and made available for offline processing, you cannot subsequently select any of the individual files in that folder to make them unavailable.

—Geoff Winslow

Customizing the Windows XP New Menu

One of the handiest features in Windows XP is the New menu, which allows you to create a new file without working within an application. In Windows Explorer, select File, New, or right-click inside the Contents pane and select New. On the submenu that appears, you'll see items that create new documents of various file types, including a folder, shortcut, bitmap image, WordPad document (or Word document, if Word is installed on the computer), text document, compressed folder, and possibly many others, depending on your system configuration and the applications you have installed.

What mechanism determines whether a file type appears on the New menu? The registry, of course. To see how this works, start the Registry Editor and open the HKEY_CLASSES_ROOT key. As we discuss in Chapter 2, the first 300 or so subkeys of HKEY_CLASSES_ROOT are the file extensions that Windows XP recognizes. Most of these keys contain only a `Default` setting that takes either of the following values:

- If the extension is registered with Windows XP, the `Default` value is a string pointing to the file type associated with the extension. For example, the default value for `.txt` is txtfile (text document).

- If the extension isn't registered with Windows XP, the `Default` value isn't set.

A few of these extension keys, however, also have subkeys. For example, open the .bmp key and you see that it has a subkey named `ShellNew`. This subkey is what determines whether a file type appears on the New menu. Specifically, if the extension is registered with Windows XP and it has a `ShellNew` subkey, the New menu sprouts a command for the associated file type.

The `ShellNew` subkey always contains a setting that determines how Windows XP creates the new file. Four settings are possible:

- **NullFile**   This setting, the value of which is always set to a null string (""), tells Windows XP to create an empty file of the associated type. Of the file types that appear on the New menu, three use the `NullFile` setting: Text Document (.txt), Bitmap Image (.bmp), and Wordpad Document (.doc).

- **FileName**   This setting tells Windows XP to create the new file by making a copy of another file. Windows XP has special hidden folders to hold these "template" files. These folders are user-specific, so you'll find them in %UserProfile%\Template. On the New menu, only the Wave Sound (.wav) file type uses the FileName setting, and its value is Sndrec.wav To see this value, you need to open the following key:

`HKCR\.wav\ShellNew`

- **Command** This setting tells Windows XP to create the new file by executing a specific command. This command usually invokes an executable file with a few parameters. Two of the New menu's commands use this setting:

  - ❏ **Shortcut** The `HKCR\.lnk\ShellNew` key contains the following value for the `Command` setting:
    rundll32.exe appwiz.cpl,NewLinkHere %1

  - ❏ **Briefcase** In the `HKCR\.bfc\ShellNew` key, you'll see the following value for the `Command` setting:
    %SystemRoot%\system32\rundll32.exe %SystemRoot%\system32\syncui.dll,Briefcase_Create %2!d! %1

- **Data** This setting contains a binary value, and when Windows XP creates the new file, it copies this binary value into the file. The New menu's Compressed (Zipped) Folder command uses this setting, which you can find here:

`HKCR\.zip\CompressedFolder\ShellNew`

Insider Secret You'll notice that some extension keys have multiple `ShellNew` subkeys. For example, in a default installation of Windows XP, the .doc key has four `ShellNew` subkeys:

```
.doc\ShellNew
.doc\Word.Document.6\ShellNew
.doc\WordDocument\ShellNew
.doc\WordPad.Document.1\ShellNew
```

Which of these subkeys does Windows XP use when constructing its New menu? The answer is: the subkey that corresponds to the registered file type. In a default installation of Windows XP, for .doc files, the registered file type is WordPad.Document.1, so it's the `.doc\WordPad.Document.1\ShellNew` subkey that Windows XP uses in the New menu.

Adding File Types to the New Menu

To make the New menu even more convenient, you can add new file types for documents you work with regularly. For any file type that's registered with Windows XP, you follow a simple three-step process:

1. Add a `ShellNew` subkey to the appropriate extension key in HKEY_CLASSES_ROOT.

2. Add one of the four settings discussed in the preceding section (`NullFile`, `FileName`, `Command`, or `Data`).

3. Enter a value for the setting.

In most cases, the easiest way to go is to use `NullFile` to create an empty file. The `FileName` setting, however, can be quite powerful because you can set up a template file containing text and other data.

Deleting File Types from the New Menu

Many Windows XP applications (such as Microsoft Office) like to add their file types to the New menu. If you find that your New menu is getting crowded, you can delete some commands to keep things manageable. To do this, you need to find the appropriate extension in the registry and delete its `ShellNew` subkey.

> **Caution**   Instead of permanently deleting a `ShellNew` subkey, you can tread a more cautious path by simply renaming the key (to, for example, ShellNewOld). This will still prevent Windows XP from adding the item to the New menu, but it also means that you can restore the item just by restoring the original key name.

Customizing Windows XP's Open With List

As mentioned in the previous chapter and again earlier in this chapter, you can use Windows XP's Open With feature to open a document in an application other than the one it's normally associated with. This is a great feature that saves a lot of file-type twiddling, and you can make this capability even better by customizing the list of programs that Open With displays in either the submenu or the dialog box.

First, however, you need to know how Windows XP compiles the list of applications that Open With displays:

■ Windows XP checks `HKCR\.ext` (where *ext* is the extension that defines the file type). If it finds an `OpenWith` subkey, the applications listed under that subkey are added to the Open With menu, and they also appear in the Open With dialog box in the Recommended Programs group.

■ Windows XP checks `HKCR\.ext` to see if the file type has a `PerceivedType` setting. If so, it means the file type also has an associated *perceived type*. This is a broader type that groups related file types into a single category. For example, the Image perceived type includes files of type BMP, GIF, and JPEG, while the Text perceived type includes the files of type TXT, HTM, and XML. Windows XP then checks HKCR\SystemFileAssociations*PerceivedType*\OpenWithList, where *PerceivedType* is the value of the file type's `PerceivedType` setting. The application keys listed under the `OpenWithList` key are added to the file type's Open With menu and dialog box.

■ Windows XP checks `HKCR\Applications`, which contains subkeys named after application executable files. If an application subkey has a `\shell\open\command` subkey, and if that subkey's `Default` value is set to the path of the application's executable file, then the application is added to the Open With dialog box.

■ Windows XP checks the following key:

```
HKCU\Software\Microsoft\Windows\CurrentVersion\Explorer
\FileExts\.ext\OpenWithList
```

Here, *ext* is the file type's extension. This key contains settings for each application that the current user has used to open the file type via Open With. These settings are named a, b, c, and so on, and there's an MRUList setting that lists these letters in the order in which the applications have been used. These applications are added to the file type's Open With menu.

Removing an Application from a File Type's Open With Menu

When you use the Open With dialog box to choose an alternative application to open a particular file type, that application appears on the file type's Open With menu (that is, the menu that appears when you select the File, Open With command). To remove the application from this menu, open the following registry key (where *ext* is the file type's extension):

```
HKCU\Software\Microsoft\Windows\CurrentVersion\Explorer
\FileExts\.ext\OpenWithList
```

Delete the setting for the application you want removed from the menu. Also, edit the MRUList setting to remove the letter of the application you just deleted. For example, if the application setting you deleted was named b, delete the letter b from the MRUList setting.

Removing a Program from the Open With List

Rather than customizing only a single file type's Open With menu, you may need to customize the Open With dialog box for all file types. To prevent a program from appearing in the Open With list, open the Registry Editor and navigate to the following key:

```
HKCR\Applications
```

Here you'll find a number of subkeys, each of which represents an application installed on your system. The names of these subkeys are the names of each application's executable file (such as notepad.exe for Notepad). To prevent Windows XP from displaying an application in the Open With list, select the application's subkey, and create a new string value named NoOpenWith. (You don't have to supply a value for this setting.) To restore the application to the Open With list, delete the NoOpenWith setting.

Insider Secret   The NoOpenWith setting works only for applications that are not the default for opening a particular file type. For example, if you add NoOpenWith to the notepad.exe subkey, Notepad will still appear in the Open With list for text documents, but it won't appear for other file types, such as HTML files.

Adding a Program to the Open With List

You can also add an application to the Open With dialog box for all file types. Again, you head for the following registry key:

```
HKCR\Applications
```

Display the subkey named after the application's executable file. (If the subkey doesn't exist, create it.) Now add the `\shell\open\command` subkey and set the `Default` value to the path of the application's executable file.

Disabling the Open With Check Box

The Open With dialog box enables you to change the application associated with a file type's Open action by selecting the Always Use The Selected Program To Open This Kind Of File check box. If you share your computer with other people, you might not want them changing this association, either accidentally or purposefully. In that case, you can clear the check box by adjusting the following registry key:

```
HKCR\Unknown\shell\openas\command
```

The Default value of this key is the following:

```
%SystemRoot%\system32\rundll32.exe %SystemRoot%\system32
\shell32.dll,OpenAs_RunDLL %1
```

To clear the check box in the Open With dialog box, append %2 to the end of the Default value:

```
%SystemRoot%\system32\rundll32.exe %SystemRoot%\system32
\shell32.dll,OpenAs_RunDLL %1 %2
```

8

Playing, Copying, and Storing Digital Media

In this chapter, you'll learn how to:

■　Control Windows Media Player playback.

■　Set options for copying tracks to and from an audio CD.

■　Get the most out of Windows Explorer's digital media features.

■　Work with digital media files.

■　Customize digital media folders.

■　Download and use the Windows Media Bonus Pack.

Microsoft Windows XP has many new and improved features, from the updated interface to fast user switching to improved support for the latest hardware gadgets. But it really seems as though the busiest of the programming bees must have been the digital media team. Windows XP is loaded with new digital media features, including a new and much improved version of Windows Media Player; dedicated and enhanced media folders (such as My Pictures and My Music); image optimization for sending files via e-mail; the ability to print digital photos online; a wizard that helps you print photos; the ability to burn recordable compact discs (CD-Rs) and rewritable compact discs (CD-RWs); and the ability to work with digital camera storage directly from Windows Explorer.

For most of these features, the basics are fairly easy to learn and don't require much coaching. But this book is dedicated to exploring the shadowy nooks of Windows XP, particularly those places that make things easier to use or more powerful. The digital media features of Windows XP have plenty of these hidden and obscure areas, and we'll take you through them in this chapter to help you get the most out of playing media, copying audio tracks, managing media files, and customizing media folders.

Tips for Working with Windows Media Player

You saw earlier that Windows supports all kinds of multimedia formats. In previous versions of Windows, the bad news was that to play those formats you had to master a passel of player programs. In Windows XP, the good news is that you need now wrestle with only a single program: Media Player. This clever chunk of software is a true one-stop multimedia shop that's capable of playing sound files, music files, audio CDs, animations, movie files, and even DVDs. It can even copy audio CD tracks to your computer, burn music files to a CD, tune in to Internet radio stations, and more.

If you don't see the Windows Media Player icon on the main Start menu, you can convince it to come out to play by selecting Start, All Programs, Windows Media Player.

Playing Media Files

You can open files directly from Media Player by selecting either Open (to launch a media file from your computer or from a network location) or Open URL (to launch a media file from the Internet) from the File menu. Use the controls at the bottom of the Media Player window to control the playback.

Windows XP also gives you many indirect ways to play media files via Media Player. Here's a summary:

■   Open Windows Explorer, find the media file you want to play, and then double-click the file.

> **Note**   To control the media file types that are associated with Media Player, click the Show Menu Bar button in the top left corner of the Media Player window, select Tools, Options and display the File Types tab. Select the check boxes for the file types that you want to open automatically in Media Player. If you don't want Media Player to handle a particular file type, clear its check box.

■ Insert an audio CD in your CD or DVD drive. If you have a hardware or software DVD decoder installed on your system, you can automatically start playing media files by inserting a DVD disc in your DVD drive.

■ If you have a CompactFlash drive, insert a CompactFlash card that contains music files. If Windows XP asks what you want to do with this disk, select Play The Music Files. If you don't want to be bothered with this dialog box each time, select the Always Do The Selected Action check box. Click OK.

■ Download media from the Internet.

Tip Here are a few Media Player shortcut keys that you may find useful while playing media files:

Ctrl+P	Play or pause the current media
Ctrl+S	Stop the current media
Ctrl+B	Go to the previous track
Ctrl+Shift+B	Rewind to the beginning of the media
Ctrl+F	Go to the next track
Ctrl+Shift+F	Fast forward to the end of the media
Ctrl+H	Toggle Shuffle playback
Ctrl+T	Toggle Repeat playback
Ctrl+E	Eject the disc from the CD or DVD drive
Ctrl+1	Switch to Full mode
Ctrl+2	Switch to Skin mode
F8	Mute sound
F9	Decrease volume
F10	Increase volume

Setting Media Player's Playback Options

Media Player comes with several options that you can work with to control various aspects of the playback. To see these options, select Tools, Options. The Player tab (see Figure 8-1 on the following page) contains several settings.

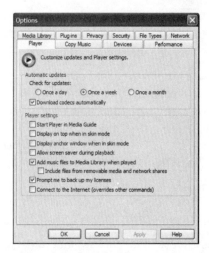

Figure 8-1 Use the Player tab to configure Media Player's playback options.

- **Check For Updates** Use this option to determine how often Media Player checks for newer versions of the program. To prevent Media Player from displaying a message that an update is available, create a string setting named **AskMeAgain** in the following registry key and set its value to **no**:

  ```
  HKLM\SOFTWARE\Microsoft\MediaPlayer\PlayerUpgrade
  ```

  You can also prevent Media Player from automatically updating itself if it detects that a newer version is available. Create the following key, and then add a DWORD value called **DisableAutoUpdate** and set its value to **1**:

  ```
  HKLM\SOFTWARE\Policies\Microsoft\WindowsMediaPlayer
  ```

- **Download Codecs Automatically** A *codec* enables Media Player to play a particular file format. If this check box is selected, Media Player will automatically attempt to download and install a codec for any file type that it doesn't recognize. If you prefer to be prompted before the download occurs, clear this check box. You can disable this check box using the Group Policy Editor. Select User Configuration, Administrative Templates, Windows Components, Windows Media Player, Playback and enable the Prevent Codec Download policy.

■ **Allow Internet Sites To Uniquely Identify Your Player**   (In Media Player 9, this check box is called Send Unique Player ID To Content Providers, and it's on the Privacy tab.) When this check box is selected, Media Player generates an identifier that is unique to your copy of Media Player. When you're listening to streaming content, this enables a remote Internet server to monitor your connection and, if necessary, make adjustments to improve the quality of the stream. No personal content is delivered to the site, but theoretically a remote site could use the unique identifier to track what you listen to and possibly display targeted ads or other unwelcome content. If you're concerned about this, clear this check box.

> **Caution**   Playing a file from an Internet site can present a more serious problem: A malicious script could be embedded within the file. To prevent Media Player from executing such scripts, add a DWORD value named **PlayerScriptCommands Enabled** to the following registry key and set its value to **0**:
>
> `HKCU\Software\Microsoft\MediaPlayer\Preferences\`
>
> In Media Player 9, this is accomplished by simply clearing Run Script Commands When Present on the Security tab. Note, too, that for users of Media Player 8 this problem has been fixed in a security patch. See the following security bulletin for more information and a link to the patch: *http://www.microsoft.com/technet/security/bulletin/MS02-032.asp*

■ **Acquire Licenses Automatically**   (In Media Player 9, this check box is called Acquire Licenses Automatically For Protected Content, and it's on the Privacy tab.) When this check box is selected, Media Player will automatically attempt to get a license for a file if it requires one. If you'd rather that Media Player not acquire licenses automatically, clear this check box.

■ **Start Player In Media Guide**   When this check box is selected, Media Player displays its Media Guide tab at startup, which requires Internet access. This can delay the startup, depending on the speed of your Internet connection, so you can disable the Media Guide startup by clearing this check box.

> **Note**   You can view the license information for a file from within Media Player. In either the Media Library or the playlist, right-click the file name, select Properties, and then select the License Information tab (the License tab, in Media Player 9). It's also a good idea to back up your licenses regularly. To do this, select Tools, License Management, choose a location for the backup, and then click Backup Now (Back Up Now, in Media Player 9).

- **Display On Top When In Skin Mode**   When this check box is selected, Media Player stays on top of other windows when you switch to Skin mode. You can configure Media Player to play only in Skin mode using the Group Policy Editor. Select User Configuration, Administrative Templates, Windows Components, Windows Media Player, User Interface, and enable the Set And Lock Skin policy. Also, use the Skin text box to specify the name of a skin file. (Note that skin files use the .wmz extension; the default skins can be found in the %ProgramFiles%\Windows Media Player\Skins folder.)

- **Display Anchor Window When In Skin Mode**   When this check box is selected, Media Player displays a small window in the lower right corner of the screen when you switch to Skin mode. You can disable this check box using the Group Policy Editor. Select User Configuration, Administrative Templates, Windows Components, Windows Media Player, User Interface, and enable the Do Not Show Anchor policy.

- **Allow Screen Saver During Playback**   When this check box is selected, the Windows XP screen saver is allowed to kick in after the system has been idle for the specified number of minutes. If you're watching streaming video content or a DVD movie, leave this check box cleared to prevent the screen saver from being activated.

Insider Secret   Media Player's File menu lists the last few media files that you opened using the File, Open and the File, Open URL commands. If you don't want these recent files to appear the next time that Media Player is opened, open the Registry Editor and delete the following keys:

```
HKCU\Software\Microsoft\MediaPlayer\Player
\RecentFileList
```

```
HKCU\Software\Microsoft\MediaPlayer\Player
\RecentURLList
```

(Note that these keys are created only after you've used the Open and Open URL commands, respectively, at least once.) Here's a VBScript that will do this (be sure to save the file with the .vbs extension):

```
On Error Resume Next
Set wshShell = WScript.CreateObject("WScript.Shell")
strKey = "HKCU\Software\Microsoft\MediaPlayer\Player\"
wshShell.RegDelete strKey & "RecentFileList\"
wshShell.RegDelete strKey & "RecentURLList\"
Set wshShell = Nothing
```

Note, too, that the Windows Media Bonus Pack (discussed later in this chapter; see "Investigating the Windows Media Bonus Pack") has a feature that will do this for you.

If you want to prevent Media Player from adding items to the recent file list, add the binary value **AddToMRU** to the following key and set its value to **00**:

```
HKCU\Software\Microsoft\MediaPlayer\Preferences
```

To reinstate Media Player's ability to add items to the recent file list, change the AddToMRU value to 01.

Media Player 9 enables you to determine up front whether you want items saved to the recent file list. During installation, when the Select Your Privacy Options screen appears, clear the Save File And URL History In The Player check box. To turn this feature back on after Media Player 9 is installed, select Tools, Options, display the Privacy tab, and select the Save File And URL History In The Player check box. The Privacy tab in Media Player 9 also enables you clear the recent file list by clicking the Clear History button. To delete the list of recent CDs and DVDs, click Clear CD/DVD.

- **Add Items To Media Library When Played** (This is called Add Music Files To Media Library When Played, in Media Player 9.) When this check box is selected, Media Player adds music files that you play to the Media Library. For example, if you play a downloaded MP3 file, Media Player adds it to the Media Library in the Audio, All Audio category. Note that by default, Media Player doesn't add media from removable media to the library.

- **Include Items From Removable Media** (This is called Include Files From Removable Media And Network Shares, in Media Player 9.) When this check box is selected, Media Player adds items from removable media, such as a CompactFlash card, to the library when played. Note that you won't be able to play these items unless the removable media is inserted.

- **Connect To The Internet (Overrides Other Commands)** When selected, this Media Player 9 check box enables the program to connect to the Internet even if the File, Work Offline command is selected. This is useful if you want a feature such as the Media Guide to access the Internet even in offline mode.

- **Prompt Me To Back Up My Licenses** When this Media Player 9 check box is selected, Media Player reminds you to back up your digital media licenses approximately two weeks after you acquire them.

Copying Music from an Audio CD

Media Player comes with the welcome ability to copy (*rip* in the vernacular) tracks from an audio CD to your computer's hard disk. While this process is straightforward, note that you'll need to take several options into account before you start copying. These options include the location of the folder in which the ripped tracks will be stored, the structure of the track file names, the file format to use, and the quality (bit rate) at which you want to copy the tracks. You control all of these settings on the Copy Music tab of the Media Player's Options dialog box (select Tools, Options to get there), shown in Figure 8-2.

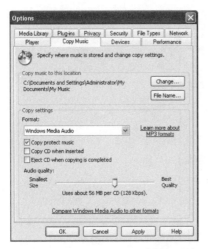

Figure 8-2   Use the Copy Music tab to specify the options you want to use when copying tracks from an audio CD.

Selecting a Location and File Name Structure

The Copy Music To This Location section of the dialog box displays the name of the folder that will be used to store the copied tracks. By default, this location is %UserProfile%\My Documents\My Music. To specify a different folder (for example, a folder on a partition with lots of free space), click Change and use the Browse For Folder dialog box to choose the new folder.

The default file names that Media Player generates for each copied track use the following structure:

Track_Number Song_Title.ext

Here, *Track_Number* is the song's track number on the CD, *Song_Title* is the name of the song, and *.ext* is the extension used by the recording format (such as .wma or .mp3). Media Player can also include additional data in the file name such as the artist name, the album name, the music genre, and the recording bit rate. To control which of these details is incorporated into the name, click the Advanced button (or the File Name button in Media Player 9) on the Copy Music tab to display the File Name Options dialog box, shown in Figure 8-3. Select the check box beside each of the details you want in the file names, and use the Move Up and Move Down buttons to determine the order of the details. Finally, use the Separator list to choose which character to use to separate each detail.

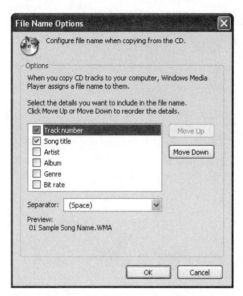

Figure 8-3   Use the File Name Options dialog box to specify the details you want in the file name assigned to each copied audio CD track.

Choosing the Recording File Format

As originally installed, Media Player supports only a single file format: WMA (Windows Media Audio). This is an excellent music format that provides good quality recordings at high compression rates. If you plan to listen to the tracks only on your computer or on a custom CD, the WMA format is all that you need. However, if you have an MP3 player or other device that doesn't recognize WMA files, you'll need to use the MP3 recording format. To get that, you need to purchase and install an MP3 encoder. On the Copy Music tab, click the MP3 Information button (in Media Player 9, click the Learn More About MP3 Formats link) to view a Microsoft Web site that has links to several third-party MP3 encoding packages.

If you have multiple encoders installed, on the Copy Music tab, use the File Format list to choose the encoder you want to use. Note that if you select Windows Media Audio, the Protect Content check box (it's called Copy Protect Music in Media Player 9) becomes enabled. Here's how this check box affects your copying:

- If Protect Content is selected, Media Player applies a license to each track that prevents you from copying the track to another computer or to any portable device that is SDMI-compliant. (SDMI is the Secure Digital Music Initiative; see *www.sdmi.org* for more information.) Note, however, that you are allowed to copy the track to a writable CD.

- If Protect Content is cleared, there are no restrictions on where or how you can copy the track. As long as you're copying tracks for personal use, clearing this check box is the most convenient route to take.

Specifying the Quality of the Recording

The tracks on an audio CD use the CD Audio Track file format (.cda extension), which represents the raw (uncompressed) audio data. You can't work with these files directly because the CDA format isn't supported by Windows XP and because these files tend to be huge (usually double-digit megabytes, depending on the track). Instead, the tracks need to be converted into a Windows XP–supported format (such as WMA). This conversion always involves compressing the tracks to a more manageable size. However, because the compression process operates by removing extraneous data from the file (that is, it's a *lossy* compression), there's a tradeoff between file size and music quality. That is, the higher the compression, the smaller the resulting file, but the poorer the sound quality. Conversely, the lower the compression, the larger the file, but the better the sound quality. Generally, how you handle this tradeoff depends on how much hard disk space you have to store the files and how sensitive your ear is to the sound quality.

The recording quality is usually measured in bits per second (this is called the *bit rate*), with higher values producing better quality and larger files. To specify the recording quality, use the Copy Music At This Quality slider (it's called Audio Quality in Media Player 9) on the Copy Music tab. Move the slider to the right for higher quality recordings, and to the left for lower quality. Note that Media Player 9 provides two new formats for copying files: Windows Media Audio (Variable Bit Rate) and Windows Media Audio Lossless. Either is available in the Format list in the Copy Settings section of the Copy Music tab. Values available on the Audio Quality slider are changed accordingly.

Copying Tracks from an Audio CD

Once you've made your recording choices, you're ready to start ripping tracks. Here are the steps to follow:

1. Insert the audio CD.

2. Click Copy From CD on the Media Player taskbar. Media Player displays a list of the available tracks. (To get the track names, connect to the Internet, click Get Names, and then click the Finish button.)

3. Select the check boxes beside the tracks you want to copy.

4. Click Copy Music. (The first time you perform this step in Media Player 9, you will encounter two additional dialog boxes that deal with copyright and media protection.) Processing these files can take some time, so monitor the progress by noting the Copy Status column in the list of tracks.

Copying Tracks to a Recordable CD or Device

Media Player can also perform the opposite task: copying media files from your computer to a CD-R, CD-RW, or portable device. Again, there are some settings you should consider before trying out this procedure.

Setting Recording Options

In Media Player's Options dialog box (select Tools, Options), choose the Devices tab, select the device you want to use, and then click Properties. In the property sheet that appears, select the recording tab. For a CD-R (or CD-RW) drive, you have four options (see Figure 8-4):

- **Enable CD Recording On This Drive**   Select this option to allow Media Player to use the CD-R drive for recording. You can prevent others from recording to this drive by clearing this check box.

- **Select A Drive Where Windows Can Store An "Image" Of The CD To Be Written**   Before doing the actual recording, Media Player converts your entire playlist into temporary .wav files that get deleted after the recording is complete. Because these are uncompressed files, a full CD's worth could take up as much as 1 GB of space. Use this list to choose a drive that has at least that much space available.

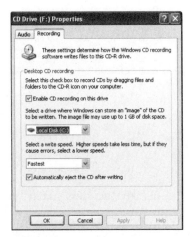

Figure 8-4   In the property sheet for a CD-R or CD-RW drive, use the Recording tab to enable and configure CD recording.

■   **Select A Write Speed**   Use this list to choose how fast you want Media Player to record to the CD. If you have trouble recording, select a slower speed.

■   **Automatically Eject The CD After Writing**   When this check box is selected, Media Player ejects the completed CD once the recording is complete. If you prefer to check the contents of the CD after the recording to ensure the process completed successfully, or if you want to play the new CD, clear this check box.

Creating a Playlist

Most people find recording is easiest if it's done from a *playlist*, a customized collection of music files. Here's how to create a new playlist in Media Player 8:

1.   Select Media Library on the Media Player taskbar.

2.   Click New Playlist to display the New Playlist dialog box.

3.   Type a name in the Enter The New Playlist Name text box and then click OK. Media Player creates the playlist and displays it in the Media Library's My Playlists branch.

4.   To add a song to the playlist, open the appropriate Audio sub-branch, select the file name in the right pane, click Add To Playlist, and then click the name of the playlist into which you want to add this song.

> **Tip**   If the music files you want to work with are on your hard disk, you can add them to the playlist using Windows Explorer. To do this, right-click a file or file selection, select Add To Playlist, choose the playlist you want to use, and then click OK.

To create a playlist in Media Player 9, follow these steps:

1. Select Media Library on the Media Player taskbar.

2. Select Playlists, New Playlist to display the New Playlist dialog box.

3. Enter a name in the Playlist Name text box. Use the View Media Library By list to select how you want to view the media. In the list below, open the appropriate sub-branch and then click the file you want to add. When you're done, click OK.

Once your playlist is created, you can edit the list by selecting it in the My Playlists branch and then right-clicking the tracks.

Recording to a CD or Device

Here are the steps to follow to record to a CD-R, CD-RW, or portable device:

1. Select Copy To CD Or Device on the Media Player taskbar.

2. Use the Music To Copy list (it's called Items To Copy in Media Player 9) to choose the playlist or specific individual titles you want to copy. Alternatively, select the Media Library item (genre, album, or artist) that contains the music you want to copy.

3. Select the check boxes beside the tracks that you want to copy. Use the selection summary (in the lower left corner of the Media Player window) to ensure that the total number of megabytes (or minutes, if you're recording to a CD-R disc) that you select isn't greater than the total number of megabytes (or minutes) available on the recording device.

4. Use the Music On Device list (Items On Device list, in Media Player 9) to select the drive or device that you want to use as the copy destination.

5. Click Copy Music (in Media Player 9, simply click Copy).

Working with Digital Media Files

Previous versions of Windows treated all documents more or less the same. Yes, we've seen innovations such as the "thumbnails" view for images and the "Web" view for folders that showed a preview of some file types in the margin, but the Windows XP designers and programmers went beyond these simple tweaks. They realized that different document types require different user actions. An image, for example, may need to be copied to a CD, set as the desktop background, e-mailed, or published to the Web. They also realized that many of today's users—especially home users—do a lot of work with digital media files: images captured from a digital camera or scanner; music files copied from an audio CD or downloaded from the Internet; and video files created via Windows Movie Maker or a third-party video editing program. The result is that Windows XP has many new features specifically designed to help users manage digital media files. We discuss these new features in this section and show you ways to improve upon them and customize them to suit the way you work.

Digging Deeper into Digital Media Files

Windows Explorer has three built-in digital media folders:

- **My Pictures**   Use this folder for images. The location of this folder is %UserProfile%\My Documents\My Pictures.

- **My Music**   Use this folder for music and audio files. The location of this folder is %UserProfile%\My Documents\My Music.

- **My Video**   Use this folder for video clips and animations. The location of this folder is %UserProfile%\My Documents\My Video. (Note that Windows XP doesn't create this folder until the first time you open an existing video file or save a new video file using Windows Movie Maker.)

> **Insider Secret**   You're free to rename and move all three digital media folders. Windows XP tracks the new names and locations using the My Pictures, My Music, and My Video settings in the following registry key:
>
> ```
> HKCU\Software\Microsoft\Windows\CurrentVersion
> \Explorer\Shell Folders
> ```

When these folders are open in Windows Explorer, the task pane on the left is customized to display tasks related to the folder. For example, when the My Pictures folder is open, the Picture Tasks section of the task pane contains the following commands:

- **View As Slide Show**   Click this command to see full-screen versions of each image in the folder. The images change every five seconds.

> **Note**   The Windows XP PowerToys have a couple of tools—the CD Slide Show Generator and the HTML Slide Show Wizard—that give you more options for creating slide shows. We discuss these utilities in Chapter 1, "Mastering Control Panel, Policies, and PowerToys."

- **Order Prints Online**   Click this link to run the Online Print Ordering Wizard, which enables you to send digital images to an online printing service, which will then mail the prints to you.

- **Print Pictures or Print The Selected Pictures or Print This Picture**   Click this link to display the Photo Printing Wizard, which enables you to choose the layout (full page, 5" × 7", and so on) that you want to use to print the selected image or images.

- **Set As Desktop Background**   Click this link to display the selected file as the desktop's background image.

- **Copy All Items To CD or Copy To CD**   Click this link to copy either all the folder's files or the selected files to a recordable CD.

- **Shop For Pictures Online**   Click this link to connect to the Windows XP Pictures Online Web site, where you can purchase and download images, photos, animations, clip art, and more.

The My Music and My Videos folders have their own customized tasks, although not as many as the My Pictures folder.

Tips for Working with Digital Media Files

Here are a few tips and techniques that you can use to get the most out of working with digital media files in Windows Explorer:

- **Take advantage of the new Filmstrip view.**   In the My Pictures folder, select the View, Filmstrip command to view the images sequentially, something like a filmstrip.

- **Customize the Details view.**   Windows Explorer's Details view (displayed when you select the View, Details command) normally shows four columns only: Name, Size, Type, and Date Modified. However, Windows XP has a number of other columns you can display, such as the dimensions of an image or the bit rate at which a music file was ripped. Select View, Choose Details to open the Choose Details dialog box (see Figure 8-5), or right-click a column heading and select the detail you want to see.

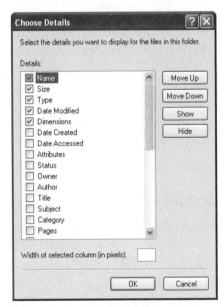

Figure 8-5   Use the Choose Details dialog box to specify the columns you want to see in Details view.

- **Hide file names in the Thumbnails and Filmstrip views.**   If you hold down the Shift key and double-click a folder, Windows Explorer opens the folder without displaying the file names in the Thumbnails and Filmstrip views. This is a toggle action; to re-enable the display of file names, click a different folder, and then hold down the Shift key and double-click the original folder.

- **Change the default thumbnail size.**   By default, the images displayed in the Thumbnails view are 96 pixels square. You can change this default by adding a DWORD value named ThumbnailSize to one of the following registry keys and setting it to a decimal value between 32 and 256:

```
HKLM\SOFTWARE\Microsoft\Windows\CurrentVersion\Explorer\
HKCU\Software\Microsoft\Windows\CurrentVersion\Explorer\
```

- **Change the default thumbnail quality.**   When you open a folder in either Thumbnails or Filmstrip view, Windows Explorer creates a file named Thumbs.db and uses it to store the thumbnail versions of each image. The size of this file depends on the quality level that Explorer uses to create the thumbnails: the higher the quality, the larger the file. You can control the quality level by adding a DWORD value named ThumbnailQuality to one of the following registry keys and setting it to a decimal value between 50 (lowest quality) and 100 (highest quality):

```
HKLM\SOFTWARE\Microsoft\Windows\CurrentVersion\Explorer\
HKCU\Software\Microsoft\Windows\CurrentVersion\Explorer\
```

> **Note**   You can change both the thumbnail size and the thumbnail quality via Tweak UI (see Chapter 1). In the Tweak UI window, open the Explorer, Thumbnails branch.

Creating a Screen Saver Using Digital Images

Rather than displaying an abstract pattern as a screen saver, Windows XP allows you to use a collection of image files. To set this up, follow these steps:

1.   Launch Control Panel's Display icon, or right-click the desktop and then select Properties.

2.   Display the Screen Saver tab.

3.   In the Screen Saver drop-down list, select My Picture Slideshow. (If the message "There were no pictures found…" is displayed, click the Settings button, and then click the Browse button to navigate to the folder of pictures to use for the slideshow.)

4. Click the Settings button to work with the following options:

❑ **How Often Should Pictures Change?**   Use this slider to set the amount of time that each picture is displayed (up to three minutes).

❑ **How Big Should Pictures Be?**   Use this slider to set the maximum size of each picture relative to the screen size. For example, if you choose 50%, the pictures are displayed at half the horizontal and vertical dimensions of the screen, resulting in 25% of the screen's area being used for this display. (By default, pictures smaller than that are displayed at full size, while pictures larger than that are shrunk to fit.)

❑ **Use Pictures In This Folder**   Click Browse to choose the folder from which the screen saver gets its images. (The default is the current user's My Pictures folder.)

❑ **Stretch Small Pictures**   When this check box is selected, Windows XP expands small pictures so that they take up the percentage of the screen specified by the How Big Should Pictures Be? slider.

> **Note**   Rather than having Windows XP stretch smaller images, you might want to change the size of an image permanently. You can do this using the Image Resizer PowerToy that we discussed in Chapter 1.

❑ **Show File Names**   When this check box is selected, the screen saver shows the path and file name of each image in the upper left corner.

❑ **Use Transition Effects Between Pictures**   When this check box is selected, the screen saver uses a random transition effect (such as a fade out and fade in) from one picture to the next.

❑ **Allow Scrolling Through Pictures With The Keyboard**   When this check box is selected, you can immediately display the next picture by pressing the Right arrow key, and you can display the previous picture by pressing the Left arrow key.

Customizing Media Folders

The features available in the My Pictures, My Music, and My Videos folders are actually based on templates that can also be applied to other folders on your system. For example, if you have images located in a folder other than My Pictures, you can set up that folder to use a template that gives it the same features as My Pictures. You can also customize a folder to show a specific image in Thumbnails view and to use an icon other than the generic folder icon.

To get started, first use Windows Explorer to display the folder you want to work with, and then select View, Customize This Folder. Windows XP opens the folder's property sheet with the Customize tab displayed.

Selecting a Folder Template

In the Use This Folder Type As A Template list, choose one of the following templates:

- **Documents**   Choose this template to give the folder the same features as a standard folder.

- **Pictures**   Choose this template to give the folder the same features as the My Pictures folder.

- **Photo Album**   Choose this template to give the folder the same features as the My Pictures folder, and also to display the folder in Filmstrip view by default.

- **Music**   Choose this template to give the folder the same features as the My Music folder.

- **Music Artist**   Choose this template for a folder that holds music by a single artist. This gives the folder the same features as the My Music folder, and it also opens the folder in Thumbnail view, which displays an album-art icon for each folder that holds an album by the artist.

- **Music Album**   Choose this template for a folder that holds music from a single artist. This gives the folder the same features as the My Music folder, and it also opens the folder in Tiles view, which displays an icon for each track from the album.

- **Video**   Choose this template to give the folder the same features as the My Videos folder.

If you want this template to be used for all the folder's subfolders, select the Also Apply This Template To All Subfolders check box.

Changing the Folder Icon

In Thumbnails view, when folders are displayed in the right pane, Windows Explorer displays a folder's icon with a picture. For example, if the folder uses the Music Album template, the folder's Thumbnails icon displays a picture of the album cover (assuming you have an Internet connection and Media Player was able to download the album cover). Similarly, for a folder that uses the Pictures or Photo Album template, its folder icon will display the first four images that reside in the folder.

To change the image, click the Choose Picture button and use the Browse dialog box to select the image file you want to appear on the folder's icon.

> **Insider Secret**   Another way to specify the image used in a folder's icon in Thumbnails view is to make a copy of the image inside the folder, and then rename that copy to Folder.jpg. Note that if you use the Choose Picture command to specify a different image, Windows XP ignores the Folder.jpg file. To use the Folder.jpg image again, click the Restore Default button.

This customization applies to folders shown in the right pane, displayed in Thumbnails view. To change the folder icon in other views, click the Change Icon button and use the Change Icon dialog box to choose a new icon.

Investigating the Windows Media Bonus Pack

The Windows Media Bonus Pack for Windows XP is a free collection of extra utilities and files designed to enhance your Windows XP digital media duties. You can learn more about the Bonus Pack and download it from the following Web site:

http://www.microsoft.com/windows/windowsmedia/download/bonuspack.asp

The Bonus Pack contains the following features:

- **Plus! MP3 Audio Converter LE**   This utility enables you to convert MP3 files to the WMA format.

> **Caution**   By default, the MP3 Audio Converter offers to add the converted files to the Media Player Media Library. This may not work, however, because applications are generally given just read-only access to the Media Library. To overcome this problem, open Media Player, select Tools, Options, and display the Media Library tab. In the Access Rights Of Other Applications section of the dialog box, select the Full Access option.

- **Windows Media Player Visualizations**   This feature installs a number of new visualizations into Media Player.

- **Windows Media Player Skins**   This feature installs a number of new skins into Media Player.

- **Windows Media Player For Windows XP Tray Control**   This feature enables you to hide Media Player entirely and operate it from the taskbar's system tray by right-clicking the tray control. Note, too, that the shortcut menu that appears has an Options menu. On this menu, select Clear MRU to clear Media Player's recent file list, and select Turn Off Media Player MRU to prevent Media Player from adding files to its recent file list.

- **Movie Maker Creativity Kit**   This component adds sound effects, title slides, and background music to Windows Movie Maker.

- **Windows Media Player For Windows XP PowerToys**   This component provides its own set of enhancements and utilities:

  - ❑ **Windows Media Player For Windows XP Tray Control** This feature enables you to hide Media Player entirely and operate it from the taskbar's system tray by right-clicking the tray control. Note, too, that the shortcut menu that appears has an Options menu. On this menu, select Clear MRU to clear Media Player's recent file list, and select Turn Off Media Player MRU to prevent Media Player from adding files to its recent file list.

  - ❑ **Media Library Management Wizard** This utility helps you organize your music files.

  - ❑ **Playlist Import To Excel Wizard** This utility enables you to export a Media Player playlist to Microsoft Excel 2002.

❑ **Windows Media Player Skin Importer**   This feature enables you to import WinAMP skins to use with Media Player.

❑ **PowerToys Skin**   This feature adds a special PowerToys skin to Media Player. When you open this skin, Media Player displays a list of seven PowerToys that you can use to perform various playlist tasks (such as converting all your albums to playlists and creating playlists for copying files to a CD).

Caution   Again, the PowerToys skin won't work unless applications are given full access to the Media Library.

9

Installing and Troubleshooting Devices

In this chapter, you'll learn how to:

- Perform nearly foolproof device installations.

- Deal with driver signatures and control their options.

- Use Device Manager to get a handle on your hardware.

- Install, update, and roll back device drivers.

- Set up hardware profiles.

- Troubleshoot devices with dexterity.

One of the roles an operating system must play is that of intermediary between your software, your hardware, and you. Any operating system worth its salt has to translate incomprehensible "device-speak" into something a person can make sense of, and it must ensure that devices are ready, willing, and able to carry out a user's commands. Given the sophistication and diversity of today's hardware market, however, that's no easy task. The good news is that Microsoft Windows XP brings to the PC world substantial support for a broad range of hardware, from everyday devices such as keyboards, mice, printers, monitors, and video, sound, and network cards to more exotic hardware fare such as IEEE 1394 (FireWire) controllers, flash storage readers (CompactFlash, Smart-Media, and so on), and infrared devices. However, while this hardware support may be broad, it's not all that deep, meaning that Windows XP doesn't have built-in support for many older devices. So although many hardware vendors have taken at least some steps toward upgrading their devices and drivers, managing hardware is still one of Windows XP's trickier areas. This chapter should help as we take you through lots of practical techniques for installing, updating, and troubleshooting devices in Windows XP.

Tips and Techniques for Installing Devices

When working with Windows 2000 and Windows NT, there was one cardinal rule for choosing a device to attach to your system: Check the hardware compatibility list! This was a list of devices that were known to work with Windows. Like its operating system predecessors, Windows XP also maintains a list of compatible hardware, only now the list is called the Windows Catalog. You can get to this Web site by selecting Start, All Programs, Windows Catalog, or by entering the following address in your Web browser:

http://www.microsoft.com/windows/catalog/

If you see your device in the hardware list, you can install the device safe in the knowledge that it will work properly with Windows XP. If you don't see the device, all is not lost because you still have two other options:

- Check the manufacturer's package for some indication that the device works with Windows XP or contains drivers for Windows XP. Seeing the "Designed For Windows XP" logo on the package is the best way to be sure that the device works with Windows XP.

- Check the manufacturer's Web site to see if it has an updated Windows XP driver or device setup program available.

Installing Plug and Play Devices

The hoped-for objective for device configuration is a setup in which you need only to insert or plug in a peripheral and turn it on (if necessary), and your system configures the device automatically. In other words, the system not only recognizes that a new device is attached to the machine, but it also gleans the device's default resource configuration and, if required, resolves any conflicts that might have arisen with existing devices. And, of course, the operating system should be able to perform all this magic without your ever having to flip a DIP switch, fiddle with a jumper, or fuss with various IRQ, I/O port, and DMA combinations.

Plug and Play is an attempt by members of the PC community to reach this Zen-like hardware state. Did they succeed? Yes, Plug and Play works like a charm, but only if your Windows XP system meets both of the following criteria:

■ **It has a Plug and Play BIOS.**   One of the first things that happens inside your computer when you turn it on (or do a hardware reboot) is that the ROM BIOS (basic input/output system) code performs a Power-On Self Test to check the system hardware. If you have a system with a Plug and Play BIOS, the initial code also enumerates and tests all the Plug and Play–compliant devices on the system. For each device, the BIOS not only selects the device, but also gathers the device's resource configuration (IRQ, I/O ports, and so forth). When all the Plug and Play devices have been isolated, the BIOS then checks for resource conflicts and, if there are any, takes steps to resolve them.

■ **It uses Plug and Play devices.**   Plug and Play devices are the extroverts of the hardware world. They're only too happy to chat with any old Plug and Play BIOS or operating system that happens along. What do they chat about? The device essentially identifies itself to the BIOS (or the operating system if the BIOS isn't Plug and Play–compliant) by sending its *configuration ID*, which tells what the device is and which resources it uses. The BIOS or operating system then configures the system's resources accordingly.

Plug and Play is built into every device that connects via a USB or IEEE 1394 port, and it comes with all PC Card devices and almost all interface cards that connect to the PCI bus. Other devices that connect via the serial, parallel, or PS/2 ports aren't necessarily Plug and Play–compliant, but almost all of them are if they were manufactured in the past few years. Interface cards that connect to the legacy ISA bus are not Plug and Play–compliant.

Before you install a Plug and Play device, check to see if the hardware came with a setup program on a floppy disk, a CD, or as part of a download package. If it did, run that program and, if you're given any setup options, be sure to install at least the device driver. Having the driver loaded on the system will help Windows XP install the device automatically.

> **Caution**   Only members of the Administrators group can install device drivers, so be sure to log on as a member of that group before installing the device.

How Windows reacts when you attach a Plug and Play device that is designed for Windows XP depends on how you attached the device:

■ If you *hot-swapped* a device such as a PC Card or a printer, Windows XP recognizes the device immediately and installs the driver for it.

■ If you turned your computer off to attach the device, Windows XP recognizes it the next time you start the machine, and installs the appropriate driver.

Either way, an icon appears in the system tray, and a balloon tip titled Found New Hardware pops up to tell you that your new hardware is installed and ready for use.

If Windows XP did not find a device driver for the new hardware, it automatically runs the Found New Hardware Wizard. You're given two choices:

■ **Install The Software Automatically (Recommended)** Choose this option if you have a floppy disk or CD that contains a Windows XP–compatible device driver for the hardware. Insert the disk or CD and click Next. Windows XP examines the system's disk drives, locates the driver, and then installs the driver. (If the wizard finds more than one driver, it asks you to choose the one you want from a list.)

■ **Install From a List or Specific Location** Choose this option if you've downloaded a driver from the Internet or if you have a disk or CD that has a driver that isn't identified as compatible with Windows XP. Click Next.

If you choose the latter option, you'll see the dialog box shown in Figure 9-1. Once again, you have two ways to proceed:

■ **Search For The Best Driver In These Locations** Choose this option if you've downloaded the device driver from the Internet. If the driver is on a floppy disk or CD, leave the Search Removable Media check box selected; otherwise, clear it. If the driver is on your hard disk or a network drive, select the Include This Location In The Search check box and then enter the full path of the folder that contains the driver. Click Next.

> **Caution**   If the downloaded driver is contained within a compressed file (such as a ZIP file), be sure to decompress the file before moving on to the next wizard step.

- **Don't Search. I Will Choose The Driver To Install**   Choose this option if you have a floppy disk or CD containing a device driver that isn't identified as compatible with Windows XP. Note that you should also choose this option if you want to use one of Windows XP's built-in drivers that you think might be a close enough match for the device. Click Next, choose the appropriate hardware type, and click Next again. In the next wizard dialog box, you have two choices:

  - ❑   If you have a floppy disk or CD, insert it, click Have Disk, enter the letter of the drive that holds the disk or CD, and click OK.

  - ❑   If you want to pick an existing Windows XP driver, select the Show Compatible Hardware check box, select the driver that most closely matches your device, and then click Next.

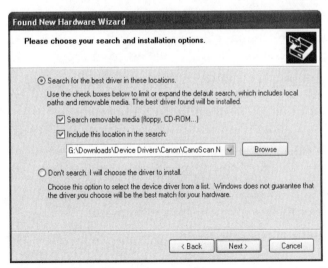

Figure 9-1   This dialog box appears if you elected to install the device driver from a list or a specific location.

Installing Legacy Devices

When it comes to installing legacy devices (that is, devices that don't support Plug and Play), your best bet by far is to run the setup program that the manufacturer supplies either on a floppy disk, on a CD, or as part of a driver download. If you're asked, choose the Windows XP driver, if one is available. If no Windows XP driver is available, the Windows 2000 driver will work in most cases. If the device has drivers only for Windows NT, Windows 9x, or Windows Me, these almost certainly will not work with Windows XP, so there's no point in installing them. Contact the manufacturer and ask for a Windows XP (or, at worst, a Windows 2000) driver.

If you don't have a setup program for the device, Windows XP may still be able to support the hardware using one of its legacy device drivers. To do this, you need to run one of Windows XP's hardware wizards. Some of these wizards are device-specific, so you should use those where appropriate:

- **Joystick or other game device** Launch Control Panel's Game Controllers icon and then click Add.

- **Modem** Launch Control Panel's Phone And Modem Options icon, select the Modems tab, and click Add.

- **Printer** Select Start, Printers And Faxes, and then click the Add A Printer link.

- **Scanner or digital camera** Launch Control Panel's Scanners And Cameras icon, and then click the Add An Imaging Device link.

For all other devices, use the Add Hardware Wizard:

1. Launch Control Panel's Add Hardware icon.

2. In the wizard's initial dialog box, click Next. The wizard searches for new Plug and Play hardware.

3. When the wizard asks if the hardware is connected, select the Yes, I Have Already Connected The Hardware option and click Next. The wizard displays a list of installed hardware.

4. At the bottom of the list, select Add A New Hardware Device and click Next.

5. You now have two choices:

❑ **Search For And Install The Hardware Automatically (Recommended)** Choose this option if you have a device that the wizard is capable of locating using hardware detection. This route often works with modems, printers, video cards, and network cards. Click Next to start the detection process. If the detection fails, the wizard will let you know. In this case, click Next and proceed with step 6.

❑ **Install The Hardware That I Manually Select From A List (Advanced)** Choose this option to pick out the device by hand. Click Next.

6 Select the hardware category that applies to your device. (If you don't see an appropriate category, select Show All Devices.) Click Next.

7. Depending on the hardware category you selected, a new wizard might appear. (For example, if you chose the Modems category, the Install New Modem Wizard appears.) In that case, follow the wizard's dialog boxes. Otherwise, a dialog box appears with a list of manufacturers and models. In this case, you have two choices:

❑ Select your device by first selecting the device's manufacturer in the Manufacturer list and then selecting the name of the device in the Model list.

❑ If you have a manufacturer's floppy disk, CD, or downloaded file, click Have Disk, enter the appropriate path and file name in the Install From Disk dialog box, and click OK.

8. Click Next.

Controlling Driver Signing Options

Device drivers that meet the Designed For Windows XP specifications have been tested for compatibility with Microsoft and then given a digital signature. This signature tells you that the driver works properly with Windows XP and that it hasn't been changed since it was tested. (For example, the driver hasn't been infected by a virus or Trojan horse program.) When you're installing a device, if Windows XP comes across a driver that has not been digitally signed, it displays a dialog box similar to the one shown in Figure 9-2.

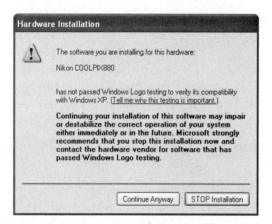

Figure 9-2 Windows XP displays a dialog box similar to this one when it comes across a device driver that does not have a digital signature.

If you click STOP Installation, Windows XP cancels the driver installation, and you won't be able to use the device. This is the most prudent choice in this situation because an unsigned driver can cause all kinds of havoc, including lock-ups, BSODs (Blue Screens of Death), and other system instabilities. You should ask the manufacturer for a Windows XP–compatible driver, or upgrade to a newer model that is supported by Windows XP.

If that's not possible, you should take some precautions:

■ Back up all your files.

■ Set a system restore point. (Windows XP will do this for you anyway whenever you elect to install an unsigned driver, but we advise you to set your own restore points, just in case something goes wrong.)

■ Test your system thoroughly after installing the driver: Use the device, open and use your most common applications, run some disk utilities. If anything seems awry, use the restore point to roll back the system to its previous configuration.

By default, Windows XP gives you the option of either continuing or canceling the installation of the unsigned driver. You can change this behavior to automatically accept or reject all unsigned drivers by following these steps:

1. Launch Control Panel's System icon.

2. Select the Hardware tab.

3. Click Driver Signing. Windows XP displays the Driver Signing Options dialog box, shown in Figure 9-3.

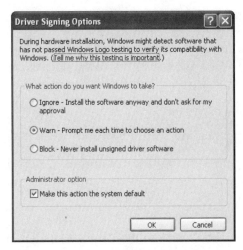

Figure 9-3   Use the Driver Signing Options dialog box to specify how Windows XP should handle unsigned device drivers.

4. Choose an option in the What Action Do You Want Windows To Take section of the dialog box:

   ❏ **Ignore**   Choose this option if you want Windows XP to install all unsigned drivers.

   ❏ **Warn**   Choose this option, shown in Figure 9-3, if you want Windows XP to warn you about an unsigned driver.

   ❏ **Block**   Choose this option if you do not want Windows XP to install any unsigned drivers.

5. If you want this action to apply to all the users of the computer, leave the Make This Action The System Default check box selected.

6. Click OK.

> **Insider Secret**   There are some device drivers that Windows XP knows will cause system instabilities. Windows XP will simply refuse to load these problematic drivers, no matter which action you choose in the Driver Signing Options dialog box. In this case, you'll see a dialog box similar to the one in Figure 9-3, except this one tells you that the driver will not be installed and your only choice is to cancel the installation.

Managing Your Hardware with Device Manager

Windows XP stores all its hardware data in the registry, but it provides the Device Manager to give you a graphical view of the devices on your system. To display the Device Manager, first use either of the following techniques:

■ Launch Control Panel's System icon.

■ Right-click My Computer and select Properties on the shortcut menu.

In the System Properties dialog box that appears, select the Hardware tab and then click Device Manager.

> **Tip** A quick way to go directly to the Device Manager snap-in is to select Start, Run, enter **devmgmt.msc**, and click OK. Note, too, that you can select the System Properties dialog box quickly by pressing ⊞+Pause/Break.

Device Manager's default display is a treelike outline that lists various hardware types. To see the specific devices, click the plus sign (+) to the left of a device type. For example, opening the DVD/CD-ROM Drives branch displays all the DVD and CD-ROM drives attached to your computer, as shown in Figure 9-4.

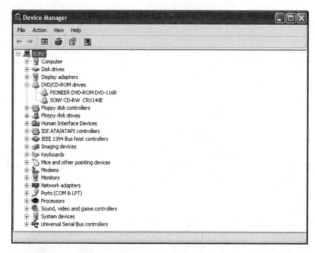

Figure 9-4 Device Manager organizes your computer's hardware in a treelike hierarchy organized by hardware type.

Controlling the Device Display

Devices Manager's default view is by hardware type (Devices By Type), but it also offers several other views, all of which are available on Device Manager's View menu:

- **Devices By Connection**   This view displays devices according to what they are connected to within your computer. For example, to see which devices are connected to the PCI bus, on most systems you'd open the ACPI branch, then the Microsoft ACPI–Compliant System branch, and then the PCI Bus branch.

- **Resources By Type**   This view displays devices according to the *hardware resources* they require. Your computer's resources are the communications channels by which devices communicate back and forth with software. There are four types:

  - ❑ **Interrupt Request (IRQ)**   This is a wire built in to the computer's motherboard or a device slot. It's used by the processor and a device to send signals to each other. In other words, the device uses the wire to send a "request" to the processor to "interrupt" whatever the processor is doing (and vice versa).

  - ❑ **Input/Output (I/O)**   This is a small block of memory (typically 8 bytes, 16 bytes, or 32 bytes) that acts as a communications channel between a device and the processor or a device driver. Each I/O port address is expressed as a range of hexadecimal numbers. For example, the first I/O port on most systems is used by the direct memory access controller, and its address is the 16-byte range 00000000–0000000F.

  - ❑ **Direct Memory Access (DMA)**   This is a connection maintained by a DMA controller chip that enables a device to transfer data directly to and from memory without going through the processor (as it does with an I/O port). The processor tells the DMA controller chip what device to work with and what data is needed. The DMA controller chip then uses the channel to perform the complete data transfer without involving the processor.

  - ❑ **Memory**   This is a portion of the computer's memory that's allocated to the device and is used to store device-dependent data.

- **Resources By Connection**   This view displays the computer's allocated resources according to how they're connected within the computer.

- **Show Hidden Devices**   When you select this command, Device Manager displays those non–Plug and Play devices that you normally don't need to adjust or troubleshoot. It also displays *non-present* devices, which are devices that have been installed but that aren't currently attached to the computer.

Viewing Device Properties

Each device listed in Device Manager has its own property sheet. You can use these properties not only to learn more about the device (such as the resources it's currently using), but also to make adjustments to the device's resources, change the device driver, alter the device's settings (if it has any), and make other changes.

To select the property sheet for a device, double-click the device or select the device and select Action, Properties. The number of tabs you see depends on the hardware, but most devices have at least the following:

- **General**   This tab gives you general information such as the name of the device, its hardware type, and the manufacturer's name. The Device Status section of the dialog box tells you whether the device is working properly, and gives you status information if it's not (see "Troubleshooting with Device Manager," later in this chapter). You use the Device Usage list to enable or disable a device (see "Managing Hardware Profiles," later in this chapter).

- **Driver**   This tab gives you information about the device driver and offers several buttons for managing the driver. See the following section, "Working with Device Drivers."

- **Resources**   This tab tells you the hardware resources used by the device.

Working with Device Drivers

For most users, device drivers exist in the nether regions of the PC world, shrouded in obscurity and the mysteries of assembly language programming. As the go-betweens who broker the dialogue between Windows XP and system hardware, however, these complex chunks of code perform a crucial task. After all, it's just not possible to unleash a system's full potential unless the hardware and the operating system coexist harmoniously and optimally. To that end, you need to ensure that Windows XP is using appropriate drivers for all your hardware. You do that by updating to the latest drivers and by rolling back drivers that aren't working properly.

Updating a Device Driver

Follow these steps to update a device driver:

1. If you have a floppy disk or CD with the updated driver, insert the disk or CD. If you downloaded the driver from the Internet, decompress the driver file, if necessary.

2. In Device Manager, select the device and select Action, Update Driver. (You can also open the device's property sheet, select the Driver tab, and click Update Driver.) The Hardware Update Wizard appears.

3. This wizard works the same way as the Found New Hardware Wizard discussed previously in this chapter, so follow the instructions given earlier (see "Installing Plug and Play Devices").

Rolling Back a Device Driver

If an updated device driver is giving you problems, you have a choice of two ways to fix things:

■   If updating the driver was the last action you performed on the system, restore the system to its most recent restore point.

■   If you've updated other things on the system in the meantime, a restore point may restore more than you need. In that case, you need to roll back just the device driver that's causing problems.

Follow these steps to roll back a device driver:

1. In Device Manager, open the device's property sheet and select the Driver tab.

2. Click Roll Back Driver.

Uninstalling a Device

When you remove a Plug and Play device, the BIOS informs Windows XP that the device is no longer present. Windows XP, in turn, updates its device list in the registry, and the peripheral no longer appears in the Device Manager display.

If you're removing a legacy device, however, you need to tell Device Manager that the device no longer exists. To do that, select the device in the Device Manager tree and then select Action, Uninstall. (Alternatively, open the device's property sheet, select the Driver tab, and click Uninstall.) If you've defined multiple hardware profiles (as described next, in the "Managing Hardware Profiles" section), Windows XP will ask whether you want to remove the device from all the profiles or just from a specific profile. Select the appropriate option. When Windows XP warns you that you're about to remove the device, click OK.

Managing Hardware Profiles

In most cases, your hardware configuration will remain relatively static. You might add the odd new device or remove a device, but these are permanent changes. Windows XP merely updates its current hardware configuration to compensate.

In some situations, however, you might need to switch between hardware configurations regularly. A good example is a notebook computer with a docking station. When the computer is undocked, it uses its built-in keyboard, mouse, and display; when the computer is docked, however, it uses a separate keyboard, mouse, and display. To make it easier to switch between these different configurations, Windows XP lets you set up a hardware profile for each setup. It then becomes a simple matter of your selecting the profile you want to use at startup; Windows XP handles the hard part of loading the appropriate drivers.

Note   Generally speaking, you don't need to bother with hardware profiles if your computer has a Plug and Play BIOS and you're using Plug and Play devices. Plug and Play detects any new Plug and Play–compliant hardware configuration automatically and adjusts accordingly. For example, Plug and Play supports hot docking of a notebook computer: While the machine is running, you can insert it into, or remove it from, the docking station, and Plug and Play handles the switch without breaking a sweat. Hardware profiles are useful when you have configurations that require major hardware changes and so you don't want to wait for the Plug and Play process to redetect each changed device.

Before creating a new hardware profile, install the drivers you need for all the hardware you'll be using. If the hardware isn't currently attached, that's fine; just be sure to specify the appropriate devices by hand in the Add New Hardware Wizard. The important thing is to make sure that all the drivers you need are installed.

After that's done, open the System Properties dialog box as described earlier and select the Hardware tab. Click the Hardware Profiles button to open the Hardware Profiles dialog box. On most systems, you see a single profile named Profile 1. This profile includes all the installed device drivers. The idea is that you create a new profile by making a copy of this configuration, and then you tell Windows XP which devices to include in that new profile.

To make a copy of the profile, click the Copy button, enter a name for the new profile in the Copy Profile dialog box, and click OK. (If you want to rename a profile, select the profile, click Rename, enter the new name in the Rename Profile dialog box, and click OK.)

Now that you have multiple profiles in place, you need to tell Windows XP which devices go with which profile. Follow these steps:

1.   If you want to work with the new profile, restart your computer and select the profile from the menu that appears at startup.

2.   Open Device Manager and find the device you want to work with.

3.   Select the device's property sheet.

4.   In the General tab's Device Usage list, choose one of the following options (you'll see one or more of the following three choices, depending on the device):

   ❑   **Use this Device (Enable)**   Select this option to include the device in the profile.

   ❑   **Do Not Use This Device In the Current Hardware Profile (Disable)**   If you choose this option, Windows XP disables the device only in the current hardware profile.

   ❑   **Do Not Use This Device In Any Hardware Profiles (Disable)**   If you choose this option, Windows XP disables the device in every hardware profile.

5.   Click OK.

Working with Device Security Policies

The Group Policy editor offers several device-related policies. To see them, open the Group Policy editor and select Local Computer Policy, Computer Configuration, Windows Settings, Security Settings, Local Policies, Security Options. Here are the policies in the Devices category:

- **Allow Undock Without Having To Log On** When this policy is enabled, users can undock a notebook computer without having to log on to Windows XP (that is, they can undock the computer by pressing the docking station's eject button). If you want to restrict who can do this, disable this policy.

> **Insider Secret** To control who can undock the computer, select Local Computer Policy, Computer Configuration, Windows Settings, Security Settings, Local Policies, User Rights Assignment. Use the Remove Computer From Docking Station policy to assign the users or groups who have this right.

- **Allowed To Format And Eject Removable Media** Use this policy to determine the groups that are allowed to format floppy disks and eject CDs and other removable media.

- **Prevent Users From Installing Printer Drivers** Enable this policy to prevent users from installing a network printer. Note that this doesn't affect the installation of a local printer.

- **Restrict CD-ROM Access To Locally Logged-On User Only** Enable this policy to prevent network users from operating the computer's CD-ROM or DVD drive at the same time as a local user. If no local user is accessing the drive, the network user can access it.

- **Restrict Floppy Access To Locally Logged-On User Only** Enable this policy to prevent network users from operating the computer's floppy drive at the same time as a local user. If no local user is accessing the drive, the network user can access it.

- **Unsigned Driver Installation Behavior** This policy determines the action Windows XP takes if it comes across an unsigned device driver. There are three choices: Silently Succeed; Warn But Allow Installation; and Do Not Allow Installation.

Troubleshooting Device Problems

Windows XP has excellent support for most newer devices, and most major hardware vendors have taken steps to update their devices and drivers to run properly with Windows XP. If you use only recent, Plug and Play–compliant devices that qualify for the Designed For Windows XP logo, you should have a trouble-free computing experience (at least from a hardware perspective). Of course, putting "trouble-free" and "computing" next to each other is just asking for trouble. Hardware is not foolproof; far from it. Things still can, and will, go wrong; when they do, you'll need to perform some kind of troubleshooting (assuming, of course, that the device doesn't have a physical fault that requires a trip to the repair shop). Fortunately, Windows XP has some handy tools to help you both identify and rectify hardware ills.

Troubleshooting with Device Manager

Device Manager not only provides you with a comprehensive summary of your system's hardware data, but it also doubles as a decent troubleshooting tool. To see what we mean, check out the Device Manager tab shown in Figure 9-5. See how the icon for the S3 ViRGE DX/GX display adapter has an exclamation mark (!) superimposed on it? This tells you that there's a problem with the device.

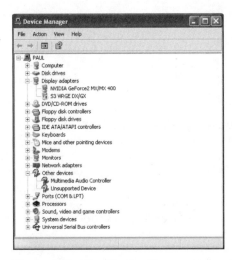

Figure 9-5 The Device Manager uses icons to warn you if there's a problem with a device.

If you examine the device's properties, as shown in Figure 9-6, the Device Status area tells you a bit more about what's wrong. As you can see in Figure 9-6, the problem here is that the device won't start. Either try Device Manager's suggested remedy, or click the Troubleshoot button to launch Windows XP's hardware troubleshooter.

> **Tip** Device Manager has several dozen error codes. See the following Microsoft Knowledge Base article for a complete list of the codes as well as solutions to try in each case:
>
> *http://support.microsoft.com/default.aspx?scid=kb;en-us;Q310123*

Figure 9-6 The Device Status area tells you if the device isn't working properly.

Device Manager uses three different icons to give you an indication of the device's current status:

- A black exclamation mark (!) on a yellow field tells you that there's a problem with the device.

- A red X tells you that the device is disabled or missing.

■   A blue i on a white field tells you that the device's Use Automatic Settings check box (on the Resources tab) is cleared and that at least one of the device's resources was selected manually. Note that the device might be working just fine, so this icon doesn't indicate a problem. If the device isn't working properly, however, the manual setting might be the cause. (For example, the device might have a DIP switch or jumper set to a different resource.)

Troubleshooting Device Driver Problems

Outside of problems with the hardware itself, device drivers are the cause of most device woes. Here are a few tips and pointers for correcting device driver problems:

■   **Reinstall the driver.**   A driver may be malfunctioning because one or more of its files have become corrupted. You can usually solve this by reinstalling the driver. Just in case a disk fault caused the corruption, you should check the partition where the driver is installed for errors before reinstalling. (See Chapter 8 "Playing, Copying, and Storing Digital Media," for instructions on checking a disk for errors.)

■   **Upgrade to a signed driver.**   Unsigned drivers are accidents waiting for a place to happen in Windows XP, so you should upgrade to a signed driver, if possible. (How can you tell if an installed driver is unsigned? Open the device's property sheet, select the Driver tab, and click Driver Details. Signed driver files have a certificate icon with a green checkmark; unsigned files have no icon.) See "Updating a Device Driver," earlier in this chapter.

■   **Disable an unsigned driver.**   If an unsigned driver is causing system instability and you can't upgrade the driver, try disabling it. On the General tab of the device's property sheet, select the appropriate Do Not Use This Device … (Disable) option in the Device Usage list.

■   **Use the Signature Verification Tool.**   This program checks your computer for unsigned drivers. See Chapter 12 "Maintaining Your System in 10 Easy Steps," to learn how to use this program.

■   **Try the manufacturer's driver supplied with the device.**   If the device came with its own driver, try either updating the driver to the manufacturer's or running the device's setup program.

■   **Download the latest driver from the manufacturer.**   Device manufacturers often update drivers to fix bugs, add new features, and tweak performance. Go to the manufacturer's Web site to see if an updated driver is available.

- **Try Windows Update.**   The Windows Update Web site often has updated drivers for downloading. Select Start, All Programs, Windows Update and select Scan For Updates to let the site scan your system. Then, in the left pane, click the Driver Updates link to see which drivers are available for your system.

- **Roll back a driver.**   If the device stops working properly after you update the driver, try rolling it back to the old driver. (See "Rolling Back a Device Driver," earlier in this chapter.)

Notes from the Real World

Finding device drivers on the Web is an art in itself. I can't tell you how much of my life I've wasted rooting around manufacturer Web sites trying to locate a device driver. Most hardware vendor sites seem to be optimized for sales rather than service, so although you can purchase, say, a new printer with just a mouse click or two, downloading a new driver for that printer can take a frustratingly long time. To help you avoid such vexation, here are some tips from my hard-won experience:

- If the manufacturer offers different sites for different locations (such as different countries), always use the company's "home" site, because most mirror sites aren't true mirrors.

- The temptation when you first enter a site is to use the search feature to find what you want. This works only sporadically for drivers, and the site search engines almost always return marketing or sales material first.

- Instead of the search engine, look for an area of the site dedicated to driver downloads. The good sites will have links to areas called "Downloads" or "Drivers," but it's far more common to first have to go through a "Support" or "Customer Service" area.

- Don't try to take any shortcuts to where you *think* the driver might be hiding. Trudge through each step the site provides. For example, it's common to have to select an overall driver category, then a device category, then a line category, then the specific model you have, and then the operating system version. This is tedious, but it almost always gets you where you want to go.

■   If the site is particularly ornery, this method may not lead you to your device. In that case, try the search engine. Note that device drivers seem to be particularly poorly indexed, so you may have to try lots of search text variations. One thing that usually works is searching for the exact file name. How can you possibly know that? A method I often use is to use Google (*www.google.com*) or Google Groups (*groups.google.com*) or some other Web search engine to search for a driver. Chances are, someone else has looked for your file and will have the file name (or, if you're really lucky, a direct link to the driver on the manufacturer's site).

■   When you get to the device's download page, be careful which file you choose. Make sure it's a Windows XP driver, and make sure you're not downloading a utility program or some other non-driver file.

■   When you finally get to download the file, be sure to save it to your computer rather than opening it. If you reformat your system or move the device to another computer, you'll be glad you have a local copy of the driver so you don't have to wrestle with the whole download rigmarole all over again.

I hope you find these tips useful the next time you head out on a driver excursion.

—Paul McFedries

Troubleshooting Resource Conflicts

On modern computer systems that support the Advanced Configuration and Power Interface (ACPI), use PCI cards, and support external Plug and Play–compliant devices, resource conflicts have become almost non-existent. That's because the ACPI is capable of managing the system's resources to avoid conflicts. For example, if a system doesn't have enough IRQ lines, ACPI will assign two or more devices to the same IRQ line and manage the devices so that they can share the line without conflicting with each other. (To see which devices are sharing an IRQ line, select Device Manager's View, Resources By Connection command, and then double-click the Interrupt Request [IRQ] entry.)

ACPI's success at allocating and managing resources is such that Windows XP doesn't allow you to change a device's resources, even if you'd want to do such a thing. If you open a device's property sheet and select the Resources tab, you'll see that none of the settings can be changed.

If you use legacy devices in your system, however, conflicts could arise because Windows XP is unable to properly manage a legacy device's resources. If that happens, Device Manager will let you know there's a problem. To solve it, first select the Resources tab on the device's property sheet. The Resource Settings list shows you the Resource Type on the left and the Resource Setting on the right. If you suspect that the device has a resource conflict, check the Conflicting Device List box to see whether any devices are listed. If the list displays only No Conflicts, the device's resources aren't conflicting with another device.

If there is a conflict, you need to change the appropriate resource. Some devices have multiple possible configurations, so one easy way to change resources is to select a different configuration. To try this, clear the Use Automatic Settings check box and then use the Setting Based On drop-down list to select a different configuration. Otherwise, you need to play around with the resource settings by hand. Here are the steps to follow to change a resource setting:

1. In the Resource Type list, select the resource you want to change.

2. Clear the Use Automatic Settings check box, if it's selected.

3. For the setting you want to change, either double-click it or select it and click the Change Setting button. (If Windows XP tells you that you can't modify the resources in this configuration, select a different configuration from the Setting Based On list.) A dialog box appears that enables you to edit the resource setting.

4. Use the Value spin box to select a different resource. Watch the Conflict Information section of the dialog box to make sure that your new setting doesn't step on the toes of an existing setting.

5. Click OK to return to the Resources tab.

6. Click OK. If Windows XP asks whether you want to restart your computer, click Yes.

> **Insider Secret** An easy way to see which devices are either sharing resources or are conflicting is via the System Information utility. Select Start, Run, enter **msinfo32**, and click OK. (Alternatively, you an select Start, All Programs, Accessories, System Tools, System Information.) Open the Hardware Resources branch and then click Conflicts/Sharing.

III

Customizing
and Optimizing

In Part III, you'll learn insider techniques to help you:

10

Customizing the Interface

In this chapter, you'll learn how to:

- Add more of your favorite programs to the Start menu.
- Customize the Start menu for easy access to programs, window icons, and documents.
- Create, display, and customize taskbar toolbars.
- Use taskbar toolbars to improve productivity.
- Make efficient use of your screen space.

In our estimation, the litmus test of any interface customization consists of a simple question: Does the modification improve productivity? We've seen far too many tweaks that fiddle uselessly with some obscure setting, resulting in little or no improvement to the user's day-to-day Microsoft Windows experience. This may be fine for people with lots of time to kill, but most of us don't have that luxury, so efficiency and productivity must be the goals of the customization process. (Note that this does not preclude aesthetic improvements to the Windows XP interface. A better-looking Windows provides a happier computing experience, and a happier worker is a more productive worker.)

To that end, we devote most of this chapter to the most common of computing tasks: launching programs and documents. This chapter is packed with useful tips and techniques for rearranging Windows XP to help you get your programs and documents up and running as quickly and as easily as possible.

Customizing the Start Menu for Easier Program and Document Launching

The whole purpose of the Start menu is, as its name implies, to start things, particularly programs and documents. Yes, you can also launch these objects via shortcut icons on the desktop, but that's not always a great alternative, since the desktop is covered most of the time by windows. So, if you want to get something going in Windows XP, most often you're going to have to do it via the Start menu. The good news is that Windows XP's new Start menu is wonderfully flexible and is geared, in fact, to launching objects with as few mouse clicks or keystrokes as possible. To get to that state, however, you have to work with a few relatively murky options and settings, which you'll learn about in the next few sections.

Getting More Favorite Programs on the Start Menu

The Start menu is divided vertically into two columns, as shown in Figure 10-1:

- **Frequent programs** This is the left side of the Start menu, which appears by default with a white background. This side includes the permanent Internet and E-mail icons at the top, and below them are shortcut icons for the six programs that you've used most frequently.

- **Built-in icons** This is the right side of the Start menu, which appears by default with a light blue background. It contains icons for various built-in Windows XP features.

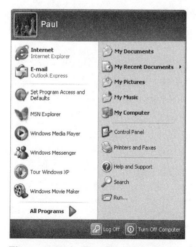

Figure 10-1 The Start menu consists of several discrete sections, each intended to improve your efficiency.

The list of frequent programs is one of the best new features in Windows XP, because it ensures that the programs you use most often are always just a couple of mouse clicks away. If there's a downside to this feature, it's that it displays a maximum of only six icons, so many frequently used programs get left off the list. However, if you have enough room, you can tell Windows XP to display up to 30 icons in this area. Here's how:

1.   Launch Control Panel's Taskbar And Start Menu icon. The Taskbar And Start Menu Properties dialog box appears.

2.   Select the Start Menu tab.

> **Tip**   A quick way to go directly to the Start Menu tab is to right-click either the Start button or an empty section of the Start menu, and then select Properties.

3.   Make sure the Start Menu option is selected and then click the Customize button to its right. The Customize Start Menu dialog box appears, as shown in Figure 10-2.

Figure 10-2   Use the Customize Start Menu dialog box to set the maximum number of shortcut icons that appear in the Start menu's list of frequent programs.

4. Use the Number Of Programs On Start Menu spin box to specify the number of frequent programs you want to display.

5. If you want to start over with a fresh list of frequent programs, click the Clear List button.

> **Tip** If you need to get rid of only one or two icons from the Start menu's frequent programs list, display the Start menu, right-click an icon you want to delete, and then select Remove From This List.

6. If you don't think you have enough screen space to display all the icons, select the Small Icons option. This significantly reduces the amount of space each icon takes up on the Start menu.

7. Click OK.

> **Insider Secret** To prevent a program from appearing on the Start menu's frequent programs list, open the Registry Editor and display the following key:
>
> `HKCR\Applications\`*`program.exe`*
>
> Here, *program.exe* is the name of the program's executable file. (If the key doesn't exist, create it.) Create a string value called `NoStartPage` and set its value to the null string (""). You can also do this via Tweak UI: Open the Taskbar, XP Start Menu branch and clear the check boxes for the programs that you don't want to appear on the Start menu.

Changing the Default Internet and E-mail Programs

Above the Start menu's frequent programs list is the *pinned programs* list, which, in addition to some items you may have intentionally added, contains two items that (by default) appear permanently on the Start menu:

- **Internet**   By default, this item launches the Microsoft Internet Explorer Web browser.

- **E-mail**   By default, this item launches the Microsoft Outlook Express e-mail client.

> **Note**   If your computer's manufacturer or reseller preinstalled Windows XP, you may notice that the manufacturer or reseller altered the default Internet and E-mail programs to support other software packaged with your computer. However, you should be able to further modify the defaults to reflect your own preferences.

If you have multiple Web browsers or e-mail clients installed on your computer, you can customize these items to launch your preferred Web browser or e-mail program. Here are the steps to follow:

1. Display the Customize Start Menu dialog box, as described in the previous section.

2. If you want the Internet item to appear on the Start menu, leave the Internet check box selected; otherwise, clear it and continue with step 4.

3. If the Internet check box is selected, use the list to its right to choose the Web browser you want associated with the Internet item.

4. If you want the E-mail item to appear on the Start menu, leave the E-mail check box selected; otherwise, clear it and continue with step 6.

5. If the E-mail check box is selected, use the list to its right to choose the e-mail client you want associated with the E-mail item.

6. Click OK.

Note, too, that it's also possible to change the text and the icon used for the Internet item on the Start menu. You do this by first displaying the following key in the Registry Editor:

```
HKLM\SOFTWARE\Clients\StartMenuInternet\client\
```

Here, *client* is the name of the executable file of the program associated with the icon (such as Iexplore.exe for Internet Explorer). The (Default) setting controls the icon text, and the (Default) setting of the DefaultIcon subkey controls the icon.

Customizing the text and icon for the E-mail item is similar. You'll find the necessary settings here:

```
HKLM\SOFTWARE\Clients\Mail\client\
```

Here, *client* is the name of the program associated with the icon (such as Outlook Express). The (Default) setting controls the icon text, and the (Default) setting of the DefaultIcon subkey controls the icon. Note that you may have to create this subkey.

Pinning a Favorite Program Permanently to the Start Menu

The Start menu's list of frequent programs is such a timesaving feature that it can be frustrating if a program drops off the list. Another aggravation is that the icons often change position because Windows XP displays the programs in order of popularity. Once you display the Start menu, this constant shifting of icons can result in a slight hesitation while you look for the icon you want. (This is particularly true if you've expanded the number of icons that can be displayed.) Contrast both of these problems with the blissfully static nature of the pinned programs list's Internet and E-mail icons, which (by default) are always where you need them, when you need them.

You can get the same effect with other shortcuts by adding—or *pinning*—them to the pinned programs list. To do this, first open the Start menu and, looking in either the frequent programs listing or the All Programs list, find the shortcut you want to work with. Then you have two choices:

- Right-click the shortcut and then select Pin To Start Menu.

- Drag the shortcut to the pinned programs list.

You can also use this technique to pin shortcuts residing on the desktop to the pinned programs list. If you decide later on that you no longer want a shortcut pinned to the Start menu's pinned programs list, right-click the shortcut and then select Unpin From Start Menu.

Insider Secret   When you display the Start menu, you can select a pinned item quickly by pressing the first letter of the item's name. If you add several shortcuts to the pinned programs list, however, you might end up with more than one item that begins with the same letter. To avoid conflicts, rename each of these items so that they begin with a number. For example, renaming "Backup" to "1 Backup" means there is no confusion if the program "Backgammon" is also pinned, and you can select this item by pressing 1 when the Start menu is displayed.

Streamlining the Start Menu by Converting Links to Menus

The right side of the Start menu contains a number of built-in Windows XP features, which are set up as links. That is, you click an item, and a window or a program runs in response. That's fine for items such as Search or Run, but it's not very efficient for an item such as Control Panel, where you're usually looking to launch a specific Control Panel icon. It seems wasteful to have to open the Control Panel window, launch the icon, and then close Control Panel.

A better approach is to convert a link into a menu of items that would normally be displayed in a separate window. For example, the Control Panel item could display a menu of its icons. One of the nicer new features in Windows XP is that it's easy to convert many of the Start menu links into menus. If you choose to convert one or more of the Start menu links to menus, here are the steps:

1. Display the Customize Start Menu dialog box as described earlier (see Figure 10-2).

2. Select the Advanced tab.

3. In the Start Menu Items section of the dialog box, find the following items and, for the links you want to convert to menus, select the Display As A Menu option:

   ❑   Control Panel

   ❑   My Computer

   ❑   My Documents

   ❑   My Music

   ❑   My Pictures

4. In the Start Menu Items section of the dialog box, select the Favorites Menu check box to add a menu of your Internet Explorer favorites to the Start menu.

5. In the Start Menu Items section of the dialog box, find the Network Connections item and select the Display As Connect To Menu option. This gives you a menu of network connections, and you can launch any connection by selecting it from the menu.

6. In the Start Menu Items section of the dialog box, find the System Administrative Tools item and select the Display On The All Programs Menu And The Start Menu option. This gives you an Administrative Tools menu that offers shortcuts to features such as the Computer Management snap-in, the Performance monitor, and the Local Security Policy editor.

7. Make sure the List My Most Recently Opened Documents check box is selected. This adds the My Recent Documents menu to the Start menu, which displays the last 15 documents that you worked with.

8. Click OK to return to the Taskbar And Start Menu Properties dialog box.

9. Click OK.

Adding, Moving, and Removing Other Start Menu Icons

Besides the main Start menu, the icons on the All Programs menu and submenus can be customized to suit the way you work. Using the techniques we discuss in this section you can perform the following Start menu productivity boosts:

■ Move important features closer to the beginning of the All Programs menu hierarchy.

■ Remove features you don't use.

■ Add new commands for features not currently available on the All Programs menu (such as the Registry Editor).

Windows XP offers three methods for adding and removing Start menu shortcuts, and we explain each of them in the next three sections.

Adding Shortcuts via the Start Button

The quickest way to add a shortcut is to drag an executable file from Windows Explorer and then do either of the following:

■ **Drop it on the Start button.**   This pins the shortcut to the bottom of the pinned programs list on the Start menu.

■ **Hover over the Start button.**   After a second or two, the main Start menu appears. Now hover over All Programs until the menu appears, and then drop the file's icon where you want the shortcut to appear.

Working with the Start Menu Folder

The All Programs shortcuts are stored in two places within %SystemDrive% \Documents and Settings\:

■ **The *user*\Start Menu\Programs subfolder, where *user* is the name of the current user.**   Shortcuts in this subfolder appear only when this user is logged on to Windows XP.

■ **The All Users\Start Menu\Programs subfolder.**   Shortcuts in this folder appear to all users.

> **Tip**   A quick way to get to the current user's Start Menu folder is to right-click the Start button and then select Explore.

By working with the Programs subfolder in Windows Explorer, you get the most control over not only where your Start menu shortcuts appear, but also the names of those shortcuts. Here's a summary of the techniques you can use:

■ Within the Programs folder and its subfolders, you can drag existing shortcuts from one folder to another.

■ To create a new shortcut, drag the executable file's name to the folder you want to use. (Remember that if you want to create a short-cut for a document or other non-executable file, right-drag the file's name and then select Create Shortcuts Here when you drop the file.)

■ You can create your own folders within the Programs folder hierar-chy and they'll appear as submenus within the All Programs menu.

- You can rename a shortcut the same way you rename any file.

- You can delete a shortcut the same way you delete any file.

Working with All Programs Menu Shortcuts Directly

Many of the chores listed in the previous section are more easily performed by working directly within the All Programs menu itself. That is, you open the All Programs menu, find the shortcut you want to work with, and then use any of these techniques:

- Drag the shortcut to another section of its current menu.

- Drag the shortcut to another menu or to the Recycle Bin.

- Right-click the shortcut and then select a command (such as Delete) from the shortcut menu.

Customizing the Taskbar for Easier Program and Document Launching

In Windows XP, the taskbar acts somewhat like a mini-application. The purpose of this "application" is to display a button for each running program and to enable you to switch from one program to another. And like most applications these days, the taskbar also has its own toolbars that, in this case, enable you to launch programs and documents.

Displaying the Built-In Taskbar Toolbars

The Windows XP taskbar comes with four default toolbars:

- **Address**   This toolbar contains a text box into which you can type a local address (such as a folder or file path), a network address (a Universal Naming Convention [UNC] path), or an Internet address. When you press Enter or click the Go button, Windows XP loads the address into Windows Explorer (if you entered a local or network folder address), an application (if you entered a file path), or Internet Explorer (if you entered an Internet address). In other words, this toolbar works just like the Address bar used by Windows Explorer and Internet Explorer.

- **Links**   This toolbar contains several buttons that link to predefined Internet sites. This is the same as the Links toolbar that appears in Internet Explorer.

- **Quick Launch**   This is a collection of one-click icons that launch Internet Explorer or Media Player, or show the desktop.

- **Desktop**   This toolbar contains all the desktop icons, as well as an icon for Internet Explorer and submenus for My Documents, My Computer, and My Network Places.

To toggle these toolbars on and off, first right-click an empty spot on the taskbar. On the shortcut menu that appears, select Toolbars and then click the toolbar you want to work with.

Setting Some Taskbar Toolbar Options

After you've displayed a toolbar, a number of options allow you to customize the look of the toolbar and make it easier to work with. Right-click an empty section of the toolbar and then select one of the following commands:

- **View**   This command displays a submenu with two options: Large Icons and Small Icons. These commands determine the size of the toolbar's icons. For example, if a toolbar has more icons than can be shown as large icons, switch to the small icons view.

- **Show Text**   This command toggles the icon titles on and off. If you turn on the text, it makes it easier to decipher what each icon does, but you'll see fewer icons in a given space.

- **Show Title**   This command toggles the toolbar title (displayed to the left of the icons) on and off.

Creating New Taskbar Toolbars

Besides the predefined taskbar toolbars, you can also create new toolbars that display the contents of any folder on your system. For example, if you have a folder of programs or documents that you launch regularly, you can get one-click access to those items by displaying that folder as a toolbar. Here are the steps to follow:

1. Right-click an empty spot on the toolbar, then select Toolbars, New Toolbar. Windows XP displays the New Toolbar dialog box.

2. Use the folder list provided to select the folder you want to display as a toolbar. (Or click Make New Folder to create a new subfolder within the currently selected folder.)

3. Click OK. Windows XP creates the new toolbar.

Putting Taskbar Toolbars to Good Use

Now that you know how to display, create, and customize taskbar toolbars, you can take advantage of them to get one-click access to large numbers of programs and documents. The basic idea is to create a toolbar, populate its folder with shortcuts to programs and documents, and then display the toolbar on the left side of the screen for easy access. Here's how it's done:

> **Note** Before you embark upon these steps, make sure the taskbar isn't locked. Right-click an empty section of the taskbar and then select Lock The Taskbar to toggle it. Also, make sure the desktop is visible by minimizing all open windows (right-click the taskbar and then select Show The Desktop).

1. Create a new folder.

2. Create shortcuts in this new folder for your favorite documents and programs.

3. Create a new taskbar toolbar that displays the contents of the new folder.

4. Drag the left edge of the new toolbar and drop it on the desktop. Windows XP displays the toolbar as a window.

5. Drag the toolbar window to the left edge of the screen and drop it when the toolbar expands to fill the left edge.

6. Right-click an empty section of the toolbar and select the Show Title, Show Text, and Always On Top commands. The Always On Top command ensures that the toolbar is always visible, even if other windows are maximized.

As you can see in Figure 10-3, the new toolbar is displayed on the left. Here are some notes about this arrangement:

- You can size the toolbar by dragging (in this case) the right edge to the left or right.

- If you prefer, you can display the toolbar on the right or top edge of the window. To move it, first drag it from the edge and drop it on the desktop. Then drag the toolbar window and drop it on the edge you want to use.

■   If you have enough room, you can display multiple toolbars on one edge of the window. For example, you could add the Quick Launch and Links toolbars for easy access to their shortcuts. To do this, display the other toolbar, drag it off the taskbar, drop it on the desktop, and then drag the toolbar window to the edge of the window and drop it on the toolbar that's already in place. You may need to drag the top edge of the toolbar up or down to see its icons.

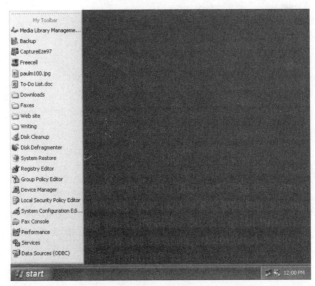

Figure 10-3   The new toolbar appears on the left edge of the screen and is visible even when other windows are maximized.

Improving Productivity by Setting Taskbar Options

The taskbar comes with a few options that can help you be more productive by either saving a few mouse clicks or by giving you more screen room to display your applications. Follow these steps to set these taskbar options:

1.   Right-click the taskbar and then select Properties. (Alternatively, launch Control Panel's Taskbar And Start Menu icon.) The Taskbar And Start Menu Properties dialog box appears with the Taskbar tab displayed, as shown in Figure 10-4 on the following page.

Figure 10-4   Use the Taskbar tab to set up the taskbar for improved productivity.

2.   Here's how the various options affect productivity:

❑   **Lock The Taskbar**   When this check box is selected, you can't resize the taskbar and you can't resize or move any task-bar toolbars. This is useful if you share your computer with other users and you don't want to waste time resetting the task-bar if it's changed by someone else.

❑   **Auto-Hide The Taskbar**   When this check box is selected, Windows XP reduces the taskbar to a thin blue line at the bot-tom of the screen when you're not using it. This is useful if you want a bit more screen room for your applications. To redisplay the taskbar, move the mouse to the bottom of the screen. Note, however, that you should consider leaving this option cleared if you use the taskbar frequently; otherwise, auto-hiding it will slow you down because it takes Windows XP a second or two to restore the taskbar when you hover the mouse over that thin blue line.

❑   **Keep The Taskbar On Top Of Other Windows**   If you clear this option, Windows XP hides the taskbar behind any window that's either maximized or moved over the taskbar. To get to the taskbar, you need to minimize or move the window, or else you need to press the 🪟 key. This isn't a very efficient way to work, so we recommend leaving this option selected.

❑   **Group Similar Taskbar Buttons**   See the next section, "Controlling Taskbar Grouping," for more information on this setting.

❑   **Show Quick Launch**   Select this check box to display the Quick Launch toolbar, discussed earlier (see "Displaying the Built-In Taskbar Toolbars"). Quick Launch is a handy way to access Internet Explorer, the desktop, and Windows Media Player (as well as any other shortcuts you add to the Quick Launch folder), so we recommend selecting this option.

❑   **Show The Clock**   Leave this check box selected to keep the clock displayed in the notification area.

❑   **Hide Inactive Icons**   When this check box is selected, Windows XP hides notification area icons that you haven't used for a while. This gives the taskbar a bit more room to display program buttons, so leave this option selected if you don't use the notification area icons all that often. If you do use the icons frequently, clear this option to avoid having to click the arrow to display the hidden icons.

> **Note**   If your notification area is crowded with icons, it's inefficient to display all the icons if you use only a few of them. Instead of showing them all, leave the Hide Inactive Icons check box selected and click Customize. For the icons you use often, click the item's Behavior column, click the arrow at the right edge of the column, and then click Always Show in the list that appears. This tells Windows XP to always display the icon in the notification area.

3.   Click OK.

Controlling Taskbar Grouping

One of the new things built into the Windows XP taskbar is the grouping feature. When the taskbar fills up with buttons, Windows XP consolidates icons from the same program into a single button, as shown in Figure 10-5 on the following page. To access one of these grouped windows, you click the button and then click the window you want.

> **Tip**   You can close all of a group's windows at once by right-clicking the group button and then selecting Close Group.

Figure 10-5   When the taskbar gets filled with buttons, Windows XP groups similar windows into a single button.

The grouping feature makes it easier to read the name of each taskbar button, but the price is a slight efficiency drop because it takes two clicks to select a window instead of one. If you don't like this tradeoff, you can disable the grouping feature by right-clicking the taskbar, selecting Properties, and then clearing the Group Similar Taskbar Buttons check box.

> **Tip**   Another way to prevent grouping is to give the taskbar more room to display buttons. The easiest way to do that is to resize the taskbar by dragging its top edge up until the taskbar expands. If this doesn't work, the taskbar is probably locked. Unlock it by right-clicking the taskbar and then clearing Lock The Taskbar.

Alternatively, you can tweak the grouping feature to suit the way you work. To do this, open the Registry Editor and head for the following key:

```
HKCU\Software\Microsoft\Windows\CurrentVersion\Explorer\Advanced\
```

Add a DWORD value called `TaskbarGroupSize` and set it to one of the following values:

- **0**   When the grouping kicks in (that is, when the taskbar gets full), Windows XP will group only the buttons from the applications that you have used the least.

- **1**   When the grouping kicks in, Windows XP will group only the buttons from the application that has the most windows open. If a second application surpasses the number of open windows in the first application, the second application's windows are grouped as well.

■   *x*   Windows XP will group any application that has at least *x* windows open, where *x* is a number between 2 and 99. Note that the grouping occurs even if the taskbar is not full.

Note that you must log off or restart Windows XP to put the new setting into effect. Note, too, that you can also change this setting via Tweak UI. Display the Taskbar, Grouping item.

Modifying the Start Menu and Taskbar with Group Policies

You've seen throughout this book that the group policies offer unprecedented control over the Windows XP interface without having to modify the registry directly. This is particularly true of the Start menu and taskbar, which boast more than 40 policies that do everything from removing Start menu links such as Run and Help to hiding the taskbar's notification area. To see these policies, launch the Group Policy editor and select User Configuration, Administrative Templates, Start Menu And Taskbar.

Most of the policies are straightforward: By enabling them, you remove a feature from the Start menu or taskbar. For example, enabling the Remove Run Menu From Start Menu policy hides the Start menu's Run command for the current user. This is a handy feature if you're trying to restrict a user to using only those programs and documents that appear on the Start menu. Here are a few policies that we think are the most useful:

■   **Remove Drag-And-Drop Context Menus On The Start Menu** Enable this policy to prevent the current user from rearranging the Start menu using drag-and-drop techniques.

■   **Prevent Changes To Taskbar And Start Menu Settings**   Enable this policy to prevent the current user from accessing the Taskbar And Start Menu Properties dialog box.

■   **Remove Access To The Context Menus For The Taskbar** Enable this policy to prevent the current user from right-clicking the taskbar and seeing the taskbar's context menus.

■   **Do Not Keep History Of Recently Opened Documents**   Enable this policy to prevent Windows XP from tracking the current user's recently opened documents.

■   **Clear History Of Recently Opened Documents On Exit**   Enable this policy to remove all documents from the current user's recent documents list whenever the user logs off.

- **Remove Balloon Tips On Start Menu Items**   Enable this policy to prevent the current user from seeing the balloon tips that Windows XP displays when it prompts you about new hardware being detected, downloading automatic updates, and so on.

- **Remove User Name From Start Menu**   Enable this policy to prevent the current user's name from appearing at the top of the Start menu. This is a good idea if you need more room on the Start menu for the pinned program or frequent program lists.

- **Hide The Notification Area**   Enable this policy to prevent the current user from seeing the taskbar's notification area.

- **Do Not Display Any Custom Toolbars In The Taskbar**   Enable this policy to prevent the current user from adding custom toolbars to the taskbar, or displaying existing custom toolbars from this taskbar.

Using Screen Space Efficiently

How images appear on your monitor, and how efficiently you use the monitor's viewable area, is a function of two measurements: the color quality and the screen resolution.

The *color quality* is a measure of the number of colors available to display images on the screen. Color quality is usually expressed in either bits or total possible colors. For example, a 4-bit display can handle up to 16 colors (since 2 to the power of 4 equals 16). The most common values are 16 bit (65,536 colors), 24 bit (16,777,216 colors), and 32 bit (4,294,967,296 colors). In Windows XP, they are known as Medium, High, and Highest, respectively.

The *screen resolution* is a measure of the density of the pixels used to display the screen image. The pixels are arranged in a row-and-column format, so the resolution is expressed as *columns* by *rows*, where *columns* is the number of pixel columns and *rows* is the number of pixel rows. For example, an 800 × 600 resolution means screen images are displayed using 800 columns of pixels and 600 rows of pixels.

How does all this affect productivity?

- In general, the greater the number of colors (and, to a lesser extent, the higher the screen resolution), the sharper your screen image will appear. Sharper images, especially text, are easier to read and put less strain on the eyes.

Tip   If you read a lot of on-screen text, select Windows XP's ClearType feature, which drastically reduces the jagged edges of screen fonts and makes text super-sharp and far easier to read than regular screen text, especially on liquid crystal display (LCD) screens (the displays used on laptops and flat-panel monitors). To use this feature, launch Control Panel's Display icon, select the Appearance tab, and click Effects. In the Effects dialog box, make sure the Use The Following Method To Smooth Edges Of Screen Fonts check box is selected and then choose ClearType from the list below it. Click OK and then click OK in the Display Properties dialog box to put the new setting into effect. Note, too, that you can customize some ClearType settings by going to the following Microsoft site:

http://www.microsoft.com/typography/cleartype /cleartypeactivate.htm

■   At higher resolutions, individual screen items—such as icons and dialog boxes—appear smaller since these items tend to have a fixed height and width, expressed in pixels. For example, a dialog box that's 400 pixels wide will appear half as wide as the screen at 800 × 600. However, it will appear to be only one quarter of the screen width at 1,600 × 1,024 (a common resolution for very large monitors). This means that at higher resolutions, your maximized windows will appear larger, so you'll get a larger work area.

The key thing to bear in mind about all this is that there's occasionally a trade-off between color quality and resolution. That is, depending on how much video memory is installed on your graphics adapter, you may have to trade higher resolution for lower color quality, or vice versa.

To change the screen resolution and color quality, follow these steps:

1.   Launch Control Panel's Display icon to display the Display Properties dialog box on-screen.

2.   Select the Settings tab, as shown in Figure 10-6.

Figure 10-6 Use the Settings tab to set the screen resolution and color quality.

3. To set the resolution, drag the Screen Resolution slider left or right.

4. To set the color quality, choose an item from the Color Quality list.

5. Click OK. Windows XP performs the adjustment and then displays a dialog box asking if you want to keep the new setting.

6. Click Yes.

> **Note** If your graphics adapter or monitor can't handle the new resolution or color quality, you'll end up with a garbled display. In this case, just wait for 15 seconds and Windows XP will restore the resolution and color quality to their original settings.

11

Optimizing Performance

In this chapter, you'll learn how to:

■ Monitor performance using Task Manager and System Monitor.

■ Reduce the time it takes for Windows XP to start up.

■ Set up Windows XP to maximize application performance.

■ Get the most out of your hard disk.

■ Tweak Windows XP's virtual memory settings for optimum performance.

We often wonder why our workaday computer chores seem to take just as long as they ever did, despite the fact that our hardware is, generally speaking, bigger, better, and faster than ever. The answer to this apparent riddle is related to Parkinson's Law of Data, which states that data expands to fill the space available for storage. On a more general level, Parkinson's Law could be restated as follows: The increase in software system requirements is directly proportional to the increase in hardware system capabilities. A slick new chip is released that promises a 30-percent speed boost; software designers, seeing the new chip gain wide acceptance, add extra features to their already bloated code to take advantage of the higher performance level; then another new chip is released, followed by another software upgrade—and the cycle continues relentlessly as these twin engines of computer progress lurch codependently into the future.

So how do you break out of the performance deadlock created by the immovable object of software-code bloat meeting the irresistible force of hardware advancement? By optimizing your system to minimize the effects of overgrown applications and maximize the native capabilities of your hardware.

Learning how to optimize memory, applications, and hard disks is the key to unleashing your system's performance potential, and that's exactly what we'll show you how to do in this chapter.

Monitoring Performance

Performance optimization is a bit of a black art in that every user has different needs, every configuration has different operating parameters, and every system can react in a unique and unpredictable way to performance tweaks. What this means is that if you want to optimize your system, you have to get to know how it works, what it needs, and how it reacts to changes. You can do this by just using the system and paying attention to how things look and feel, but a more rigorous approach often is called for. To that end, the next few sections take you on a brief tour of Microsoft Windows XP's performance monitoring capabilities.

Using Task Manager

The Task Manager utility is excellent for getting a quick overview of the current state of the system. To display it, press Ctrl+Alt+Delete. (If you are using the Classic logon screen, the Windows Security dialog box will appear; click the Task Manager button.)

> **Tip** To bypass the Windows Security dialog box, right-click an empty section of the taskbar and then select Task Manager.

The Processes tab, shown in Figure 11-1, displays a list of the programs, services, and system components that are currently running on your computer. The processes are displayed in the order in which they were started, but you can change the order by clicking the column headings. (Note that to get back to the original, chronological display of processes, you will need to close and reopen Task Manager.) Besides the name of each process and the user who started the process, you also see two performance measures:

■ **CPU**   This value tells you the percentage of CPU resources that the process is using. If your system seems sluggish, look for a process that is consuming all or nearly all of the CPU's resources. Most programs will occasionally monopolize the CPU for short periods, but a program that is stuck at 100 (percent) for a long time most likely has some kind of problem. In this case, try shutting down the program. If that doesn't work, click the program's process and then click End Process. Click Yes when Windows XP asks if you're sure you want to do this.

■ **Mem Usage**   This value tells you approximately how much memory the process is using. This value is less informative, since a process may genuinely require a lot of memory in order to function. However, if this value is increasing steadily for a process that you're not using, a problem may be present, and you should shut down the process.

> **Insider Secret**   The four default columns on the Processes tab aren't the only data available to you. Select the View, Select Columns command to see a list of more than two dozen items that you can add to the Processes tab.

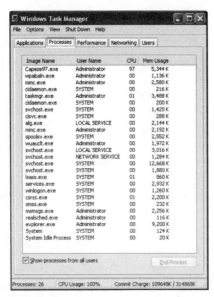

Figure 11-1   The Processes tab lists your system's running programs and services.

The Performance tab, shown in Figure 11-2, offers a more substantial collection of performance data, particularly for that all-important component: your system's memory.

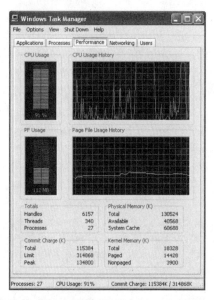

Figure 11-2   The Performance tab lists various numbers related to your system's memory and CPU components.

The graphs show you both the current value and the values over time for CPU usage and page file usage.

What is a page file? Your computer can address memory beyond what is physically installed on the system. This non-physical memory is called *virtual memory*, and it's implemented by using a piece of your hard disk that's set up to emulate physical memory. This hard disk storage is actually a single file called a *page file* (or sometimes a *paging file* or a *swap file*). When physical memory is full, Windows XP makes room for new data—either program code or document contents—by taking some infrequently used data that's currently in memory and swapping it out to the page file. The PF Usage graph shows the current utilization of the page file, and the Page File Usage History graph shows the relative size of the page file over time.

Below the graphs are various numbers. The items in the Totals section of the window appeal only to programmers, so we'll skip them. Here's what the other values mean:

> **Note** The memory values are listed in kilobytes. To convert to mega-bytes, divide by 1,024.

- **Physical Memory Total** The total amount of physical random access memory (RAM) in your system.

- **Physical Memory Available** The amount of physical RAM that Windows XP has available for your programs. Note that the system cache (see the next item) is not included in this total.

- **Physical Memory System Cache** The amount of physical RAM that Windows XP has set aside to store recently used programs and documents.

- **Commit Charge Total** The combined total of physical RAM and virtual memory the system is using.

- **Commit Charge Limit** The combined total of physical RAM and virtual memory available to the system.

- **Commit Charge Peak** The maximum combined total of physical RAM and virtual memory the system has used so far in this session.

- **Kernel Memory Total** The total amount of RAM used by the Windows XP system components and device drivers.

- **Kernel Memory Paged** The amount of kernel memory that is mapped to pages in virtual memory.

- **Kernel Memory Nonpaged** The amount of kernel memory that cannot be mapped to pages in virtual memory.

Here are some notes related to these values that will help you monitor memory-related performance issues:

- If the Physical Memory Available value approaches zero, it means your system is starved for memory. You may have too many programs running, or a large program may be using lots of memory.

- If the Physical Memory System Cache value is much less than half the Physical Memory Total, it means your system isn't operating as efficiently as it could because Windows XP can't store enough recently used data in memory. Because Windows XP gives up some of the system cache when it needs RAM, close down programs you don't need.

- If the Commit Charge Total value remains higher than the Physical Memory Total value, it means Windows XP is doing a lot of work swapping data to and from the page file, which greatly slows performance.

- If the Commit Charge Peak is higher than the Physical Memory Total value, it means at some point in the current session Windows XP had to use the page file. If the Commit Charge Total is currently less than Physical Memory Total, the peak value may have been a temporary event, but you should monitor the peak over time, just to make sure.

In all of these situations, the quickest solution is to reduce the system's memory footprint either by closing documents or by closing applications. For the latter, use the Processes tab to determine which applications are using the most memory and then shut down the ones you can live without for now. The better, but more expensive, solution is to add more physical RAM to your system. This decreases the likelihood that Windows XP will need to use the paging file, and it also enables Windows XP to increase the size of the system cache, which greatly improves performance.

Using System Monitor

For more advanced performance monitoring, Windows XP offers the System Monitor tool, which you can get to by selecting Start, Run, entering **perfmon.msc**, and clicking OK. System Monitor appears in the Performance window, as shown in Figure 11-3.

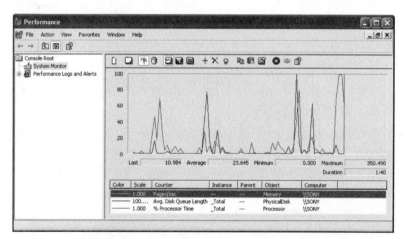

Figure 11-3 Use System Monitor to keep an eye on various system settings and components.

System Monitor's job is to provide you with real-time reports on how various system settings and components are performing. Each item is called a *counter,* and the displayed counters are listed at the bottom of the window. Each counter is assigned a different colored line, and that color corresponds to the colored lines shown in the graph. Note, too, that you can get specific numbers for a counter—the most recent value, the average, the minimum, and the maximum—by clicking a counter and reading the boxes just below the graphs.

The idea is that you should configure System Monitor to show the processes you're interested in (page file size, free memory, and so on) and then keep System Monitor running while you perform your normal chores. By examining the System Monitor readouts from time to time, you gain an appreciation of what is "typical" on your system. Then, if you run into performance problems, you can check System Monitor to see whether you've run into any bottlenecks or anomalies.

By default, System Monitor shows only the Kernel Processor Usage setting, which tells you the percentage of time the processor is busy. To add another setting to the System Monitor window, follow these steps:

1. Right-click a counter and then select Add Counters. The Add Counters dialog box appears.

2. Use the Performance Object list to select a counter category (such as Memory, Paging File, or Processor).

3. Choose the Select Counters From List option.

4. Select the counter you want and then click Add. (If you need more information about the item, click the Explain button.)

5. Repeat step 4 to add any other counters you want to monitor.

6. Click Close.

Fine-Tuning Performance

Now that you know how to monitor performance, it's time to get practical with a few specific optimizations. The rest of this chapter shows you how to optimize items such as the Windows XP startup, applications, the hard disk, virtual memory, and more.

Optimizing Startup

One of the longest-running debates in computer circles involves the question of whether or not to turn off the computer when you're not using it. The "off" camp believes that shutting down the computer reduces hard disk wear-and-tear (because the disk's platters spin full-time, even when the computer is idle), prevents damage from power surges or power failures that occur while the machine is off, and saves energy. The "on" camp believes that cold starts are hard on many computer components, that energy can be saved by taking advantage of power-saving features, and that leaving the computer running is more productive because it avoids the lengthy startup process.

In the end, I believe it's the overall boot time that usually determines which of these camps one belongs to. If the startup time is just unbearably long, you'll certainly be more inclined to leave your computer running all the time. Fortunately, Windows XP has made great strides in improving startup times, which are now routinely measured in seconds instead of minutes. However, if you're convinced that turning off the computer is a sensible move, but you hate waiting even for Windows XP's faster startup process, here are a few tips for improving startup performance even more:

- **Reduce or eliminate BIOS checks.**   Many computers run through one or more diagnostic checks at system startup. For example, it's common for machines to check the integrity of the system memory chips. That seems like a good idea, but it can take an interminable amount of time to complete on a system with a great deal of memory. Access your system's BIOS settings and turn off these checks to reduce the overall time of the computer's Power-On Self Test.

- **Reduce OS Choices menu timeout.**   If you have two or more operating systems on your computer, you see Windows XP's OS Choices menu at startup. If you're paying attention to the startup, you can press Enter as soon as this menu appears, and your system will boot the default operating system. If your mind is focused elsewhere, however, the startup will be delayed 30 seconds until the default choice is selected automatically. If this happens to you frequently, you can reduce that 30-second timeout to speed up the startup. There are four ways to do this:

  ❑   Edit the Boot.ini file. In the [boot loader] section, change the timeout value.

  ❑   Select Start, Run, enter **msconfig -4**, and click OK. On the System Configuration Utility's BOOT.INI tab, modify the value in the Timeout text box.

❑ Launch Control Panel's System icon to get to the System Properties dialog box. Select the Advanced tab, click Settings in the Startup And Recovery section of the dialog box, and then adjust the value of the Time To Display List Of Operating Systems spin box.

❑ At the command prompt, enter the following command (replace *ss* with the number of seconds you want to use for the timeout):

```
BOOTCFG /Timeout ss
```

> **Tip** If your system has multiple hardware profiles, the Hardware Profile menu also appears for 30 seconds before choosing the default profile. You can reduce this timeout by launching Control Panel's System icon, selecting the Hardware tab, and then clicking Hardware Profiles. In the Hardware Profiles dialog box, choose the Select The First Profile Listed If I Don't Select A Profile In option and use the spin box below it to set the reduced timeout.

■ **In BOOT.INI, use the /NOGUIBOOT switch.** This prevents the Windows XP splash screen from appearing, which will shave a small amount of time off the startup.

> **Caution** Using /NOGUIBOOT also means that you won't see any startup blue-screen errors. In other words, if a problem occurs, all you'll know for sure is that your system has hung, but you won't know why. For this reason, the small performance improvement you'll experience by using /NOGUIBOOT is likely not enough to offset the lack of startup error messages.

■ **Upgrade to Windows XP device drivers.** Device drivers designed to work with Windows XP generally will load faster than older drivers.

- **Use an automatic logon.** One of the best ways to reduce startup time frustration is to ignore the startup altogether by doing something else (such as getting a cup of coffee) while the boot chores occur. This strategy is foiled if the startup is interrupted by the logon process. If you're the only person who uses your computer, you can overcome this problem by setting up Windows XP to log you on automatically. We discussed this in **Chapter 5**, "Managing Logons and Users."

- **Don't require Ctrl+Alt+Delete.** If you must log on, and if you're using the Classic logon method (that is, you're not using the new Welcome screen), Windows XP usually asks you to press Ctrl+Alt+Delete before it displays the Log On To Windows dialog box. You can save a startup step by eliminating this usually unnecessary procedure. We show you how to do this in **Chapter 5**.

- **Reduce or eliminate startup programs.** By far the biggest startup bottleneck is the array of programs scheduled to launch automatically when Windows XP loads. Loading many small programs or just a couple of large programs can slow the startup to an excruciating crawl. Use the techniques we discussed in **Chapter 4** to reduce the number of startup programs to only those you absolutely need to get going first thing.

- **Use hibernation mode.** Hibernation mode, which is supported by most new PCs, saves the current contents of memory (running programs, open documents, and so on) to a file on your hard disk and then shuts down the computer. When you turn the machine back on, Windows XP bypasses the usual startup routines and just restores the memory contents from the hibernation file. The result is that your system is back on its feet in just a few seconds. Before you can use hibernation, you need to make sure it's enabled on your system by first launching Control Panel's Power Options icon. In the Power Options Properties dialog box, display the Hibernate tab and select the Enable Hibernation check box. For users of the Welcome logon screen to put the computer into hibernation, select Start, Turn Off Computer, hold down the Shift key, and then select Hibernate. Similarly, for users of the Classic logon screen, select Start, Shut Down and then select Hibernate from the list.

Caution   The contents of your system's memory are stored in a file called Hiberfil.sys in the root folder of whatever drive Windows XP is installed on. This is hardwired into the system and can't be changed. Therefore, before enabling hibernation, make sure you have plenty of free space on the Windows XP drive. Note that Hiberfil.sys will be as large as the amount of RAM on your system. If you have 256 MB of RAM, the hibernation file will also be approximately 256 MB.

■ **Configure the prefetcher.**   Prefetching is a new Windows XP performance feature that analyzes disk usage and then reads into memory the data that you or your system accesses most frequently. The prefetcher can be used to speed up booting, application launching, or both. You configure the prefetcher using the following registry setting:

```
HKLM\SYSTEM\CurrentControlSet\Control\SessionManager
\Memory Management\PrefetchParameters\EnablePrefetcher
```

Set this value to 1 for application-only prefetching; 2 for boot-only prefetching; or 3 for both application and boot prefetching. We recommend setting this value to 2 for boot-only prefetching. This will improve boot performance and, on most systems, will have little or no effect on application performance (because the files commonly used to launch application files are probably in the RAM cache anyway).

As a final startup tweak, we also recommend downloading and running Microsoft's Bootvis tool. Bootvis is a handy tool that not only helps you visualize the startup, but can also help optimize your startup based on *traces* that it makes of your system's boot sequence. You can get this tool here:

http://www.microsoft.com/hwdev/platform/performance/fastboot/BootVis.asp

When you launch the downloaded file, be sure to unpack it either in the default Temp folder or in your Desktop folder. Then double-click the Bootvis.exe file to launch Bootvis. The Bootvis window offers several check boxes for items such as CPU Usage and Disk I/O that Bootvis will trace during startup. In most cases, you'll want to select all the check boxes. For a boot visualization, follow these steps:

1. Select Trace, Next Boot. The Trace Repetitions dialog box appears, as shown in Figure 11-4.

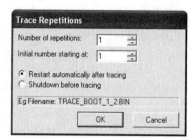

Figure 11-4   You see this dialog box when you select the Trace, Next Boot command.

2. Click OK. Bootvis displays a countdown.

3. Wait for the countdown to finish or click Reboot Now. Bootvis reboots the system.

When the system reboots, Bootvis launches again automatically. The program displays various charts that document the boot process, as shown in Figure 11-5.

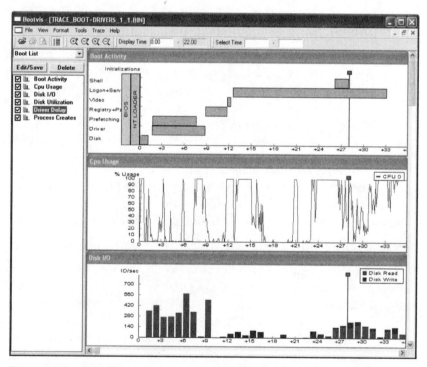

Figure 11-5   The charts give you a visual display of the resources used during the boot process.

To optimize your system's boot process, follow these steps:

1. Select Trace, Optimize System. Bootvis displays a countdown.

2. Wait for the countdown to finish or click Reboot Now. Bootvis reboots the system.

When the system reboots, Bootvis rearranges various startup files on disk so that they can be accessed optimally, thus improving boot performance.

Optimizing Applications

Running applications is the reason we use Windows XP, so it's a rare user who doesn't want his or her applications to run as fast as possible. Here are some pointers for improving the performance of applications under Windows XP:

- **Add more memory.**   All applications run in RAM, of course, so the more RAM you have, the less likely it is that Windows XP will have to store excess program or document data in the page file on the hard disk, which is a real performance killer. In Task Manager or System Monitor, watch the Available Memory value. If this starts to get too low, you should consider adding RAM to your system.

- **Install to the fastest hard drive.**   If your system has multiple hard drives, install your applications on the fastest drive. This will enable Windows XP to access the application's data and documents faster.

- **Set the prefetcher to optimize application launching.**   As discussed in the previous section, Windows XP's new prefetcher component can optimize disk files for booting, application launching, or both. It probably won't make much difference, but experiment with setting the registry's EnablePrefetcher value to 1 or 3 to optimize application launching.

- **Get the latest device drivers.**   If your application works with a device, check with the manufacturer or Windows Update to see if a newer version of the device driver is available. In general, the newer the driver, the faster its performance. We show you how to update device drivers in **Chapter 9**, "Installing and Troubleshooting Devices."

- **Make sure Windows XP is optimized for programs.**   Launch Control Panel's System icon, select the Advanced Tab, and then click Settings in the Performance section of the dialog box. In the Performance Options dialog box, select the Advanced tab, shown in Figure 11-6. In both the Process Scheduling and the Memory Usage sections of the dialog box, select the Programs option.

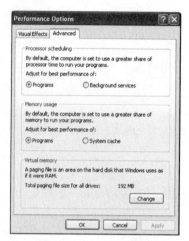

Figure 11-6 Use the Advanced tab to optimize Windows XP for programs.

■ **Set the program priority in Task Manager.** To maximize a program's performance under Windows XP, tell the system to give the program a higher priority than other applications. To do this, first make sure your program is running. Then run Task Manager and select the Processes tab. Right-click your application's process, select Set Priority, and then select (from highest priority to lowest) Realtime, High, or AboveNormal.

Insider Secret If you're not sure which process belongs to your program, select the Task Manager's Applications tab, right-click the program's name, and then select Go To Process.

Optimizing the Hard Disk

Windows XP accesses the hard disk to fetch application code and documents as well as to store data temporarily in the page file. Therefore, optimizing your hard disk can greatly improve Windows XP's overall performance.

If you're looking to add another drive to your system, your starting point should be the drive itself, specifically its theoretical performance specifications. Compare the drive's average seek time with other drives of the same capacity (the lower the value the better). Also, pay attention to the rate at which the drive spins the disk's platters. A 7200-RPM (or higher) drive will have noticeably faster performance than, say, a 5400-RPM drive.

For an existing drive, optimization is the same as maintenance, so you should implement the maintenance plan we discuss in Chapter 12, "Maintaining Your System in 10 Easy Steps." For a hard disk, this means you should attend to the following:

■   Keep an eye on the disk's free space to make sure it doesn't get too low.

■   Periodically clean out any unnecessary files on the disk.

■   Uninstall any programs or devices you no longer use.

■   Check all partitions frequently for errors.

■   Defragment partitions on a regular schedule.

Also, don't use compression or encryption on a partition if you don't have to. Both technologies slow down disk accesses because of the overhead involved in both the compression/decompression and the encryption/decryption processes. Finally, consider turning off the Indexing Service for a drive if you don't do much file searching. To do this, right-click the drive in Windows Explorer and then select Properties. On the General tab, clear the Allow Indexing Service To Index This Disk For Fast File Searching check box.

Insider Secret   You should also make sure your hard disk has *write caching* enabled. Write caching means that Windows XP doesn't flush changed data to the disk until the system is idle, which improves performance. The downside is that a power outage or system crash means the data never gets written, so the changes are lost. The chances of this happening are minimal; we recommend leaving write caching enabled, which is the Windows XP default. To make sure, click Start, Control Panel, double-click System, click Hardware, Device Manager, open the Disk Drives branch, and double-click your hard disk. On the Policies tab, make sure the Enable Write Caching On The Disk check box is selected.

Converting FAT16 and FAT32 Partitions to NTFS

The Windows NT file system (NTFS) is your best choice if you want optimal hard disk performance since, in most cases, NTFS outperforms both FAT16 and FAT32. (This is particularly true with large partitions and with partitions that have numerous files.) Note, however, that for best NTFS performance, you should format a partition as NTFS and then add files to it. If this isn't possible, Windows XP offers the CONVERT utility for converting a FAT 16 or FAT32 drive to NTFS:

```
CONVERT volume /FS:NTFS [/V] [/CvtArea:filename] [/NoSecurity] [/X]
```

volume	Specifies the drive letter (followed by a colon) or volume name you want to convert.
/FS:NTFS	Specifies that the volume is to be converted to NTFS.
/V	Uses verbose mode, which gives detailed information during the conversion.
/CvtArea:filename	Specifies a contiguous placeholder file in the root directory that will be used to store the NTFS system files.
/NoSecurity	Specifies that the default NTFS permissions are not to be applied to this volume. All the converted files and folders will be accessible by all users.
/X	Forces the volume to dismount first if it currently has open files.

For example, running the following command at the command prompt converts drive C to NTFS:

```
convert c: /FS:NTFS
```

Note, however, that if Windows XP is installed on the partition you're trying to convert, you'll see the following message:

```
Convert cannot gain exclusive access to the C: drive, so it cannot
convert it now. Would you like to schedule it to be converted the
next time the system restarts? <Y/N>
```

In this case, press **Y** to schedule the conversion.

Optimizing NTFS

If you make the move to NTFS, either via formatting a partition during Setup or by using the CONVERT utility, you can implement a couple of other tweaks to maximize NTFS performance:

- **Turn off 8.3 file name creation.**   To support legacy applications that don't understand long file names, NTFS keeps track of both the long name for each file as well as a shorter name that conforms to the old 8.3 standard used by the original DOS file systems. The overhead involved in tracking two names for one file isn't much for a small number of files, but it can become onerous if a folder has a huge number of files (300,000 or more). To disable the tracking of an 8.3 name for each file, enter the following statement at the command prompt:

```
FSUTIL BEHAVIOR SET DISABLE8DOT3 1
```

Note, too, that you can do the same thing by changing the value of the following registry setting to 1 (note that the default value is 0):

```
HKLM\SYSTEM\CurrentControlSet\Control\FileSystem
\NtfsDisable8dot3NameCreation
```

- **Disable Last Access timestamp.**   For each folder and file, NTFS stores an attribute called Last Access Time that tells you when the folder or file was last accessed by the user. If you have folders that have a large number of files and if you use programs that access the files frequently, writing the Last Access Time data can slow down NTFS. To disable writing of the Last Access Time attribute, enter the following statement at the command prompt:

```
FSUTIL BEHAVIOR SET DISABLELASTACCESS 1
```

You can achieve the same effect by creating the following DWORD setting and changing its value to 1 (note that the default value is 0):

```
HKLM\SYSTEM\CurrentControlSet\Control\FileSystem
\NtfsDisableLastAccessUpdate
```

Optimizing Virtual Memory

No matter how much main memory your system boasts, Windows XP still creates and uses a page file for virtual memory. To maximize page file performance, you should make sure that Windows XP is working with the page file optimally. Here are some techniques that help you do just that:

- Store the page file on the hard disk that has the fastest access time. You'll see later in this section that you can indicate which hard disk to use for the page file. If you have multiple hard disks (not just multiple partitions of a single disk), you should store the page file on the disk that has the fastest access time.

■ Store the page file on an uncompressed hard disk. Windows XP is happy to store the page file on a compressed hard disk. However, as with all file operations on a compressed disk, the performance of page file operations suffers thanks to the compression and decompression required. Therefore, you should store the page file on an uncompressed disk.

■ Store the page file on the hard disk that has the most free space. Windows XP expands and contracts the page file dynamically depending on the system's needs. To give Windows XP the most flexibility, make sure the page file resides on a hard disk that has a lot of free space.

■ Split the page file over two or more physical drives. If you have two or more physical drives (not just two or more partitions on a single physical drive), splitting the page file over each drive can improve performance because it means Windows XP can extract data from each drive's page file simultaneously. For example, if your current initial page file size is 384 MB, then on one drive you'd set up a page file with a 192-MB initial size, and on a second drive you'd set up another page file with a 192-MB initial size.

■ Customize the page file size. By default, Windows XP sets the initial size of the page file to 1.5 times the amount of RAM in your system, and it sets the maximum size of the page file to three times the amount of RAM. For example, on a system with 256 MB of RAM, the page file's initial size will be 384 MB and its maximum size will be 768 MB. The default values work well on most systems, but you may want to customize these sizes to suit your own configuration. Here are some notes about custom page file sizes:

    ❑ The less RAM you have, the more likely it is that Windows XP will use the page file, so the Windows XP default page file sizes make sense. If your computer has less than 512 MB of RAM, you should leave the page file sizes as is.

    ❑ The more RAM you have, the less likely it is that Windows XP will use the page file. Therefore, the default initial page file size is too large and the disk space reserved by Windows XP is wasted. On systems with 512 MB of RAM or more, you should set the initial page file size to half the RAM size, while leaving the maximum size at three times RAM, just in case.

❏   If disk space is at a premium and you can't move the page file to a drive with more free space, set the initial page file size to 2 MB (the minimum size supported by Windows XP). This should eventually result in the smallest possible page file, but you'll see a bit of a performance drop because Windows XP will often have to dynamically increase the size the page file as you work with your programs.

❏   You might think that setting the initial size and the maximum size to the same (relatively large—say, two or three times RAM) value would improve performance since it would mean that Windows XP would never resize the page file. In practice, however, it has been shown that this trick does *not* improve performance, and in some cases can actually decrease performance.

❏   If you have a large amount of RAM (at least 1 GB), you might think that Windows XP would never need virtual memory, so that it would be okay to turn off the page file. This won't work, however, because Windows XP needs the page file anyway, and some programs may crash if no virtual memory is present.

■   Watch the page file size. Start up all the programs you normally use (and perhaps a few extra, for good measure) and then watch System Monitor's Process\Page File Bytes and Process\Page File Bytes Peak counters.

Changing the Paging File's Location and Size

The page file is named Pagefile.sys, and it's stored in the root folder of the drive on which Windows XP is installed. Here's how to change the hard disk that Windows XP uses to store the page file as well as the page file sizes:

1.   If necessary, defragment the hard disk that you'll be using for the page file. See Chapter 12, "Maintaining Your System in 10 Easy Steps."

2.   Launch Control Panel's System icon to display the System Properties dialog box.

3.   In the Advanced tab's Performance section of the dialog box, click Settings to display the Performance Options dialog box.

4.   In the Performance Options dialog box, within the Advanced tab's Virtual Memory section of the dialog box, click Change. Windows XP displays the Virtual Memory dialog box, shown in Figure 11-7.

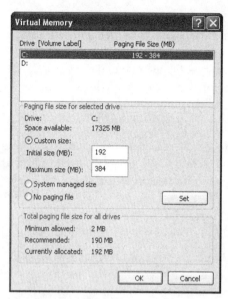

Figure 11-7 Use the Virtual Memory dialog box to select a different hard disk to store the page file.

5. Use the Drive list to select the hard drive you want to use.

6. Select a page file size option:

❑ **Custom Size** Choose this option to set your own page file sizes using the Initial Size (MB) and Maximum Size (MB) text boxes. Ensure that Windows XP is able to dynamically resize the page file as needed by entering a maximum size that's larger than the initial size.

❑ **System Managed Size** Choose this option to let Windows XP manage the page file sizes for you.

❑ **No Paging File** Choose this option to disable the page file on the selected drive.

7. Click Set.

Close all the dialog boxes. If you changed the drive, or if you decreased either the initial size or the maximum size, you need to restart your computer to put the changes into effect.

Insider Secret   If you want to move the page file to another drive, first select the original drive and then choose the No Paging File option to remove the page file from that drive. Then select the other drive and choose either Custom Size or System Managed Size to add a new page file to that drive.

If you want to split the page file over a second drive, leave the original drive as is, select the second drive, and choose either Custom Size or System Managed Size to create a second page file on that drive. If Custom Size is specified for either or both drives, set the new values now.

Defragmenting the Paging File

As Windows XP dynamically sizes the page file, it's possible that it can become fragmented, resulting in a small performance hit. Windows XP manipulates the page file in relatively large blocks, so the fragmentation rarely occurs. However, if you're looking to eke out every last drop of performance on your machine, you should probably ensure that the page file is defragmented.

Unfortunately, Windows XP Disk Defragmenter tool does not defragment the page file. To accomplish this, you have to temporarily move or disable the page file. Here are the steps to follow:

1. Display the Virtual Memory dialog box as described in the previous section.

2. You have two ways to proceed:

    ❑   If you have a second hard drive on your system, first set up a page file on the other hard drive using the same initial and maximum values of the original page file. Then select the original drive, select Custom Size, and reduce the initial and maximum sizes to 0 for the page file.

    ❑   If you have only one hard drive, note the current values, and then select No Paging File to disable the page file.

3. Restart your computer.

> **Insider Secret** To determine whether the page file is defragmented, run Disk Defragmenter and analyze the partition that contains the page file. View the analysis report and, in the Volume Information list, find the Pagefile Fragmentation item. The Total Fragments value tells you the number of fragments used by the page file.

4. Defragment the hard drive that contained the original page file.

5. Display the Virtual Memory dialog box and restore the original page file settings.

6. Restart your computer.

Adjusting Power Options

Windows XP's power management options can shut down your system's monitor or hard disk to save energy. Unfortunately, it takes a few seconds for the system to power up these devices again, which can be frustrating when you want to get back to work. You can do two things to eliminate or reduce this frustration:

- **Don't let Windows XP turn off the monitor and hard disk.** Launch Control Panel's Power Options icon to display the Power Options Properties dialog box. On the Power Schemes tab, use the Power Schemes list to select the Always On item (this is optional) and select Never in the Turn Off Monitor and Turn Off Hard Disks lists. For good measure, you should also make sure Never is selected in the System Standby and System Hibernates lists.

- **Don't use a screen saver.** Again, it can take a few seconds for Windows XP to recover from a screen saver. To ensure you're not using one, launch Control Panel's Display icon, display the Screen Saver tab, and choose (None) in the Screen Saver list. (If you're worried about monitor wear-and-tear, use the Blank or Windows XP screen savers, which are relatively lightweight and can be exited quickly.)

Turning Off Fast User Switching

Windows XP's Fast User Switching feature enables multiple users to keep programs and documents running concurrently, which makes it easy to quickly switch from one user to another. Of course, having multiple sets of running programs and open documents adds to the memory and resource requirements of your system, which slows down performance for all users. In other words, the time saved by switching users quickly is most likely lost several times over by overall slower performance.

Therefore, you should disable Fast User Switching by following these steps:

1. Launch Control Panel's User Accounts icon.

2. Click the Change The Way Users Log On Or Off link.

3. Clear the Use Fast User Switching check box.

4. Click Apply Options.

Reducing the Use of Visual Effects

Windows XP uses a large number of visual effects to enhance the user's overall Windows experience. For example, Windows XP animates the movement of windows when you minimize or maximize them; it fades or scrolls in menus and tooltips; and it adds small visual touches such as shadows under menus and the mouse pointer. Most of these effects serve merely cosmetic purposes and are drains (albeit small ones) on system performance. If you don't need some or all of these effects, you can choose to turn them off:

■   Launch Control Panel's Display icon, display the Appearance tab, and click Effects. In the Effects dialog box (see Figure 11-8), clear the following check boxes:

- ❑   Use The Following Transition Effect For Menus And Tooltips

- ❑   Use The Following Method To Smooth Edges Of Screen Fonts

- ❑   Show Shadows Under Menus

- ❑   Show Window Contents While Dragging

■   While you have the Display Properties dialog box open, display the Settings tab and choose Medium (16 bit) in the Color Quality list. Using fewer colors gives your graphics card less to do, which should speed up video performance. Also, click Advanced, display the Troubleshooting tab, and make sure the Hardware Acceleration slider is set to Full.

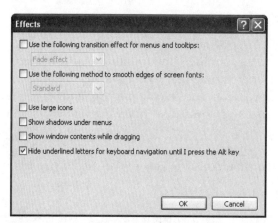

Figure 11-8 Clear most of the check boxes in the Effects dialog box to improve performance.

- Launch Control Panel's System icon, display the Advanced tab, and click Settings in the Performance section of the dialog box. On the Visual Effects tab of the Performance Options dialog box (see Figure 11-9), either select the Adjust For Best Performance option (which clears all the check boxes) or choose Custom and then clear the check boxes for the effects you want to disable.

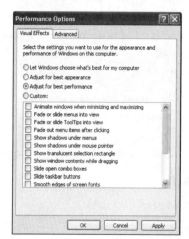

Figure 11-9 Clear the check boxes on the Visual Effects tab to improve performance.

- Launch Tweak UI and select the Mouse branch. Move the Menu Speed slider all the way to the left (Fast). This eliminates the delay when you hover the mouse over a menu item that displays a submenu. This is equivalent to setting the following registry value to 0:

```
HKCU\Control Panel\Desktop\MenuShowDelay
```

12

Maintaining Your System in 10 Easy Steps

In this chapter, you'll learn how to:

- Maintain your hard disk by checking for errors, deleting unnecessary files, and defragmenting files.

- Set up your system for easier recovery by creating restore points and by backing up your files.

- Keep your system up-to-date by checking for updates, patches, and security vulnerabilities.

- Set up a maintenance schedule to keep your system running in peak form without burdening your schedule.

Computer problems, like the proverbial death and taxes, seem to be one of those constants in life. Whether it's a hard disk biting the dust, a power failure that trashes your files, or a virus that invades your system, the issue isn't *whether* something will go wrong, but rather *when* will it happen. Instead of waiting to deal with these difficulties after they occur (what we call *pound-of-cure mode*), you need to become proactive and perform maintenance on your system in advance (*ounce-of-prevention mode*). This will not only reduce the chances that something will go wrong, but it will also set up your system to more easily recover from any problems that do occur. This chapter shows you how various Microsoft Windows XP utilities and techniques can help you do just that. In particular, we give you a step-by-step plan for maintaining your system and checking for the first signs of problems.

Step 1—Check Your Hard Disk for Errors

Our hard disks store our programs and, most important, our precious data, so they have a special place in the computing firmament. They ought to be pampered and coddled to ensure a long and trouble-free existence, but, unfortunately, that's rarely the case. Just consider everything that a modern hard disk has to put up with:

- **Wear and tear**   If your computer is running right now, its hard disk is spinning away at between 5,400 and 10,000 revolutions per minute. That's right— even though you're not doing anything, the hard disk is hard at work. Because of this constant activity, most hard disks simply wear out after a few years.

- **Bumps and thumps**   Your hard disk includes "read/write heads" that are used to read data from, and write data to, the disk. These heads float on a cushion of air just above the spinning hard disk platters. A bump or jolt of sufficient intensity can send them crashing onto the surface of the disk, which could easily result in trashed data. If the heads happen to hit a particularly sensitive area, the entire hard disk could crash.

- **Power surges**   The current that is supplied to your PC is, under normal conditions, reasonably constant. The possibility exists, however, for your computer to be assailed by massive power surges (for example, during a lightning storm). These surges can wreak havoc on a carefully arranged hard disk.

So what can you do about these flies in the ointment? Windows XP comes with a program called Check Disk that can check your hard disk for problems and repair them automatically. It might not be able to recover a totally trashed hard disk, but it can at least let you know when a hard disk might be heading for trouble.

Check Disk has two versions: a GUI version and a command-line version, both of which we discuss in the next two sections.

Running the Check Disk GUI

Here are the steps to follow to run the GUI version of Check Disk:

1.   In Windows Explorer, right-click the drive you want to check and then select Properties.

2.   On the drive's property sheet, select the Tools tab.

3.   Click the Check Now button. The Check Disk window appears, as shown in Figure 12-1.

Figure 12-1   Use Check Disk to scan a hard disk partition for errors.

4.   You have two options:

❑   **Automatically Fix File System Errors**   If you select this check box, Check Disk will automatically repair any file system errors that it finds. If you leave this option cleared, Check Disk just reports any errors it finds.

❑   **Scan For And Attempt Recovery Of Bad Sectors**   If you select this check box, Check Disk performs a sector-by-sector surface check of the hard disk surface. If Check Disk finds a bad sector, it automatically attempts to recover any information stored in the sector and marks the sector as defective so no information can be stored there in the future.

5.   Click Start.

6.   If you selected the Automatically Fix File System Errors check box and are checking a partition that has open system files, Check Disk will tell you that it can't continue because it requires exclusive access to the disk, and it will ask if you want to schedule the scan to occur the next time you boot the computer. Click Yes to schedule the disk check.

7.   When the scan is complete, Check Disk displays both a message letting you know that it has finished and a report on the errors it found, if any.

Insider Secret If you click Yes when Check Disk asks if you want to schedule the scan for the next boot, the program adds the AUTOCHK utility to the following registry setting:

```
HKLM\SYSTEM\CurrentControlSet\Control\Session Manager
\BootExecute
```

This setting specifies the programs that Windows XP should run at boot time when the Session Manager is loading. AUTOCHK is the automatic version of Check Disk that runs at system startup. When AUTOCHK is scheduled, you see the following the next time you restart the computer:

```
A disk check has been scheduled.
To skip disk checking, press any key within 10 second(s).
```

You can bypass the check by pressing a key before the timeout expires. Note that you can change the timeout value by creating a DWORD value named AutoChkTimeOut in the following registry key:

```
HKLM\SYSTEM\CurrentControlSet\Control\Session Manager
\BootExecute
```

Set this to the number of seconds you want to use for the timeout. Another way to do this is to use the CHKNTFS /T:[*time*] command, where *time* is the number of seconds to use for the timeout. (If you exclude *time*, CHKNTFS returns the current timeout setting.) For example, the following command sets the timeout to 60 seconds:

```
CHKNTFS /T:60
```

Running Check Disk from the Command Line

Here's the syntax for Check Disk's command-line version:

```
CHKDSK [volume [filename]] [/F] [/V] [/R] [/X] [/I] [/C] [/L:[size]]
```

volume	The drive letter (followed by a colon) or volume name.
filename	On FAT16 and FAT32 disks, the name of the file to check for fragmentation. Include the path if the file isn't in the current folder.
/F	Tells Check Disk to automatically fix errors. This is the same as running the Check Disk GUI with the Automatically Fix File System Errors option selected.

/V	Runs Check Disk in verbose mode. On FAT16 and FAT32 drives, Check Disk displays the path and name of every file on the disk; on NTFS drives, it displays cleanup messages, if any.
/R	Tells Check Disk to scan the disk surface for bad sectors and recover data from the bad sectors, if possible. This is the same as running the Check Disk GUI with the Scan For And Attempt Recovery Of Bad Sectors option selected.
/X	On NTFS non-system disks that have open files, forces the volume to dismount, invalidates the open file handles, and then runs the scan (the /F switch is implied).
/I	On NTFS disks, tells Check Disk to check only the file system's index entries.
/C	On NTFS disks, tells Check Disk to skip the checking of cycles within the folder structure. A *cycle* is a corruption in the file system whereby a subfolder's parent folder is listed as the subfolder itself. (For example, a folder named C:\Data should have C:\ as its parent; if C:\Data is a cycle, then C:\Data—the same folder—is listed as the parent, instead.) This creates a kind of loop in the file system that can cause the cycled folder to "disappear." This is a rare error, so using /C to skip the cycle check can speed up the disk check.
/L:*size*	On NTFS disks, tells Check Disk to set the size of its log file to the specified number of kilobytes. The default size is 65,536, which is plenty big enough for most systems, so you should never need to change the size. Note that if you include this switch without the *size* parameter, CHKDSK tells you the current size of the log file.

Step 2—Check Free Disk Space

Hard disks with capacities measured in the tens of gigabytes are commonplace nowadays, so disk space is much less of a problem than it used to be. Still, you need to keep track of how much free space you have on your disk drives, particularly the Windows XP system drive, which usually stores the virtual memory page file.

One way to check disk free space is to view My Computer using the Details view, which includes columns for Total Size and Free Space, as shown in Figure 12-2. Alternatively, right-click the drive in Windows Explorer and then select Properties. The disk's total capacity as well as its current used and free space appear on the General tab of the disk's property sheet.

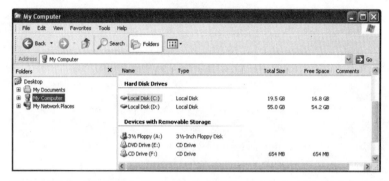

Figure 12-2 Display My Computer in Details view to see the total size and free space on your system's disks.

Here's a VBS script that displays the status and free space for each drive on your system:

```
Option Explicit
Dim objFSO, colDiskDrives, objDiskDrive, strMessage

' Create the File System Object
Set objFSO = CreateObject("Scripting.FileSystemObject")

' Get the collection of disk drives
Set colDiskDrives = objFSO.Drives

' Run through the collection
strMessage = "Disk Drive Status Report" & vbCrLf & vbCrLf
For Each objDiskDrive in colDiskDrives

    ' Add the drive letter to the message
    strMessage = strMessage & "Drive: " _
& objDiskDrive.DriveLetter & vbCrLf

    ' Check the drive status
    If objDiskDrive.IsReady = True Then

        ' If it's ready, add the status and the free space to the message
        strMessage = strMessage & "Status: Ready" & vbCrLf
        strMessage = strMessage & "Free space: " & objDiskDrive.FreeSpace
        strMessage = strMessage & vbCrLf & vbCrLf
    Else

        ' Otherwise, just add the status to the message
        strMessage = strMessage & "Status: Not Ready" & vbCrLf & vbCrLf
    End If
Next

' Display the message
Wscript.Echo strMessage
```

This script creates a FileSystemObject and then uses its Drives property to return the system's collection of disk drives. Then a For Each...Next loop runs through the collection, gathering the drive letter, the status, and, if the disk is ready, the free space. It then displays the drive data, as shown in Figure 12-3.

Figure 12-3   The script displays the status and free space for each drive on your system.

Step 3—Delete Unnecessary Files

If you find that a hard-disk partition is getting low on free space, you should delete any unneeded files and programs. Windows XP comes with a Disk Cleanup utility that enables you to remove certain types of files quickly and easily. Before discussing this utility, let's look at a few methods you can use to perform a spring cleaning on your hard disk by hand:

■   **Uninstall programs you don't use.**   If you have an Internet connection, you know it's easier than ever to download new software for a trial run. Unfortunately, that also means it's easier than ever to clutter your hard disk with unused programs. Use Control Panel's Add Or Remove Programs icon to uninstall these and other rejected applications.

■   **Delete downloaded program archives.**   Speaking of program downloads, your hard disk is probably also littered with ZIP files or other downloaded archives. For those programs you use, you should consider moving the archive files to a removable medium for storage. For programs you don't use, consider deleting the archive files.

- **Remove Windows XP components that you don't use.** If you don't use some Windows XP components (such as MSN Explorer, Paint, and some or all of the Windows XP games), in Control Panel, select Add Or Remove Programs, Add/Remove Windows Components to remove those components from your system.

- **Delete application backup files.** Applications often create backup copies of existing files and name the backups using either the .bak or .old extension. Use Windows Explorer's Search utility to locate these files and delete them.

Once you've completed these tasks, you next should run the Disk Cleanup utility, which can automatically remove several other types of files. Here's how it works:

1. Select Start, All Programs, Accessories, System Tools, Disk Cleanup. The Select Drive dialog box appears.

2. Choose the disk drive you want to work with and then click OK. Disk Cleanup scans the drive to see which files can be deleted and then displays a window similar to the one shown in Figure 12-4.

Figure 12-4 Disk Cleanup can automatically and safely remove certain types of files from a disk drive.

> **Tip**   Windows XP offers two methods for bypassing the Select Drive dialog box. One is to right-click the disk drive in Windows Explorer and then click the Disk Cleanup button on the General tab of the drive's property sheet. The other is to select Start, Run, and enter **cleanmgr /d***drive*, where *drive* is the letter of the drive you want to work with (for example, cleanmgr /dc).

3.   In the Files To Delete list, select the check box beside each category of file you want to remove. If you're not sure what an item represents, select it and read the text in the Description box. Note, too, that for most of these items you can click View Files to see what you'll be deleting.

4.   Click OK. Disk Cleanup asks if you're sure you want to delete the files.

5.   Click Yes. Disk Cleanup deletes the selected files.

> **Insider Secret**   It's possible to save your Disk Cleanup settings and run them again at any time. This is handy if you want to, say, delete all your downloaded program files and temporary Internet files at shutdown. Launch the command prompt and then enter the following command:
>
> ```
> cleanmgr /sageset:1
> ```
>
> Note that the number 1 in the command is arbitrary: you can enter any number between 0 and 65535. This launches Disk Cleanup with an expanded set of file types to delete. Make your choices and click OK. What this does is save your settings to the registry; it doesn't delete the files. To delete the files, open the command prompt and run the following command:
>
> ```
> cleanmgr /sagerun:1
> ```
>
> Note that you can also create a shortcut for this command, add it to a batch file, or schedule it with the Task Scheduler.

Step 4—Defragment Your Hard Disk

Windows XP comes with a utility called Disk Defragmenter that's an essential tool for tuning your hard disk. Disk Defragmenter's job is to rid your hard disk of *file fragmentation*, which occurs when a file is stored in multiple places on a partition. Defragmenting files stores them contiguously, which greatly improves hard-disk performance because Windows XP can load each file from a single location on the disk.

Before using Disk Defragmenter, you should perform a couple of house-keeping chores:

■ Delete any files from your hard disk that you don't need, as described in the previous section. Defragmenting junk files only slows down the whole process.

■ Check for file-system errors by running Check Disk as described in Step 1 of this chapter.

Running the Disk Defragmenter Tool

Follow these steps to use Disk Defragmenter:

1. Select Start, All Programs, Accessories, System Tools, Disk Defragmenter. Alternatively, in Windows Explorer, right-click the drive you want to defragment, select Properties, and then select the Tools tab in the dialog box that appears. Click the Defragment Now button. Either way, the Disk Defragmenter window appears, as shown in Figure 12-5.

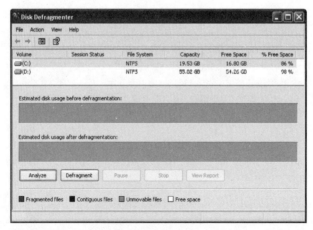

Figure 12-5 Use Disk Defragmenter to eliminate file fragmentation and improve hard disk performance.

2. Select the drive you want to defragment.

3. Click Analyze. Disk Defragmenter analyzes the fragmentation of the selected drive and then displays its recommendation (for example, `You should defragment this volume`).

4. Click View Report for fragmentation details in the Analysis Report window. If you don't want to defragment the drive, click Close; if you want to defragment the drive, click Defragment.

Defragmenting from the Command Line

If you want to schedule a defragment or perform this chore from a batch file, you need to use the DEFRAG command-line utility. Here's the syntax:

```
DEFRAG volume [-a] [-f] [-v]
```

`volume`	Specifies the drive letter (followed by a colon) of the disk you want to defragment.
`-a`	Tells DEFRAG to only analyze the disk.
`-f`	Forces DEFRAG to defragment the disk, even if it doesn't need defragmenting or if the disk has less than 15 percent free space. (DEFRAG normally requires at least that much free space because it needs an area in which to sort the files.)
`-v`	Runs DEFRAG in verbose mode, which displays both the analysis report and the defragmentation report.

Step 5—Set System Restore Points

One of the biggest causes of Windows instability in the past was the tendency for some newly installed programs to simply not get along with Windows. It could be an executable file that didn't mesh with the Windows system or a registry change that brought chaos to other programs or to Windows itself. Similarly, hardware installations often caused problems by adding faulty device drivers to the system or by corrupting the registry.

To help recover from software or hardware installations that bring down the system, Windows XP offers the System Restore feature. Its job is straightforward, yet clever: It takes periodic snapshots—called *restore points* or *checkpoints*—of your system, each of which includes the currently installed program files, registry settings, and other crucial system data. The idea is that if a program or device installation causes problems on your system, you use System Restore to revert your system to the most recent restore point before the installation.

System Restore creates restore points automatically under the following conditions:

- **Every 24 hours**   This is called a *system checkpoint*, and it's set to occur once a day as long as your computer is running. (If your computer isn't running, the system checkpoint is created the next time you start your computer, assuming it has been at least 24 hours since the previous system checkpoint was set.)

> **Insider Secret**   The RPGlobalInterval setting governs the system checkpoint interval via the following registry key:
>
> HKLM\SOFTWARE\Microsoft\Windows NT\CurrentVersion\SystemRestore
>
> The value is in seconds, and the default is 86400 (24 hours). If you often change your system configuration, you might prefer a shorter interval of, say, 28800 (8 hours). Note, too, that you can also adjust the RPSessionInterval value, which controls the intervals in seconds, that System Restore waits before a system checkpoint is created during each Windows XP session (the default is 0, meaning that the feature is turned off). Finally, the RPLifeInterval value determines the number of days that Windows XP maintains restore points. The default is 7776000 (90 days).

- **Before installing certain applications**   Some newer applications—notably Microsoft Office 2000 and later—are aware of System Restore and will ask it to create a restore point prior to installation.

- **Before installing a Windows Update patch**   System Restore creates a restore point before you install a patch either manually via the Windows Update site, or via the Automatic Updates feature.

- **Before installing an unsigned device driver**   Windows XP warns you about installing unsigned drivers. If you choose to go ahead, the system creates a restore point prior to installing the driver.

- **Before restoring backed-up files**   When you use the Windows XP Backup program to restore one or more backed-up files, System Restore creates a restore point just in case the restoration causes problems with system files.

■   **Before reverting to a previous configuration using System Restore**   Sometimes reverting to an earlier configuration doesn't fix the current problem, or it creates its own set of problems. In these cases, System Restore creates a restore point before reverting so that you can undo the restoration.

It's also possible to create a restore point manually using the System Restore user interface. Here are the steps to follow:

1.   Select Start, All Programs, Accessories, System Tools, System Restore. The System Restore window appears.

2.   Select the Create A Restore Point option and click Next.

3.   Use the Restore Point Description text box to enter a description for the new checkpoint, and then click Create. System Restore creates the restore point and displays the Restore Point Created window.

4.   Click Close.

Insider Secret   To change how much disk space System Restore uses to store checkpoints, launch Control Panel's System icon and select the System Restore tab. Select the drive you want to work with and then click Settings. Use the Disk Space Usage slider to specify the amount of disk space you want to reserve for the exclusive use of System Restore. Note that for any drive, except the drive on which Windows XP is installed, you can toggle System Restore on and off using the Turn Off System Restore On This Drive check box.

Step 6—Back Up Your Files

The Backup program that comes with Windows XP does a fine job of making all-important backup copies of your important files. (If you're using Windows XP Home Edition, note that you need to install Backup from the Windows XP Home Edition CD. In the VALUEADD\MSFT\NTBACKUP folder, launch the Ntbackup.msi file.) Here are the steps to follow to define and run a backup job:

1.   Select Start, All Programs, Accessories, System Tools, Backup. The Backup Or Restore Wizard appears.

2.   Click the Advanced Mode link to display the Backup Utility window.

3. Select the Backup tab.

4. Select Tools, Options, make sure the Backup Type tab is displayed, and then use the Default Backup Type list to choose one of the following options (click OK when you're done):

  ❏ **Normal** Backs up all the files in the backup job. Each file is marked (that is, its archive bit is turned off) to indicate that the file has been backed up.

  ❏ **Incremental** Backs up only those files that have changed since the last normal or incremental backup. This is the fastest type because it includes only the minimum number of files. Again, the files are marked to indicate that they've been backed up.

  ❏ **Differential** Backs up only those files that have changed since the last non-differential backup. Files are not marked to indicate they've been backed up. So, if you run this type of backup again, the same files get backed up (plus any others that have been added or changed in the meantime).

  ❏ **Copy** Makes copies of the selected files. This type of backup does not mark the files as having been backed up.

  ❏ **Daily** Backs up only those files that were modified on the day you run the backup. Files are not marked as having been backed up.

5. Use the folder and file lists to select the check boxes for the drives, folders, and files you want to include in the backup job.

6. Use the Backup Destination list to choose a backup device.

7. If you chose File in step 6, use the Backup Media Or File Name text box to enter the drive, path, and file name for the backup file.

8. Select Job, Save Selections. If you're creating a new backup job, enter a name in the Save As dialog box and then click Save.

9. Click Start Backup to perform the backup.

Notes from the Real World

It's a rare computer user these days who doesn't know that backing up is important. So why do so many of us put off backing up? I think the main reason is that it's often a difficult or inconvenient process. However, there are a few things you can do to make backing up easier. Here are some ideas that I use to make my backup chores more palatable:

- **Forget floppies, if possible.** Backing up to floppy disks ranks just above "root canal" on the Top 10 Most Unpleasant Chores list. The reason, of course, is that a standard 3.5-inch floppy disk holds a mere 1.39 MB (*not* 1.44 MB) of data. If your hard disk contains hundreds of megabytes, you'll have to back up to hundreds of floppy disks, which hurts just to think about it.

- **Try a tape drive.** Tape drives are the de facto backup standard, and they come in many different capacities. You can back up hundreds of megabytes or even multiple gigabytes for a relatively low cost.

- **Try other backup media.** The big downfall for tape drives is their relatively slow access times. Fortunately, there are much faster media available. These include CD-R and CD-RW drives or the even more capacious DVD-R, DVD-RW, DVD+R, and DVD+RW drives; removable media such the Iomega Zip or Jaz drives; a second hard disk (*not* a second partition on the same hard disk!); and a network folder.

- **Consider online backups.** If your ISP provides you with disk space for a Web site, use it to back up your most important files. Note, too, that there are also companies that will sell you online disk space for backups.

- **Back up data, not programs.** Although a full system backup can come in handy, it isn't strictly necessary. The only irreplaceable files on your system are those you created yourself, so they're the ones you should spend the most time protecting.

(continued)

Notes from the Real World   *(continued)*

- **Keep data together.** You save an immense amount of backup time if you store all your data files in one place. It could be the My Documents folder, a separate partition, or a separate hard disk. In each case, you can select all the data files for backup simply by selecting a single folder or drive check box.

- **Back up downloaded archives.** If space is at a premium, you can leave program files out of your backup job because they can always be reinstalled from their source disks. The exceptions to this are downloaded programs. To avoid having to find and download these files again, make backup copies of the archives.

- **Don't always run the full backup.** You can speed up your backup times by running differential or incremental backups.

—Paul McFedries

Step 7—Run the Automated System Recovery Preparation Wizard

The worst-case scenario for PC problems is a system crash that renders your hard disk or system files unusable. Your only recourse here is to start from scratch, either with a reformatted hard disk or a new hard disk. This usually means that you have to reinstall Windows XP and then reinstall and reconfigure all your applications. In other words, you're looking at the better part of a day or, more likely, a few days to recover your system.

However, Windows XP comes with a utility called Automated System Recovery that, with a little advance planning on your part, can help you recover from a crash in just a few steps. What kind of advance planning is required? Just two things:

- You must run the Automated System Recovery Preparation Wizard. This wizard backs up your system files and creates a disk that enables you to restore your system.

- You must run a full backup of all your data and application files.

> **Tip**   If you're not replacing your hard disk and if you have your application files and data files on a separate partition, you don't have to back up that partition because you won't be formatting it.

Because your system, application, and data files change regularly, to ensure a smooth recovery, you need to do both of these things regularly. Here are the steps to follow to run the Automated System Recovery Preparation Wizard:

1. In the Backup Utility window, select Tools, ASR Wizard. The Automated System Recovery Preparation Wizard appears.

2. Click Next. The wizard prompts you for a backup destination for your system files.

3. Choose the backup media type and then enter the backup media or file name. Click Next.

> **Caution**   Don't back up the system files to the %SystemDrive% partition because this is the partition you'll be formatting as part of your recovery effort.

4. Click Finish. The wizard backs up your system files. When it's done, it prompts you to insert a floppy disk in drive A.

5. Insert a blank, formatted disk and click OK. The wizard copies the files Asr.sif, Asrpnp.sif, and Setup.log to the disk and lets you know when it has finished.

6. Click OK.

To learn how to recover your system using Automated System Recovery, see Chapter 13, "Troubleshooting and Recovering from Problems."

Step 8—Check For Updates and Security Patches

Microsoft is working constantly to improve Windows XP with bug fixes, security patches, new program versions, and device driver updates. All of these new and improved components are made available online, so you should check for updates and patches often.

Checking the Windows Update Web Site

The main online site for Windows XP updates is the Windows Update Web site, which you load into your Web browser by selecting Start, All Programs, Windows Update. Click Scan For Updates to look for crucial new components that can make Windows XP more reliable and more secure. This process should become a regular part of your routine.

Windows XP also comes with a vastly improved automatic updating feature, which can download and install updates automatically. If you prefer to know what's happening with your computer, it's possible to control the automatic updating by following these steps:

1.   Launch Control Panel's System icon to display the System Properties dialog box.

2.   Select the Automatic Updates tab, shown in Figure 12-6.

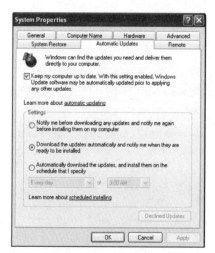

Figure 12-6   Use the Automatic Updates tab to configure Windows XP's automatic updating.

3.   If you don't want Windows XP to use automatic updating, clear the Keep My Computer Up To Date check box.

4. If you left the Keep My Computer Up To Date option selected, use the Settings section of the dialog box to determine how Windows XP performs the updating:

   ❑ **Notify Me Before Downloading Any Updates And Notify Me Again Before Installing Them On My Computer**   This option gives you the most control because it lets you reject the update either before the download or before the installation.

   ❑ **Download The Updates Automatically And Notify Me When They Are Ready To Be Installed**   This option gives Windows XP control over the downloading of the updates.

   ❑ **Automatically Download The Updates, And Install Them On The Schedule That I Specify**   This option lets you control when the downloaded updated are installed. For example, you might prefer to choose a time when you won't be using your computer.

5. If you've taken control of the updates and have declined to download or install one or more of them, you can get notified about these updates again by clicking the Declined Updates button. When Windows XP asks if you want to be notified again about the declined updates, click Yes.

6. Click OK to put the new settings into effect.

Checking for Security Vulnerabilities

Microsoft regularly finds security vulnerabilities in components such as Microsoft Internet Explorer and Windows Media Player. Fixes for these problems are usually made available via Windows Update. However, to ensure that your computer is safe, you should download and regularly run the Microsoft Baseline Security Analyzer. This tool not only scans your system for missing security patches, but it also looks for things such as weak passwords and other Windows vulnerabilities. Download the tool here:

http://www.microsoft.com/technet/security/tools/Tools/mbsahome.asp

After you install the tool, follow these steps to use it:

1. Select Start, All Programs, Microsoft Baseline Security Analyzer. The program's Welcome screen appears.

2. Click Scan A Computer.

3. Your computer should be listed in the Computer Name list. If not, choose it from that list. (Alternatively, use the IP Address text boxes to enter your computer's IP address.)

4. Use the Options check boxes to specify the security components you want to check. For most scans you should leave all the options selected.

5. Click Start Scan. The program checks your system and displays a report on your system's security (and usually offers remedies for any vulnerabilities it finds).

Step 9—Verify Digitally Signed Files

In Chapter 9, "Installing and Troubleshooting Devices," you learned that digitally unsigned drivers are often the cause of system instabilities. To ensure you don't accumulate unsigned drivers on your system (particularly if you share your computer with other users), you should regularly run the Signature Verification Tool. This program scans your entire system (or, optionally, a specific folder) for unsigned drivers. Follow these steps to run this tool:

1. Select Start, Run, enter **sigverif**, and click OK. The File Signature Verification window appears.

2. Click Advanced to display the Advanced File Signature Verification Settings dialog box.

3. Select the Look For Other Files That Are Not Digitally Signed option.

4. In the Look In This Folder text box, enter *SystemRoot***System32** **drivers**, where *SystemRoot* is the folder in which Windows XP is installed (such as C:\WINDOWS).

5. Click OK.

6. Click Start to begin the verification process.

When the verification is complete, the program displays a list of the unsigned driver files. (The results for all the scanned files are copied to the log file Sigverif.txt, which is located in the %SystemRoot% folder. In the Status column, look for files listed as "Not Signed.")

Step 10—Review Event Viewer Logs

Windows XP constantly monitors your system for unusual or noteworthy occurrences. It might be a service that doesn't start, the installation of a device, or an application error. These occurrences are called *events,* and Windows XP tracks them in three different event logs:

- **Application**   This log stores events related to applications, including Windows XP programs and third-party applications.

- **Security**   This log stores events related to system security, including logons, user accounts, and user privileges. Note that this log doesn't record anything until you turn on Windows XP's security auditing features. You do this by opening the Group Policy Editor and selecting Computer Configuration, Windows Settings, Local Policies, Audit Policy. You can then enable auditing for any of the several polices listed.

- **System**   This logs stores events generated by Windows XP and components such as system services and device drivers.

> **Note**   The System log lists device driver errors, but remember that Windows XP has other tools that make it easier to see device problems. As we discussed in Chapter 9, "Installing and Troubleshooting Devices," Device Manager displays an icon on devices that have problems, and you can view a device's property sheet to see a description of the problem. Also, the System Information utility (Msinfo32.exe) reports hardware woes in the System Information, Hardware Resources, Conflicts/Sharing branch and the System Information, Components, Problem Devices branch.

You should scroll through the Application and System event logs regularly to look for existing problems or for warnings that could portend future problems. (The Security log isn't as important for day-to-day maintenance. You need to use it only if you suspect a security issue with your machine; for example, if you want to keep track of who logs on to the computer.) To examine these logs, you use the Event Viewer snap-in, available either via selecting Start, Run and entering **Eventvwr.msc** or by launching Control Panel's Administrative

Tools icon and selecting Event Viewer. Figure 12-7 shows a typical Event Viewer window. Use the tree in the left pane to select the log you want to view: Application, Security, or System.

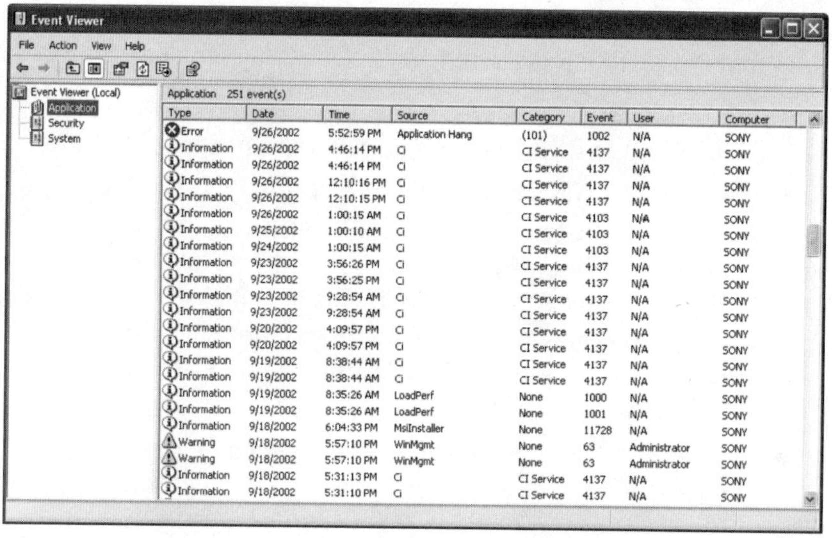

Figure 12-7   Use the Event Viewer to monitor events generated by applications and Windows XP.

When you select a log, the right pane displays the available events, including the event's date, time, and source, its type (Information, Warning, or Error), and other data. To see a description of an event, double-click it or select it and press Enter.

Insider Secret   Rather than monitoring the event logs by hand, Windows XP comes with a couple of tools that can help automate the process. The Eventquery.vbs script enables you to query the log files for specific event types, IDs, sources, and more. Search Windows XP's Help And Support Center for "eventquery" to get the script's command-line syntax. Also, you can set up an *event trigger* that will perform some action when a particular event occurs. You do this using the Eventtriggers.exe utility. Search the Help And Support Center for "eventtriggers" to get the full syntax for this tool.

Setting Up a Maintenance Schedule

Maintenance is effective only if it's done regularly, but there's a fine line to be navigated here. If maintenance is performed too often, it can become a burden and interfere with more interesting tasks; if it's performed too seldom, it becomes ineffective. So how often should you perform the maintenance steps listed in this chapter? Here are our schedule guidelines:

- **Check your hard disk for errors.**   Run a basic scan about once a week. Run the more thorough disk surface scan once a month. (The surface scan takes a long time, so run it when you won't be using your computer for a while.)

- **Check free disk space.**   Do this once about once a month. If you have a drive in which the free space is getting low, check it about once a week.

- **Delete unnecessary files.**   If free disk space isn't a problem, run this chore about once every two or three months.

- **Defragment your hard disk.**   How often you defragment your hard disk depends on how often you use your computer. If you use it every day, you should run Disk Defragmenter about once a week. If your computer doesn't get heavy use, you probably need to run Disk Defragmenter only once a month or so.

- **Set restore points.**   Windows XP already sets regular system checkpoints, so you need only create your own restore points when you're installing a program or device or making some other major change to your system.

- **Back up your files.**   Perform a full backup of all your documents, as well as a backup of the system state, about once a month. Do a differential backup of modified files once a week. Do an incremental backup of modified files every day.

- **Check Windows Update.**   If you've turned off automatic updating, you should check in with the Windows Update Web site about once a month.

- **Check for security vulnerabilities.**   Run the Microsoft Baseline Security Analyzer once a month. You should also pay a monthly visit to Microsoft's Security And Privacy site to keep up to date on the latest security news, get security and virus alerts, and more:

  http://www.microsoft.com/security/

- **Verify digitally signed files.** If other people use your computer regularly, you should run the Signature Verification Tool every couple of months.

- **Review event viewer logs.** If your system appears to be working fine, you need to check the Application and System log files just weekly or every couple of weeks. If the system has a problem, check the logs daily to look for Warning or Error events.

Remember as well that Windows XP offers a number of options for running most of these maintenance steps automatically:

- If you want to run a task every day, you can set it up to launch automatically at startup, as we describe in Chapter 4, "Starting Up and Shutting Down."

- Use the Task Scheduler (Start, All Programs, Accessories, System Tools, Scheduled Tasks) to set up a program on a regular schedule. Note that some programs, particularly Disk Defragmenter, can't be scheduled in their GUI form. You need to use the command-line version instead.

- The Backup program enables you to schedule backup jobs. In the Backup Utility window, select the Schedule Jobs tab and click Add Job.

- Use the automatic updating feature instead of checking for Windows updates by hand.

13

Troubleshooting and Recovering from Problems

- Determine the source of a problem.
- Use general troubleshooting strategies to solve common problems.
- Troubleshoot problems using Web sites and newsgroups.
- Use Windows XP's recovery tools: Last Known Good Configuration, System Restore, Recovery Console, and Automated System Recovery.
- Reinstall Windows XP.

A long time ago, somebody proved mathematically that it is impossible to make any reasonably complex software program problem-free. As the number of variables increase, as the interactions of subroutines and objects become more complex, and as the underlying logic of a program grows beyond the ability of a single person to grasp all at once, errors inevitably creep into the code. Given Microsoft Windows XP's status as one of the most complex software packages ever created, almost certainly problems are lurking in the weeds. (Actually, considering the richness, depth, and immense intricacy of Windows XP—its lines of code are numbered in the tens of millions—the fact that to date relatively few problems have been reported borders on miraculous.) And, the good news is that the great majority of these problems are extremely obscure and will appear only under rare circumstances.

However, this doesn't mean you're guaranteed a glitch-free computing experience. Far from it. The majority of computer woes are caused by third-party programs and devices, either because they have inherent problems themselves or because they don't get along well with Windows XP. Using software, devices, and device drivers designed for Windows XP can help tremendously, as can the maintenance program we outline in Chapter 12, "Maintaining Your System in 10 Easy Steps." Nonetheless, you need to know how to troubleshoot and resolve the computer problems that invariably will come your way. In this chapter, we help you do just that by showing you our favorite techniques for determining problem sources, and by taking you through all of Windows XP's recovery tools.

> **Note**   Software glitches are traditionally called *bugs*, although many developers shun the term because it comes with too much negative baggage these days. However, there's a popular and appealing tale of how this sense of the word *bug* came about. As the story goes, in 1947 an early computer pioneer named Grace Hopper was working on a system called the Mark II. While investigating a problem, she found a moth hiding out among the machine's vacuum tubes, so from then on glitches were called bugs. A great story, to be sure, but this tale was not the source of the "computer glitch" sense of "bug." In fact, engineers had already been referring to mechanical defects as "bugs" for at least 60 years before Ms. Hopper's actual moth came on the scene. As proof, the *Oxford English Dictionary* offers the following quotation from an 1889 edition of the *Pall Mall Gazette*:
>
> *Mr. Edison, I was informed, had been up the two previous nights discovering "a bug" in his phonograph—an expression for solving a difficulty, and implying that some imaginary insect has secreted itself inside and is causing all the trouble.*

Determining the Source of the Problem

One of the ongoing mysteries that all computer users experience at one time or another is what might be called the now-you-see-it-now-you-don't problem. This is a glitch that plagues you for a while and then mysteriously vanishes without any intervention on your part. (This also tends to occur when you ask a nearby user or someone from the IT department to look at the problem. Like the automotive problem that goes away when you take the car to a mechanic, computer problems will often resolve themselves as soon as a knowledgeable user sits down at the keyboard.) When this happens, most people just shake their heads and resume working, grateful to no longer have to deal with the problem.

Unfortunately, most computer ills don't get resolved so easily. For these more intractable problems, your first order of business is to track down the source of the snag. This is, at best, a black art, but it can be done if you take a systematic approach. Over the years, we've found that the best method is to ask a series of questions designed to gather the required information and/or to narrow down clues to the culprit. Here are the questions:

- **Did you get an error message?**   Most computer error messages are obscure and do little to help you resolve a problem directly. However, error codes and error text can help you down the road, either by giving you something to search for in an online database (see "Troubleshooting Using Online Resources," later in this chapter) or by providing information to a tech support person. Therefore, you should always write down the full text of any error message that appears.

Tip   If the error message is lengthy and you can still use other programs on your computer, don't bother writing down the full message. Instead, while the message is displayed, press Print Screen to place an image of the current screen on the clipboard. Then open Paint or some other graphics program, paste the screen into a new image, and save the image. If you think you'll be sending the image via e-mail to a tech support employee or someone else who can help with the problem, consider saving the image as a monochrome or 16-color bitmap to keep the image size small.

Insider Secret   If the error message appears before Windows XP starts, but you don't have time to write it down, press the Pause/Break key to pause the startup. After you record the error, press Ctrl+Pause/Break to resume the startup.

- **Does an error or warning appear in the Event Viewer logs?** Open the Event Viewer and examine the Application and System logs for errors or warnings. See Chapter 12 for more information on the Event Viewer.

- **Does an error appear in System Information?** Select Start, All Programs, Accessories, System Tools, System Information to launch the System Information utility. In the Hardware Resources\Conflicts/Sharing category, look for device conflicts. See if any devices are listed in the Components\Problem Devices category.

- **Does the onset of the error coincide with a past hardware or software change?** In the System Information utility, select View, System History. This displays a history of the changes made to your system in each of the main categories: Hardware Resources, Components, and Software Environment. If you know when the problem began, you can look through the history items to see if a change occurred at the same time and so might be the cause of the problem.

- **Did you recently edit the registry?** Improper registry modifications can cause all kinds of mischief. If the problem occurred after editing the registry, try restoring the changed key or setting. (Ideally, if you have previously exported a backup of the now-offending key, you should import the backup. See Chapter 2, "Getting the Most Out of the Registry," to learn how to back up the registry.)

- **Did you recently change any Windows settings?** If the problem started after you changed your Windows configuration, try reversing the change. Even something as seemingly innocent as starting the screen saver can cause problems, so don't rule anything out.

- **Did Windows XP "spontaneously" reboot?** This apparently random behavior is actually built into the system in the event of a system failure (also called a *stop error* or a *blue screen of death*). By default, Windows XP writes an error event to the System log, dumps the contents of memory into a file, and then reboots the system. So if your system reboots, check the Event Viewer to see what happened. You can control how Windows XP handles system failures by launching Control Panel's System icon, selecting the Advanced tab, and then clicking Settings in the Startup And Recovery section of the

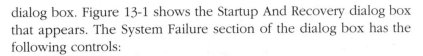

dialog box. Figure 13-1 shows the Startup And Recovery dialog box that appears. The System Failure section of the dialog box has the following controls:

❑   **Write An Event To The System Log**   Leave this check box selected in order to have the system failure recorded in the System log.

❑   **Send An Administrative Alert**   If you're on a network and this option is selected, Windows XP sends an alert message to the administrator of the network when a system failure occurs.

❑   **Automatically Restart**   This is the option that, when selected, causes your system to reboot when a stop error occurs. Clear this check box to avoid the reboot.

❑   **Write Debugging Information**   This list determines what information Windows XP saves to disk (in the folder specified in the text box below the list) when a system failure occurs. This information—called a *memory dump*—contains data that can help a tech-support employee determine the cause of the problem. You have four choices:

◆   **None**   No debugging information is written.

◆   **Small Memory Dump (64 KB)**   This option writes the minimum amount of useful information that could be used to identify what caused the stop error. This 64-KB file includes the stop error number and its description, the list of running device drivers, and the processor state.

◆   **Kernel Memory Dump**   This option writes the contents of the kernel memory to the disk. (The *kernel* is the Windows XP component that manages low-level functions for processor-related activities such as scheduling and dispatching threads, handling interrupts and exceptions, and synchronizing multiple processors.) This dump includes memory allocated to the kernel, the hardware abstraction layer, and the drivers and programs used by the kernel. Unallocated memory and memory allocated to user programs are not included in the dump. This information is the most useful for troubleshooting, so we recommend using this option.

◆   **Complete Memory Dump**   This option writes the entire contents of RAM to the disk.

Caution Windows XP first writes the debugging information to the paging file—Pagefile.sys in the %SystemDrive%. (Note that this is not affected if you choose to purge the contents of the paging file at shutdown, as we discuss in Chapter 4.) When you restart the computer, Windows XP then transfers the information to the dump file. Therefore, you need to have a large enough paging file to handle the memory dump. This is particularly true for the Complete Memory Dump option, which requires the paging file to be as large as the physical RAM, plus one megabyte. The file size of the Kernel Memory Dump is typically about a third of physical RAM, although it may be as large as 800 MB. We show you how to check and adjust the size of the paging file in Chapter 11, "Optimizing Performance."

◆ **Overwrite Any Existing File** When this option is selected, Windows XP overwrites any existing dump file with the new dump information. If you clear this check box, Windows XP creates a new dump file with each system failure. Note that this option is enabled only for the Kernel Memory Dump and the Complete Memory Dump (which write to the same file by default: %SystemRoot% \Memory.dmp).

Figure 13-1 Use the Startup And Recovery dialog box to configure how Windows XP handles system failures.

- **Did you recently change any application settings?**   If so, try reversing the change to see if it solves the problem. If that doesn't help, check to see if an upgrade or patch is available. Also, some applications come with a "Repair" option that can fix corrupted files. Otherwise, try reinstalling the program.

> **Note**   If a program freezes, you won't be able to shut it down using conventional methods. If you try, you may see a dialog box warning you that the program is not responding. If so, click End Now to force the program to close. Alternatively, right-click the taskbar and then select Task Manager. When you select the Applications tab, you should see your stuck application listed, and the Status column will likely say `Not responding`. Click the program and then click End Task.

- **Did you recently install a new program?**   If you suspect a new program is causing system instability, restart Windows XP and try operating the system for a while without using the new program. (If the program has any components that load at startup, be sure to clear them, as we describe in Chapter 4, "Starting Up and Shutting Down.") If the problem doesn't reoccur, the new program is likely the culprit. Try using the program without any other programs running. You should also examine the program's "readme" file (if it has one) to look for known problems and possible workarounds. It's also a good idea to check for a Windows XP–compatible version of the program. Again, you can also try the program's "Repair" option, or you can reinstall the program.

> **Insider Secret**   One common cause of program errors is having one or more program files corrupted because of bad hard-disk sectors. Before you reinstall a program, run a surface check on your hard disk to identify and block off bad sectors. We show you how to do a hard-disk surface scan in Chapter 12.

- **Did you recently upgrade an existing program?** If so, try uninstalling the upgrade.

> Tip When a program crashes, Windows XP displays a dialog box to let you know and asks whether you want to send an error report to Microsoft. If you never choose to send the report, this dialog box can be annoying. To turn it off, launch Control Panel's System icon, select the Advanced tab, and then click Error Reporting. Select the Disable Error Reporting option. To continue informing Microsoft of problems in Windows XP, but not problems in application programs, leave the Enable Error Reporting option selected and clear the Programs check box.

- **Did you recently install a new device or update a device driver?** If so, check Device Manager to see if there's a problem with the device. Follow our troubleshooting suggestions in Chapter 9, "Installing and Troubleshooting Devices."

- **Did you recently install a device driver that is not Windows XP–compatible?** As we explain in Chapter 9, Windows XP allows you to install drivers that aren't Windows XP–certified, but it also warns you that this is a bad idea. Incompatible drivers are one of the most common sources of system instability, so whenever possible you should uninstall the driver and install one that is designed for Windows XP. Windows XP automatically sets a system restore point before it installs the driver, so if you can't uninstall the driver, you should use that to restore the system to its previous state. (See "Recovering Using System Restore," later in this chapter.)

- **Did you recently apply an update from Windows update?** Before you install an update from the Windows Update site, Windows XP creates a system restore point (usually called Windows Update V4). If your system becomes unstable after installing the update, use System Restore to revert to the preupdate configuration.

Insider Secret   If you have Windows XP set up to perform automatic updating, you can keep tabs on the changes made to your system by examining the Windows Update.log file, which you'll find in the %SystemRoot% folder. You can also review your Windows Update changes by going to the Windows Update site (select Start, All Programs, Windows Update) and clicking the View Installation History link.

■ **Did you recently install a Windows XP hotfix or service pack?**   It's ironic that hotfixes and service packs that are designed to increase system stability will occasionally do the opposite and cause more problems than they fix.

❑ If you've applied a hotfix, you can often remove it using Control Panel's Add Or Remove Programs icon. Look for a "Windows XP Hotfix" entry in the Change Or Remove Programs list. If you have multiple hotfixes listed, make sure you remove the correct one. To be sure, check with either the Microsoft Security site or the Microsoft Knowledge Base, both of which we discuss later. Note, however, that many hotfixes cannot be uninstalled. You can try using System Restore to revert to a recent restore point, but there's no guarantee this will work.

❑ If you installed a service pack and you elected to save the old system files, then you can uninstall the service pack using Control Panel's Add Or Remove Programs icon. Look for a "Windows XP Service Pack" entry in the Change Or Remove Programs list.

General Troubleshooting Tips

Figuring out the cause of a problem is often the hardest part of troubleshooting, but by itself it doesn't do you much good. Once you know the source, you need to parlay that information into a fix for the problem. We discussed a few solutions in the previous section, but here are a few other general fixes you need to keep in mind.

■ **Close all programs.** You can often fix flaky behavior by shutting down all your open programs and starting again. This is a particularly useful fix for problems caused by low memory or low system resources.

■ **Log off Windows XP.** Logging off clears the RAM and so gives you a slightly cleaner slate than merely closing all your programs.

■ **Reboot the computer.** If problems exist with some system files and devices, logging off won't help because these objects remain loaded. By rebooting the system, you reload the entire system, which is often enough to solve many computer problems.

■ **Turn off the computer and restart.** You can often solve a hardware problem by first shutting your machine off. Wait for 30 seconds to give all devices time to spin down, and then restart.

■ **Check connections, power switches, and so on.** Some of the most common (and some of the most embarrassing) causes of hardware problems are the simple physical things: making sure a device is turned on, checking that cable connections are secure, and ensuring that insertable devices are properly inserted.

■ **Use the Help And Support Center.** Microsoft greatly improved the quality of the Help system in Windows XP. The Help And Support Center (select Start, Help And Support) is awash in articles and advice on using Windows XP. However, the real strength of Help And Support is, in our opinion, the "Support" side. On the Help And Support Center home page, click the Fixing A Problem link to see more links for general troubleshooting and for fixing specific problems related to software, multimedia, e-mail, networking, and more. Note, too, that the Help And Support Center offers a number of troubleshooter guides that take you step by step through troubleshooting procedures.

Troubleshooting Using Online Resources

The Internet is home to an astonishingly wide range of information, but its forte has always been computer knowledge. Whatever problem you may have, there's a good chance that someone out there has run into the same thing, knows how to fix it, and has posted the solution on a Web site or newsgroup, or would be willing to share it with you if asked. True, finding what you need is sometimes difficult, and you often can't be sure how accurate some of the solutions are. However, if you stick to the more reputable sites and if you get second opinions on solutions offered by complete strangers, then you'll find the online world an excellent troubleshooting resource. Here's our list of favorite online resources to check out:

- **Microsoft Product Support Services**   This is Microsoft's main online technical support site. Through this site you can access Windows XP frequently asked questions, see a list of known problems, download files, and send questions to Microsoft support personnel.

  http://support.microsoft.com/

- **Microsoft Knowledge Base**   The Microsoft Product Support Services site has links that enable you to search the Microsoft Knowledge Base, which is a database of articles related to all Microsoft products, including, of course, Windows XP. These articles provide you with information about Windows XP and the use of its features. But the most useful aspect of the Knowledge Base is its help in troubleshooting problems. Many of the articles were written by Microsoft support personnel. By searching for error codes or keywords, you can often get specific solutions to your problems.

Notes From the Real World

Quite often in my efforts to troubleshoot or research a problem, I find the assistance of the Microsoft Knowledge Base to be invaluable. This database of tips, how-tos, and workarounds is a gold mine of information. However, like any gold mine, you have to dig deep into the Knowledge Base to get the best nuggets, and that means knowing how to search for what you need.

First, make sure you choose the Advanced Search And Help link. This displays a form that gives you much greater search precision. Then be sure to use the Select A Microsoft Product list to choose which product you're working with (such as Windows XP).

(continued)

Notes from the Real World *(continued)*

After you enter your search text, use the Using list to choose the option that determines how the search engine should interpret your text: All Of The Words Entered acts like a Boolean AND search; Any Of The Words Entered acts like a Boolean OR; The Exact Phrase Entered treats the search text as a single phrase; and Boolean (Text Contains AND/OR) enables you to enter your own Boolean search operators. If you choose the last option, note that the search engine supports the AND, OR, and AND NOT operators. (Use the last one to match articles that do *not* contain the search text that appears after the AND NOT operator.)

Next, use the Search Type options to choose what part of the articles is to be searched. You can search the full text, the title only, or only the article ID number. Searching the full text takes a little longer but will generally result in a larger number of hits and a more successful search. Finally, use the Date Range list to match only articles that were published within a certain time frame (or select the Anytime value to search all the articles).

Note that if you're searching by article number, it's a good idea to get in the habit of inputting the number only (omit the leading "Q"). As of November 7, 2002, the Knowledge Base began phasing out prefix letters in an effort to standardize the numbering schemes for articles across multiple languages. Microsoft promises that existing URLs to Knowledge Base articles will continue to function for two years after the changeover date, but new articles will no longer be published using the old naming conventions.

—Geoff Winslow

- **Microsoft TechNet** This Microsoft site is designed for IT professionals and power users. It contains a huge number of articles on all Microsoft products. These articles give you technical content, program instructions, tips, scripts, downloads, and troubleshooting ideas.

  http://www.microsoft.com/technet/

- **Windows Update** Check this site for the latest device drivers, security patches, service packs, and other updates.

  http://windowsupdate.microsoft.com/

■ **Microsoft Security and Privacy**   Check this site for the latest information on Microsoft's security and privacy initiatives, particularly security patches.

http://www.microsoft.com/security/

■ **Vendor Web sites**   All but the tiniest hardware and software vendors maintain Web sites with customer support sections that you can peruse for upgrades, patches, workarounds, frequently asked questions, and sometimes chat or bulletin board features.

■ **Newsgroups**   Computer-related newsgroups exist for hundreds of topics and products. Microsoft maintains its own newsgroups via the msnews.microsoft.com server, and Usenet has a huge list of groups in the alt. and comp. hierarchies. Before asking a question in a newsgroup, be sure to search Google Groups to see if your question has been answered in the past.

http://groups.google.com/

Recovering from a Problem

Ideally, solving a problem will require a specific tweak to the system: a registry setting change, a driver upgrade, a program uninstall. But sometimes you need to take more of a "big picture" approach that reverts your system to some previous state in the hope that you'll leap past the problem and get your system working again. Windows XP offers four tools that enable you to try this approach: Last Known Good Configuration, System Restore, Recovery Console, and reinstalling Windows XP, which should be used in that order. The next four sections discuss these tools.

Booting Using the Last Known Good Configuration

Each time Windows XP starts successfully in normally mode, the system makes a note of which *control set* (the system's drivers and hardware configuration) was used. Specifically, it enters a value in the following registry key:

```
HKLM\SYSTEM\Select\LastKnownGood
```

For example, if this value is 1, it means that control set 1 was used to start Windows XP successfully:

```
HKLM\SYSTEM\ControlSet001
```

If you make driver or hardware changes and then find that the system won't start, you can have Windows XP load using the control set that worked the last time (that is, the control set that doesn't include your most recent hardware changes). This is called the *Last Known Good Configuration*, and the theory is that by using the previous working configuration, your system should start since it's bypassing the changes that caused the problem. Here's how to start Windows XP using the last known good configuration:

1. Restart your computer.

2. When the OS Choices menu appears, press F8 to display the Windows Advanced Options menu. (If your system doesn't display the OS Choices menu, press F8 immediately after your system finishes the Power-On Self Test, which is usually indicated by a single beep.)

3. Select the Last Known Good Configuration option.

Recovering Using System Restore

The Last Known Good Configuration is most useful when your computer won't start and you suspect that a hardware change is causing the problem. You might think that you can also use the Last Known Good Configuration if Windows XP starts but is unstable, and you suspect a hardware change is causing the glitch. Unfortunately, that won't work because once you start Windows XP successfully in normal mode, the hardware change is added to the Last Known Good Configuration. To revert the system to a previous configuration when you can start Windows XP successfully, you need to use the System Restore feature.

We show you how to use System Restore to set restore points in Chapter 12. Remember, too, that Windows XP creates automatic restore points each day and when you perform certain actions (such as installing an uncertified device driver). To revert your system to a restore point, follow these steps:

1. Select Start, All Programs, Accessories, System Tools, System Restore.

2. Make sure the Restore My Computer To An Earlier Time option is selected and click Next. The Select A Restore Point window appears, as shown in Figure 13-2.

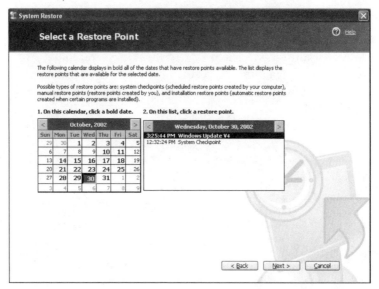

Figure 13-2   Use the Select A Restore Point window to choose the restore point you want to revert to.

3. Use the calendar to click the date on which the restore point was made. System Restore displays that day's restore points in a box to the right of the calendar.

4. Click the restore point you want to restore. (Note that the System Checkpoint items are the restore points created automatically.)

5. Click Next. System Restore asks you to close all open programs and warns you not to do anything with your computer until the restoration is done.

6. Click Next. System Restore begins reverting to the restore point. When it's done, it restarts your computer and displays the Restoration Complete window.

7. Click OK.

> **Insider Secret**   System Restore is available in safe mode. So if Windows XP won't start properly, and if using the Last Known Good Configuration doesn't work, perform a safe mode startup and run System Restore from there.

Recovering Using the Recovery Console

If Windows XP won't start normally, your first troubleshooting step is almost always to start the system in safe mode. Once you make it to Windows XP, you can then investigate the problem and make the necessary changes (such as disabling or rolling back a device driver). But what if your system won't even start in safe mode?

Your next step should be booting with the Last Known Good Configuration. And if that doesn't work either? Don't worry, there's still hope in the form of the Recovery Console, a command-line tool that enables you to launch recovery tools, stop and start services, access files, and replace corrupted system files. Here's how to use it:

1. Insert the Windows XP Professional CD-ROM.

2. Restart your computer. If your system prompts you to boot from the CD, press the required key or key combination.

> **Tip** If your system won't boot from the Windows XP CD, you need to adjust the system's BIOS settings to allow this. Restart the computer and look for a startup message that prompts you to press a key or key combination to modify the BIOS settings (which might be called Setup or something similar). Find the boot options and either enable a CD-based boot or make sure the option to boot from the CD comes before the option to boot from the hard disk. Note that many Intel motherboards designed for the P4 processor require that you open the computer and move a jumper to enable access to the BIOS settings. (However, most of these machines will allow you to choose a boot device from a list of supported devices if you hold down the F8 key during the BIOS self-check during boot.)

3. When the Windows XP Professional Setup, Welcome To Setup screen appears, press R to choose the To Repair A Windows XP Installation Using Recovery Console option. The Recovery Console displays a list of the Windows installations on your computer.

4. Type the number that corresponds to your main Windows XP installation and press Enter. The Recovery Console prompts you to enter the Administrator password.

5. Type the password and press Enter. The Recovery Console command-line prompt appears.

The Recovery Console is similar to the Windows XP command prompt, but it offers only limited access to the files and folders: the %SystemRoot% folder; the root folder of any partition; and the contents of any floppy disk, CD-ROM, or other removable disk.

Here are some troubleshooting notes to bear in mind when working at the Recovery Console:

- You have a large but limited set of commands at your disposal. To see a list of those commands, type **Help** and press Enter.

- If Windows XP won't start because the Boot.ini file is corrupted or improperly configured, you can repair it by running the BOOTCFG /REBUILD command.

- To repair bad sectors on the hard disk, run the CHKDSK command. Note, however, that CHKDSK only has two switches when you run it from the Recovery Console: /P and /R. In most cases, you'll use /R (which also implies /P) to repair any bad sectors. Be aware that the /P switch is available only in the Recovery Console; there is no equivalent in the normal command-line version of CHKDSK.

- If Windows XP won't start because a system file is corrupted, use the COPY command to copy the file from the Windows XP CD's I386 folder to the appropriate folder in the %SystemDrive%. This works for both regular and compressed files. If the file exists within a compressed cabinet (.cab) file, use the EXPAND command, instead.

- If another operating system has taken over the partition boot sector, or if you suspect the partition boot sector is corrupt, you can fix the problem by running the FIXBOOT command.

- If you suspect that your computer won't start because the Master Boot Record is corrupted, you can repair it by running the FIXMBR command.

- You can display a list of all the available device drivers and services by running the LISTSVC command. If a driver or service is preventing Windows XP from starting, you can work around this by disabling the driver or service. You do this by running the DISABLE *servicename* command, where *servicename* is the name of the driver or service. Run ENABLE *servicename* to enable the driver or service.

- When you're finished working with the Recovery Console, type **exit** and press Enter.

Insider Secret   If you run the SET command in the Recovery Console, you'll see a list of four environment variables that control your ability to access and copy data while in the Recovery Console:

- **AllowWildCards**   This variable determines whether you can use the ? and * wildcard characters in Recovery Console commands.

- **AllowAllPaths**   This variable determines whether you can use the CD command to change to any folder on the hard disk.

- **AllowRemovableMedia**   This variable determines whether you can copy files from the hard disk to a removable disk.

- **NoCopyPrompt**   This variable determines whether the Recovery Console warns you when the COPY command will overwrite an existing file.

Each variable is set to FALSE, by default. Unfortunately, if you attempt to use SET to change the value of any variable, the Recovery Console tells you that the SET command is disabled. To enable this command, you need to adjust a group policy setting. (Of course, if you can't start Windows XP, this won't do you much good now. However, we're letting you know about it just in case you need it for future troubleshooting missions.) In the Group Policy Editor, open the Computer Configuration, Windows Settings, Security Settings, Local Policies, Security Options branch. Select the Recovery Console: Allow Floppy Copy And Access To All Drive And All Folders policy. Note, too, that you can also select the Recovery Console: Allow Automatic Administrative Logon policy. Doing this prevents you from being prompted for a password when you start the Recovery Console. (This is quite dangerous, of course, so select this policy only if you're sure no one else has access to your computer.)

Reinstalling Windows XP

If you can't get Windows XP back on its feet using the Recovery Console, you may be able to fix things by reinstalling Windows XP over the existing installation. This won't affect your data or any personal settings you've adjusted, but it may cure what's ailing Windows XP either by reverting the system to its default settings or by installing fresh copies of corrupted system files. Here are the steps to follow to reinstall Windows XP:

1.   Insert the Windows XP Professional CD-ROM.

2.   Restart your computer. If your system prompts you to boot from the CD, press the required key or key combination.

3.   When the Windows XP Professional Setup, Welcome To Setup screen appears, press Enter to choose the To Set Up Windows XP Now option.

4.   When the Licensing Agreement appears, press F8 to accept it. Setup then displays a list of Windows XP installations on your computer.

5.   If you have more one Windows XP installation, select the one you want to fix.

6.   Press R to choose the To Repair The Selected Windows XP Installation option.

Recovering Using Automated System Recovery

If nothing can get Windows XP up and running again, you have no choice but to start with a clean slate. This means either formatting the %SystemDrive% partition or, if hard disk errors are the culprit, replacing your hard disk. This will be less catastrophic if you followed our advice and used the Automated System Recovery Preparation Wizard to make backups of your system files (see Chapter 12). If so, here are the steps to follow to recover your system:

1.   Insert the Windows XP Professional CD-ROM.

2.   Restart your computer. If your system prompts you to boot from the CD, press the required key or key combination. Watch the bottom of the screen for the following prompt:

    `Press F2 to run Automated System Recovery (ASR)...`

3.   Press F2. Setup asks you to insert the ASR disk.

4.   Insert the disk and then press any key. Setup continues the Windows XP installation. Note that, along the way, Setup automatically formats the %SystemDrive% partition.

From here, the Setup program proceeds normally, except that it uses the information on the ASR disk to restore your system files and settings from the backup you made using the ASR Preparation Wizard. If you also backed up your application and data files, use the Backup Utility to restore those now.

IV

Mastering Internet and Networking Features

In Part IV, you'll learn insider techniques to help you:

14

Implementing Internet Security and Privacy

In this chapter, you'll learn how to:

■ Guard against e-mail viruses.

■ Set up Outlook Express to automatically delete spam messages.

■ Get and use a digital ID for secure e-mail.

■ Keep intruders at bay with Internet Connection Firewall.

■ Work with security zones and other Internet Explorer security settings.

■ Protect online privacy by managing cookies.

If you made a list of the various tenets that constitute the Internet ethos, one tenet would be that information should be free and easily accessible to all. This admirably egalitarian view is one of the reasons the Internet has been so successful. The composition of the Internet's building blocks (the software that enables the various networks to communicate with each other and exchange data) is public knowledge, so it's relatively easy to write software that performs functions over the Internet. The downside to all this openness is that it also makes it easy for the malicious and the malevolent to get into all kinds of mischief. By studying the published standards for how the Internet works, crackers (as hackers who've succumbed to the dark side of the Force are called) can apply their knowledge of programming and computer systems to compromise these systems and bypass the normal Internet operating procedures.

In other words, although being online is generally quite secure and relatively private, you should never take your security and privacy for granted. In this chapter, we show you how to wield various Microsoft Windows XP tools to enhance your online safety and privacy without slowing you down or making the entire online experience more trouble than it's worth.

Working with E-mail Safely and Securely

E-mail is by far the most popular online activity, but it can also be the most frustrating in terms of security and privacy. E-mail viruses are legion; spam gets worse every day; and messages that should be secret are really about as secure as if they were written on the back of a postcard. Fortunately, it doesn't take much to remedy these and other e-mail problems, as you'll see over the next few sections.

Protecting Yourself Against E-mail Viruses

Until just a few years ago, the primary method that computer viruses used to propagate themselves was the floppy disk. A user with an infected machine would copy some files to a floppy, and the virus would surreptitiously add itself to the disk. When the recipient inserted the disk, the virus copy would come to life and infect yet another computer.

When the Internet became a big deal, viruses adapted and began propagating either via malicious Web sites or via infected program files downloaded to users' machines.

Over the past couple of years, however, by far the most productive method for viruses to replicate has been the humble e-mail message. Melissa, I Love You, BadTrans, Sircam, Klez—the list of e-mail viruses and Trojan horses is a long one, but they all operate more or less the same way: They arrive as a message attachment, usually from someone you know. When you open the attachment, the virus infects your computer and then, without your knowledge, uses your e-mail client and your address book to ship out messages with more copies of itself attached. The nastier versions will also mess with your computer; they might delete data or corrupt files, for example.

You can avoid getting infected by one of these viruses by implementing a few commonsense procedures:

■   Never open an attachment that comes from someone you don't know.

■   Even if you know the sender, if the attachment isn't something you're expecting, assume the sender's system is infected. Write back and confirm that he or she sent the message.

■   Install a top-of-the-line anti-virus program, particularly one that checks incoming e-mail.

Besides these general procedures, Microsoft Outlook Express also comes with its own set of virus protection features. Here's how to use them:

1.   In Outlook Express, select Tools, Options.

2.   Select the Security tab.

3.   In the Virus Protection section of the dialog box, you have the following options:

❏   **Select The Internet Explorer Security Zone To Use**   Later in this chapter we describe the security zone model used by Outlook Express (see "Surfing the Web Securely"). From the perspective of Outlook Express, you use the security zones to determine whether active content inside an HTML-format message is allowed to run:

◆   **Internet Zone**   If you choose this zone, active content is allowed to run.

◆   **Restricted Sites Zone**   If you choose this option, active content is disabled. This is the default setting, and it's the one we recommend.

❏   **Warn Me When Other Applications Try To Send Mail As Me.**   As we mentioned earlier, it's possible for programs and scripts to send e-mail messages without your knowledge. This is done using Simple MAPI calls (MAPI is an acronym for Messaging Application Programming Interface), which can be used to send messages via the default mail client, and it's all hidden from the user. When this check box is selected, Outlook Express displays a warning dialog box (see Figure 14-1) when a program or script attempts to send a message using Simple MAPI. Click Send to allow the message; click Do Not Send to cancel the message.

Figure 14-1 Outlook Express warns you if a program or script uses Simple MAPI to attempt to send a message.

> **Caution** Selecting the Warn Me When Other Applications Try To Send Mail As Me option protects you against scripts that attempt to send surreptitious messages using Simple MAPI calls. However, there's another way to send messages behind the scenes. It's called Collaboration Data Objects (CDO), and it's installed by default in Windows XP. Here's a sample script that uses CDO to send a message:
>
> ```
> Dim objMessage
> Set objMessage = CreateObject("CDO.Message")
> With objMessage
>     .To = "you@there.com"
>     .From = "me@here.com"
>     .Subject = "CDO Test"
>     .TextBody = "Just testing..."
>     .Send
> End With
> Set objMessage = Nothing
> ```
>
> The Warn Me When Other Applications Try To Send Mail As Me option does *not* trap this kind of script, so bear in mind that your system is still vulnerable to Trojan horses that send mail via your Windows XP accounts.

❏ **Do Not Allow Attachments To Be Saved Or Opened That Could Potentially Be A Virus** When this check box is selected, Outlook Express monitors attachments to look for file types that could contain viruses or destructive code. If it detects such a file, it halts the ability to open or save that file, and it displays a note at the top of the message to let you know about the unsafe attachment, as shown in Figure 14-2.

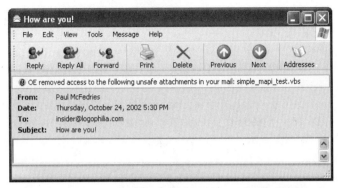

Figure 14-2   If Outlook Express detects an unsafe file attachment, it displays a notice at the top of the message to let you know that you do not have access to the file.

Insider Secret   The file types that Outlook Express disables are defined by Microsoft Internet Explorer's built-in *unsafe-file list*. This list includes file types associated with the following extensions: .ad, .ade, .adp, .bas, .bat, .chm, .cmd, .com, .cpl, .crt, .exe, .hlp, .hta, .inf, .ins, .isp, .js, .jse, .lnk, .mdb, .mde, .msc, .msi, .msp, .mst, .pcd, .pif, .reg, .scr, .sct, .shb, .shs, .url, .vb, .vbe, .vbs, .vsd, .vss, .vst, .vsw, .wsc, .wsf, .wsh.

4.   Click OK to put the new settings into effect.

Filtering Out Spam

Spam—unsolicited commercial messages—has become a plague upon the earth. Unless you've done a masterful job at keeping your address secret, you probably receive at least a few spam e-mail messages every day, and it's more likely that you receive a few dozen. The bad news is most experts agree that it's only going to get worse. And why not? Spam is one of the few advertising mediums where the costs are substantially borne by the users, not the advertisers.

Insider Secret The best way to avoid spam is to not get on a spammer's list of addresses in the first place. That's hard to do these days, but there are some steps you can take. First, never use your actual e-mail address in a newsgroup account. The most common method that spammers use to gather addresses is to harvest them from newsgroup posts. Many people *munge* their e-mail address by adding text that invalidates the address but is still obvious for other people to figure out:

user@myisp.remove_this_to_email_me.com

Also, when you sign up for something online, use a fake address if possible. If you need or want to receive e-mail messages from the company and so must use your real address, make sure you clear any options that ask if you want to receive promotional offers. Alternatively, enter the address from a free Web-based account (such as an MSN Hotmail account), so that any spam you receive will go there instead of to your main address. Finally, if you create Web pages, never put your e-mail address on a page, because spammers use *crawlers* that harvest addresses from Web pages. If you must put an address on a page, hide it using some simple JavaScript code:

```
<script language="JavaScript" type="text/javascript">
<!--
var add1 = "webmaster"
var add2 = "@"
var add3 = "whatever.com"
document.write(add1 + add2 + add3)
//-->
</script>
```

There are a host of commercial "spam-killers" on the market, but with a bit of work you should be able to eliminate most spam by using nothing more than the built-in tools available in Outlook Express. We're talking specifically about using *rules*: conditions that look for messages with specific characteristics—for example, certain words in the subject or body—and actions that do something with the matching messages—such as delete them.

To filter spam, your rules need to look for incoming messages that meet one or more of the following criteria:

- **Specific words in the Subject line**   The sneakier spammers hide their messages behind innocuous Subject lines such as "Here's the information you requested." But most spam comes with fairly obvious Subject lines: "Make $$$Money Now!!!" or "FREE Business Cards." Instead of creating a rule based on an entire Subject line, you need only to watch for certain key words. Here are a few that we use (we've removed some of the more explicit terms that filter out pornographic spam):

  !!!!!!, $, %, .name, 18+, adult, adv, are you in debt, bargain, be 18, bulk, buy recommendation, cartridges, casino, collect your money, credit card, credit rating, creditor, debts, dieting, diploma, double your money, dvd movies, e-mail marketing, erotic, excite game, f r e e, find out anything, flash alert, free cell, free credit, free pda, free phone, free trial, free vacation, free!, freee, get out of debt, got debt, guaranteed!, hair loss, hormone, how to make money, increase your sales, klez, loans, lose up to, lose weight, lose while you sleep, losing sleep, low on funds, marketing services, maximize your income, millionaire, mlm, mortgage, new car, over 18, over 21, printer cartridge, promote your business, reach millions, reduce your debt, refinance, refinancing, s e x, satellite, saw your site, secure your future, seen on tv, sex, singles, snoring, steroids, stock alert, thinning hair, too good to be true, trading alert, trading report, uncover the truth, urgent notice, viagra, web traffic, work at home, work from home, xxx, years younger, you are a winner, you have to see this

- **Specific words in the message body**   The message body is where the spammer makes his or her pitch, so there's rarely any subterfuge here. You can filter on the same terms as you used for the Subject line, but there are also a few telltale terms that appear only in spam messages. Here are some that we use:

  //////////////, 100% satisfied, adult en, adult web, adults only, cards accepted, check or money order, dear friend, extra income, for free!, for free?, satisfaction guaranteed, money-back guarantee, one-time mail, order now!, removal instructions, special promotion

- **Specific names in the From line**   Many spammers *spoof* their From address by using a random address or, more likely, an address plucked from their distribution list. However, some use addresses that have a common theme, such as "sales@" (for example, sales@blah.com). Here are some common From line names to filter:

@mlm, @public, @savvy, ebargains, free, hello@, link2buy, mail@, profits@, sales@, success, success@

■ **Specific names in the To line**   The To line of spam messages usually contains either an address from the distribution list or "Undisclosed Recipients." You can't filter on the latter, however, because many legitimate mailings also use that "address." However, there are a few common To line names to watch for:

anyone@, creditcard@, free@, friend, friend@, nobody@, opportunity@, public@, success@, winners@

If you notice that a particular address is the source of much spam, the easiest way to block the spam is to block all incoming messages from that address. You can do this using the Outlook Express Blocked Senders list, which watches for messages from a specific address and deletes them automatically. To use this feature, follow these steps:

1. Select a message that comes from the address you want to block.

2. Select Message, Block Sender. Outlook Express adds the address to the Blocked Senders list and asks if you want to delete all messages from that address.

3. Click Yes to delete the messages, or click No to leave them in the folder.

To view the Blocked Senders list, select Tools, Message Rules, Blocked Senders List. Outlook Express opens the Message Rules dialog box and displays the Blocked Senders tab. From here, you can Add another blocked sender, or Modify or Remove an existing blocked sender.

For other types of spam, you need to set up mail rules. Here's how:

1. Select the Tools, Message Rules, Mail command. Outlook Express displays the New Mail Rule dialog box.

2. In the Select The Conditions For Your Rule list, select the check box beside the rule condition you want to use to label a message as spam. Outlook Express adds the condition to the Rule Description text box, as shown in Figure 14-3. Note that you're free to select multiple conditions.

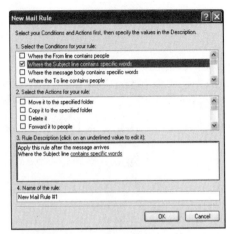

Figure 14-3   Use the New Mail Rule dialog box to set up a mail rule for filtering incoming messages.

3.   The condition shown in the Rule Description text box will probably have some underlined text. You need to replace that underlined text with the specific criterion you want to use (such as a word or an address). To do that, click the underlined text to display the Type Specific Words dialog box.

4.   Enter the word or phrase and click Add. Most conditions support multiple criteria (such as multiple addresses or multiple words in a Subject line), so repeat this step as necessary. When you're done, click OK.

> **Insider Secret**   You can make a condition adhere to Boolean principles such as AND, OR, and NOT. To do this, click the Options button in the Type Specific Words dialog box. To make a NOT condition, select the Message Does Not Contain The Words Below option. If you entered multiple words or phrases, you can make an AND criterion by selecting the Message Matches All Of The Words Below option; to make an OR criterion, select the Message Matches Any One Of The Words Below option.

5. In the Select The Actions For Your Rule list, select the check box beside the action you want Outlook Express to take with messages that meet your criteria. With spam, for example, you'll probably want to choose the Delete It option. Again, you may have to click underlined text in the Rule Description text box to complete the action. Also, you can select multiple actions.

6. If you selected multiple conditions, Outlook Express assumes that all the conditions must be true before invoking the rule (Boolean AND). To change this, click the And link in the Rule Description text box, select the Messages Match Any One Of The Criteria option, and click OK.

7. Use the Name Of The Rule text box to enter a descriptive name for the rule.

8. Click OK. Outlook Express displays the Mail Rules tab of the Message Rules dialog box. Click OK to close the dialog box and enable your e-mail filter.

Here are a few notes to bear in mind when working with the list of rules on either the Mail Rules tab or the News Rules tab:

■ **Toggling rules on and off**   Use the check box beside each rule to turn the rule on and off.

■ **Setting rule order**   Some rules should be processed before others. For example, if you have a rule that deletes spam, you want Outlook Express to process that rule before sending out, say, a vacation reply. To adjust the order of a rule, select it and then click either Move Up or Move Down.

■ **Modifying a rule**   To edit a rule, select it and click Modify.

■ **Applying a rule**   If you want to apply a rule to existing Inbox messages or to messages in a different folder, click Apply Now in the Message Rules dialog box. Select the rule you want to apply (or click Select All to apply them all). To choose a different folder, click Browse. When you're ready, click Apply Now in the Apply Mail Rules Now dialog box.

■ **Deleting a rule**   Select the rule and click Remove. When Outlook Express asks if you're sure, click Yes.

Maintaining Your Privacy While Reading E-mail

You wouldn't think that the simple act of reading an e-mail message would have privacy implications, but you'd be surprised. There are actually two scenarios that compromise your privacy:

- **Read receipts**   A *read receipt* is an e-mail notification that tells the sender that you've opened the message that he or she sent you. If the sender requests a read receipt and you either select the message (so that the message text appears in the preview pane) or double-click the message to open it, by default Outlook Express displays the dialog box shown in Figure 14-4. Click Yes to send the receipt, or click No to skip it. Many people like asking for read receipts because they offer "proof of delivery." It has been our experience, however, that getting a read receipt back starts a kind of internal clock that the sender uses to "measure" how long it takes you to respond after reading the message. Because of this annoyance, and because we feel it's nobody's business to know when one reads a message, we always click No when asked to send a read receipt. In fact, you can go one better and tell Outlook Express to never send a read receipt. To do this, select Tools, Options and select the Receipts tab. In the Returning Read Receipts section of the dialog box, select the Never Send A Read Receipt option.

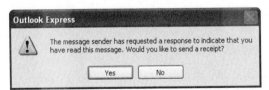

Figure 14-4   You see this dialog box when you open a message for which the sender has requested a read receipt.

- **Web bugs**   A *Web bug* is an image that resides on a remote server and is added to an HTML-formatted e-mail message by referencing a URL on the remote server. When you open the message, Outlook Express uses the URL to download the image for display within the message. That sounds harmless enough, but if the message is junk e-mail, it's likely that the URL will also contain either your e-mail address or a code that points to your e-mail address. When the remote server gets a request for this URL, it knows not only that you've opened their message but also that your e-mail address is legitimate. If you've installed Internet Explorer 6 Service Pack 1 or later, there's a way to thwart Web bugs. In Outlook Express, select Tools, Options and select the Read tab. Select the Read All Messages In Plain Text check box. This prevents Outlook Express from downloading any Web bugs because it displays all messages in plain text.

Sending and Receiving Secure E-mail

When you connect to a Web site, your browser sets up a direct connection—called a *channel*—between your machine and the Web server. Because the channel is a direct link, implementing security is relatively easy because all you have to do is secure the channel, which is what Private Communication Technology (PCT) and Secure Sockets Layer (SSL) do.

However, e-mail security is entirely different and much more difficult to set up. The problem is that e-mail messages don't have a direct link to a Simple Mail Transfer Protocol (SMTP) server. Instead, they must usually "hop" from server to server until the final destination is reached. Combine this with the open and well-documented e-mail standards used on the Internet, and you end up with three e-mail security issues.

- **The privacy issue**   Because messages often pass through other systems and can even end up on a remote system's hard disk, it isn't that hard for someone with the requisite know-how and access to the remote system to read a message.

- **The tampering issue**   Because a user can read a message passing through a remote server, it comes as no surprise that he or she can also change the message text.

- **The authenticity issue**   With the Internet e-mail standards an open book, it isn't difficult for a savvy user to forge or *spoof* an e-mail address.

To solve these issues, the Internet's gurus came up with the idea of *encryption*. When you encrypt a message, a complex mathematical formula scrambles the message content to make it unreadable. In particular, a *key value* is incorporated into the encryption formula. To unscramble the message, the recipient feeds the key into the decryption formula.

This *single-key encryption* works, but its major drawback is that the sender and the recipient must both have the same key. *Public-key encryption* overcomes that limitation by using two related keys: a *public key* and a *private key*. The public key is available to everyone, either by sending it to them directly or by offering it in an online key database. The private key is secret and is stored on the user's computer.

Here's how public-key cryptography solves the issues discussed earlier:

- **Solving the privacy issue**   When you send a message, you obtain the recipient's public key and use it to encrypt the message. The encrypted message can now be decrypted only by using the recipient's private key, thus assuring privacy.

- **Solving the tampering issue**   An encrypted message can still be tampered with, but only randomly because the content of the message can't be seen. This thwarts the most important skill used by tamperers: making the tampered message look legitimate.

- **Solving the authenticity issue**   When you send a message, you use your private key to digitally sign the message. The recipient can then use your public key to examine the digital signature to ensure the message came from you.

If there's a problem with public-key encryption, it is that the recipient of a message must obtain the sender's public key from an online database. (The sender can't just send the public key because the recipient would have no way to prove that the key came from the sender.) Therefore, to make all this more convenient, a *digital ID* is used. This is a digital certificate that states the sender's public key has been authenticated by a trusted certifying authority. The sender can then include his or her public key in outgoing messages.

Setting Up an E-mail Account with a Digital ID

To send secure messages using Outlook Express, you first have to obtain a digital ID. Here are the steps to follow:

1.   In Outlook Express, select Tools, Options and then select the Security tab.

2.   Click Get Digital ID. Internet Explorer loads and takes you to the Outlook Express digital ID page on the Web.

3.   Click a link to the certifying authority (such as VeriSign) you want to use.

4.   Follow the authority's instructions for obtaining a digital ID. (Note that digital IDs are not free; they typically cost about US$15 per year.)

With your digital ID installed, the next step is to assign it to an e-mail account:

1. In Outlook Express, select Tools, Accounts to open the Internet Accounts dialog box.

2. Use the Mail tab to select the account you want to work with and then click Properties. The account's dialog box appears.

3. Select the Security tab.

4. In the Signing Certificate section of the dialog box, click Select. Outlook Express displays the Select Default Account Digital ID dialog box.

5. Make sure the certificate you installed is selected and then click OK. Your name appears in the Security tab's first Certificate box.

6. Click OK to return to the Internet Accounts dialog box.

7. Click Close.

Insider Secret To make a backup copy of your digital ID, open Internet Explorer and select Tools, Internet Options. Select the Content tab and click Certificates to see a list of your installed certificates (be sure to use the Personal tab). Click your digital ID and then click Export.

Obtaining Another Person's Public Key

Before you can send an encrypted message to another person, you must obtain his or her public key. How you do this depends on whether you have a digitally signed message from that person.

If you do have a digitally signed message, open the message, as described later in this chapter in the "Receiving a Secure Message" section. Outlook Express adds the digital ID to the Address Book automatically:

■   If you have one or more contacts whose e-mail addresses match the address associated with the digital ID, the digital ID is added to each contact. (To see it, open the Address Book, open the contact, and then select the Digital IDs tab.)

■   If there are no existing matches, a new contact is created.

> **Insider Secret**   If you don't want Outlook Express to add digital IDs automatically, select Tools, Options, select the Security tab, and click Advanced. In the dialog box that appears, clear the Add Senders' Certificates To My Address Book check box.

If you don't have a digitally signed message for the person you want to work with, you have to visit a certifying authority's Web site and find the person's digital ID. For example, you can go to the VeriSign site (*www.verisign.com*) to search for a digital ID and then download it to your computer. After that, follow these steps:

1. Open the Address Book.

2. Open the person's contact info, or create a new contact.

3. Enter one or more e-mail addresses, and fill in the other data as necessary.

4. Select the Digital IDs tab.

5. In the Select An E-Mail Address list, select the address that corresponds with the digital ID you downloaded.

6. Click the Import button to choose the Select Digital ID File To Import dialog box.

7. Find and select the downloaded digital ID file, and then click Open.

8. Click OK.

Sending a Secure Message

After your digital ID is installed, you can start sending out secure e-mail messages. You have two options:

■ **Digitally sign a message to prove that you're the sender.**   Start a new message and then either select the Tools, Digitally Sign command or click the Sign toolbar button. A small red "seal" icon appears to the right of the header fields.

■ **Encrypt a message to avoid snooping and tampering.**   In the New Message window, either select the Tools, Encrypt command or click the Encrypt toolbar button. A blue lock icon appears to the right of the header fields.

> **Tip** You can tell Outlook Express to digitally sign and/or encrypt all your outgoing messages. Select Tools, Options and select the Security tab. To encrypt all your messages, select the Encrypt Contents And Attachments For All Outgoing Messages check box. To sign all your messages, select the Digitally Sign All Outgoing Messages check box.

Receiving a Secure Message

The technology and mathematics that underlie the digital ID are complex, but there's nothing complex about dealing with incoming secure messages. Outlook Express handles everything behind the scenes, including the authentication of the sender (if the message was digitally signed) and the decryption of the message (if the message was encrypted). For the latter, a dialog box tells you that your private key has been used to decrypt the message.

As you can see in Figure 14-5, the preview pane gives you a few visual indications that you're dealing with a secure message:

- The message text doesn't appear in the preview pane.

- The preview pane title is Security Help, and the subtitle tells you the type of security used: Digitally Signed and/or Encrypted.

- The preview pane text describes the security used in the message.

To read the message, click the Continue button at the bottom. (If you don't want to see this security preview in the future, select the Don't Show Me This Help Screen Again check box.)

> **Insider Secret** If you change your mind and decide you want to see the preview screen, you have to edit the registry. Open the Registry Editor and head for the key named HKCU\Identities. Open your 32-character identity key and then open the Software\Microsoft\Outlook Express\5.0\Dont Show Dialogs subkey. Open the Digital Signature Help setting and change its value to 0.

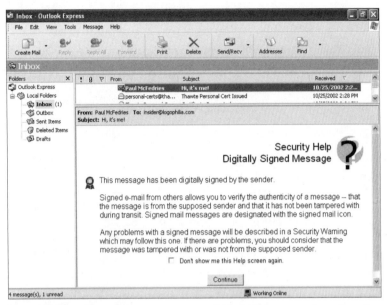

Figure 14-5   For a secure message, the preview pane describes the type of security used.

Keeping Intruders Out of Your System

If you access the Internet using a broadband—cable modem or digital sub-scriber line (DSL)—service, chances are that you have an "always on" connection, which means there's a much greater chance that a malicious hacker could find your computer and have his or her way with it. You might think that with millions of people connected to the Internet at any given moment, there would be little chance of a "script kiddy" finding you in the herd. Unfortunately, one of the most common weapons in a black-hat hacker's arsenal is a program that runs through millions of IP addresses automatically, looking for "live" connections. The problem is compounded by the fact that many cable systems and some DSL systems use IP addresses in a narrow range, thus making it easier to find "always on" connections. However, having a cracker locate your system isn't a big deal as long as he or she can't get into your system. There are two ways to prevent this:

■   Turn off file and printer sharing on your Internet connection.

■   Turn on Windows XP's Internet Connection Firewall.

File and printer sharing is used to enable network users to see and work with shared files and printers on your computer. Obviously, you don't way to share your system with strangers on the Internet! By default, Windows XP turns off file and printer sharing for Internet connections. To make sure of this, however, follow these steps:

1.   Launch Control Panel's Network Connections icon.

2.   Right-click the icon for the connection that gets you on the Internet and then select Properties.

3.   Select the Networking tab and make sure the File And Printer Sharing For Microsoft Networks check box is cleared.

Although disabling file and printer sharing is a must, it's not enough. That's because when a hacker finds your IP address, he or she has many other avenues with which to access your computer. Specifically, your Transmission Control Protocol/Internet Protocol (TCP/IP) connection uses many different "ports" for sending and receiving data. For example, Web data and commands typically use port 80, e-mail uses ports 25 and 110, file transfer protocol (FTP) uses ports 20 and 21, Domain Name System (DNS) uses port 53, and so on. In all, there are dozens of these ports, and every one is an opening through which a clever cracker can gain access to your computer.

As if all this weren't enough, hackers also can check your system to see if some kind of Trojan horse virus is installed. (Those nasty e-mail virus attachments we discussed earlier in this previous chapter sometimes install these programs on your machine.) If the hacker finds one, he or she can effectively take control of your machine and either wreak havoc on its contents or use your computer to attack other systems (in which case, your machine becomes what's called a *zombie computer*).

Again, if you think your computer is too obscure or worthless for someone else to bother with, think again. A typical computer connected to the Internet all day long will get "probed" for vulnerable ports or installed Trojan horses at least a few times a day. If you want to see just how vulnerable your computer is, several good sites on the Web will test your security:

- Gibson Research (Shields Up): *http://grc.com/default.htm*

- DSL Reports: *http://www.dslreports.com/secureme_go*

- HackerWhacker: *http://www.hackerwhacker.com/*

The good news is that Windows XP includes a *personal firewall* tool called Internet Connection Firewall that can lock down your ports and prevent unauthorized access to your machine. In effect, your computer becomes invisible to the Internet (although you can still surf the Web and work with e-mail normally). Follow these steps to fire up Internet Connection Firewall:

1. Launch Control Panel's Network Connections icon.

2. Right-click the icon for the connection that gets you on the Internet and then select Properties.

3. Select the Advanced tab and select the Protect My Computer And Network By Limiting Or Preventing Access To This Computer From The Internet check box.

4. Click OK.

> **Insider Secret** You should also turn off Windows XP's Messenger Service. This service (which is not to be confused with the Windows Messenger instant messaging program) is used by network administrators to broadcast messages to users. However, some advertisers have figured out how to use this service to have ads pop up on your computer. You can block these ads by turning off the service. To do this, launch Control Panel's Administrative Tools icon and then launch the Services icon. Double-click the Messenger service and then click Stop to shut it down. To prevent it from starting in future Windows XP sessions, select Manual from the Startup Type list.

Notes from the Real World

Once you have machines connected to the Internet via broadband, other Internet users begin to regularly scan your network to try to gain access to it. This means that a firewall is a necessity for any broadband connection. I use a hardware firewall at the edge of my broadband connection, along with enabling Windows XP's Internet Connection Firewall on each machine on my network.

(continued)

Notes from the Real World *(continued)*

I like to have access to files on my home network while I'm away from home but also want to keep the number of open firewall ports (and thus potential entry points to my network) as small as possible. The method I use to accomplish this is Windows XP's Remote Desktop. I open one port on my firewall to allow Remote Desktop connections to a single machine on my network. From within that Remote Desktop session, I have access to the other machines and files on my home network, as well as the local hard disk of the laptop I'm using to make the connection. This allows me to easily copy files to and from my home network, while not directly allowing file sharing over the Internet. To add another layer of security, I've modified the port that Remote Desktop uses to listen for incoming connections. I did that by altering the following registry value:

```
HKLM\SYSTEM\CurrentControlSet\Control\TerminalServer\WinStations
\RDP-Tcp\PortNumber
```

I set this to a decimal number other than 3389, which is the default port number. This makes it difficult for a person using a port scanner against my broadband connection to tell that the purpose of the open port is for a Remote Desktop connection. In turn, this makes it much less likely that he or she will try to make a Remote Desktop connection into my network.

—Austin Wilson

Surfing the Web Securely

When implementing security for Internet Explorer, Microsoft realized that different sites have different security needs. For example, it makes sense to have fairly stringent security for Internet sites, but you can probably scale the security back a bit when browsing pages on your corporate intranet.

To handle these different types of sites, Internet Explorer defines various *security zones*, and you can customize the security requirements for each zone. The current zone is displayed in the status bar.

To work with these zones, either select Tools, Internet Options in Internet Explorer, or launch Control Panel's Internet Options icon. In the Internet Options dialog box that appears, select the Security tab, shown in Figure 14-6.

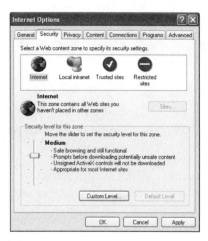

Figure 14-6   Use the Security tab to set up security zones and customize the security options for each zone.

> **Tip**   Another way to display the Security tab is to double-click the security zone shown at the right end of the Internet Explorer status bar.

The list at the top of the dialog box shows icons for the four types of zones available:

- **Internet**   This zone includes Web sites that aren't in any of the other three zones. The default security level is Medium.

- **Local Intranet**   This zone includes the Web pages on your computer and your network (intranet). The default security level is Medium-low.

- **Trusted Sites**   This zone encompasses Web sites that implement secure pages and that you're sure have safe content. The default security level is Low.

- **Restricted Sites**   This zone is the umbrella for Web sites that don't implement secure pages or that you don't trust, for whatever reason. The default security level is High.

Adding and Removing Zone Sites

Three of these zones, Local Intranet, Trusted Sites, and Restricted Sites, enable you to add sites. To do this, follow these steps:

1. Select the zone you want to work with and then click Sites.

2. If you selected Trusted Sites or Restricted Sites, skip to step 4. Otherwise, if you selected the Local Intranet zone, you see a dialog box with three check boxes:

   - **Include All Local (Intranet) Sites Not Listed In Other Zones** When selected, this option includes all intranet sites in the zone. If you add specific intranet sites to other zones, those sites aren't included in this zone.

   - **Include All Sites That Bypass The Proxy Server** When this check box is selected, sites that you've set up to bypass your proxy server (if you have one) are included in this zone.

   - **Include All Network Paths (UNCs)** When this check box is selected, all network paths that use the Universal Naming Convention (UNC) are included in this zone. (UNC is a standard format used with network addresses. They usually take the form *server**resource*, where *server* is the name of the network server and *resource* is the name of a shared network resource.)

3. To add sites to the Local Intranet zone, click Advanced.

4. Enter the site's address in the Add This Web Site To The Zone text box and then click Add.

> **Note** When entering an address, you can include an asterisk as a wildcard character. For example, the address *http://*.microsoft.com* adds every microsoft.com domain, including *www.microsoft.com, windowsupdate.microsoft.com, support.microsoft.com*, and so on.

5. If you make a mistake and enter the wrong site, select it in the Web Sites list and then click Remove.

6.   Two of these dialog boxes (Local Intranet and Trusted Sites) have a Require Server Verification (https:) For All Sites In This Zone check box. If you select this option, each site you enter must use the secure https protocol.

7.   Click OK.

Changing a Zone's Security Level

To change the security level for a zone, first select it in the Security tab's Select A Web Content Zone To Specify Its Security Settings list. Then use the Security Level For This Zone slider to set the level. To set up your own security settings, click Custom Level. This displays the Security Settings dialog box shown in Figure 14-7.

Figure 14-7   Use the Security Settings dialog box to set up customized security levels for the selected zone.

The Security Settings dialog box provides you with a long list of possible security issues, and your job is to specify how you want Internet Explorer to handle each issue. You usually have three choices:

■   **Disable**   Security is turned on. For example, if the issue is whether to run an ActiveX control, the control is not run.

■   **Enable**   Security is turned off. For example, if the issue is whether to run an ActiveX control, the control is run automatically.

■ **Prompt**   You're asked how you want to handle the issue. For example, you decide whether you want to accept or reject an ActiveX control.

Enhancing Online Privacy by Managing Cookies

A *cookie* is a small text file that's stored on your computer. It's used by Web sites to "remember" information about your session at that site: shopping cart data, page customizations, passwords, and so on. No other site can access the cookie, so it's safe and private under most—but definitely not all—circumstances. To understand why cookies can sometimes compromise your privacy, you need to understand the different cookie types that exist.

■ **Temporary cookie**   This type of cookie lives just as long as you have Internet Explorer running. When you shut down the program, all the temporary cookies are deleted.

■ **Persistent cookie**   This type of cookie remains on your hard disk through multiple Internet Explorer sessions. The cookie's duration depends on how it's set up, but it can be anything from a few seconds to a few years.

■ **First-party cookie**   This is a cookie that's set by the Web site that you're viewing.

■ **Third-party cookie**   This is a cookie that's set by a site other than the one you're viewing. Most third-party cookies are created and stored by advertisers who have placed an ad on the site you're viewing.

Given these cookie types, your privacy can be compromised in two ways:

■ A site might store *personally identifiable information*—your name, e-mail address, home address, phone number, and so on—in a persistent first- or third-party cookie and then use that information in some way (such as filling in a form) without your consent.

■ A site might store information about you in a persistent third-party cookie and then use that cookie to track your online movements and activities. It can do this because it might have (for example) an ad on dozens or hundreds of Web sites, and that ad is the mechanism that enables the site to set and read its cookies. Such sites are supposed to come up with *privacy policies* stating that they won't engage in surreptitious monitoring of users, they won't sell user data, and so on.

To help you handle these scenarios, Windows XP implements a privacy feature that gives you extra control over whether sites can store cookies on your machine. To check out this feature, select Internet Explorer's Tools, Internet Options command, and then select the Privacy tab, shown in Figure 14-8.

Figure 14-8   Use the Privacy tab to configure how Internet Explorer handles cookies.

You set your cookie privacy level by using the slider in the Settings section of the dialog box. First, let's look at the two extreme settings:

- **Accept All Cookies**   This setting (it's at the bottom of the slider) tells Internet Explorer to accept all requests to set and read cookies.

- **Block All Cookies**   This setting (it's at the top of the slider) tells Internet Explorer to reject all requests to set and read cookies.

> **Caution**   Blocking all cookies may sound like the easiest way to maximize your online privacy. However, numerous sites rely on cookies to operate properly, so if you block all cookies, you may find that your Web surfing isn't as convenient or as smooth as it used to be.

In between are four settings that offer more detailed control. Table 14-1 shows you how each setting affects the three types of privacy issues.

Table 14-1   Cookie settings and privacy issues

Setting	Third-Party Cookies With No Compact Privacy Policy	Third-Party Cookies Using Personally Identifiable Information Without The Type Of Consent	First-Party Cookies Using Personally Identifiable Information Without The Type Of Consent
Low	Restricted	Restricted (implicit consent)	OK
Medium	Blocked	Blocked (implicit consent)	Restricted (implicit consent)
Medium High	Blocked	Blocked (explicit consent)	Blocked (implicit consent)
High	Blocked	Blocked (explicit consent)	Blocked (explicit consent)

Here are some notes about the terminology in this table:

- *Restricted* means that Internet Explorer doesn't allow the site to set a persistent cookie, just a temporary one.

- A *compact privacy policy* is a shortened form of a privacy policy that can be sent along with the cookie and that can be read by the browser.

- *Implicit consent* means that on one or more pages leading up to the cookie, you were warned that your personally identifiable information would be used and you agreed that it was okay.

- *Explicit consent* means that on the page that reads the cookie, you were warned that your personally identifiable information would be used and you agreed that it was okay.

> **Note**   If you decide to change the privacy setting, you should first delete all your cookies because the new setting won't apply to any cookies already on your computer. To delete your cookies, select Tools, Internet Options, select the General tab, and then click Delete Cookies. (If you prefer to delete individual cookies, click Settings, click View Files, and then look for file names that begin with Cookie:.)

15

Getting the Most Out of Internet Explorer

In this chapter, you'll learn how to:

- Launch and navigate Web pages.

- Take full advantage of the Address bar.

- Customize the Links bar to allow one-click surfing.

- Change Internet Explorer's default search engine.

- Work with Internet Explorer's advanced options.

As we write this, Microsoft Internet Explorer is by far the most dominant Web browser—depending on which source you use—for anywhere from 85 percent to 95 percent of the worldwide market. And because most computer-savvy people have also been on the Internet for a number of years, it's safe to say that Internet Explorer is probably one of the most familiar applications available today. Or perhaps we should say that the *basics* of Internet Explorer are familiar to most people. However, as with the Internet Explorer security and privacy issues that you saw in the previous chapter, there are hidden pockets of the browser that most people don't know about. Significantly, many of these seldom seen areas are not as obscure as you might think. Lots of these features can be put to good use immediately to make your Web surfing easier, more efficient, and more productive. In this chapter, we take you on a tour of a few of our favorite Internet Explorer nooks and crannies and we show you how they can improve your Web experience.

Tips and Techniques for Better Web Surfing

Surfing Web pages with Internet Explorer is straightforward and easy, but even experienced users might not be aware of all the ways that they can open and navigate pages. Here's a review of all the techniques you can use to open a Web page in Microsoft Windows XP:

- **Type a URL in any Address bar.** By default, all Internet Explorer and all Windows Explorer windows have an Address bar. To open a page, type the URL in the Address bar and press Enter.

- **Type a URL in the Run dialog box.** Select Start, Run, type the URL you want in the Run dialog box, and click OK.

- **Select a URL from the Address bar.** Internet Explorer's Address bar doubles as a drop-down list that holds the last 15 addresses you entered.

- **Use the Open dialog box for remote pages.** In Internet Explorer, select File, Open (or press Ctrl+O) to display the Open dialog box, type the URL, and click OK.

- **Use the Open dialog box for local pages.** If you want to view a Web page that's on your computer, display the Open dialog box, enter the full path (drive, folder, and file name), and click OK. Alternatively, click Browse, find the page, click Open, and then click OK.

- **Select a favorite.** Open the Favorites menu and click the site you want to open.

- **Click a Links bar button.** The Links bar contains several buttons that take you to predefined Web pages. (You can add buttons to the Links bar, remove existing buttons, and more. See "Customizing the Links Bar for One-Click Surfing," later in this chapter.)

- **Click a Web address in an Outlook Express message.** When Microsoft Outlook Express recognizes a Web address in an e-mail message (that is, an address that begins with *http://, https://, ftp://, www.,* and so on), it converts the address into a link. Clicking the link opens the address in Internet Explorer. Note, too, that many other programs are URL-aware, including the Microsoft Office suite of programs.

Once you've opened a page, you usually move to another page by clicking a link: either a text link or an image map. However, there are more techniques you can use to navigate to other pages:

■ **Open a link in another window.**   If you don't want to leave the current page, you can force a link to open in another Internet Explorer window by right-clicking the link and then selecting Open In New Window. (You can open a new window for the current page by selecting File, New, Window, or by pressing Ctrl+N.)

> **Tip**   Hold down Shift and click a link to open that link in a new browser window.

■ **Retrace the pages you've visited.**   Click Internet Explorer's Back button to return to a page you visited previously in this session. Alternatively, select View, Go To, Back (or press Alt+Left arrow). Once you've gone back to a page, click the Forward button to move ahead through the visited pages. You can also select View, Go To, Forward (or press Alt+Right arrow.) Note, too, that the Back and Forward buttons also serve as drop-down lists. Click the downward-pointing arrow to the right of each button to see the list.

■ **Return to the home page.**   By default, when you launch Internet Explorer without specifying a URL, you end up at MSN, Internet Explorer's default start page (*http://www.msn.com/*). You can return to Internet Explorer's home page at any time by selecting View, Go To, Home Page, or by clicking the Home button on the toolbar (you can also press Alt+Home).

> **Tip**   To change the home page, first surf to the page you want to use. Then select Tools, Internet Options, select the General tab, and in the Home Page section of the dialog box, click Use Current. Alternatively, drag the icon from the Address bar and drop it on the Home toolbar button. When Internet Explorer asks if you want to set your home page to the current page, click Yes.

- **Use the History bar.** If you click the toolbar's History button or select the View, Explorer Bar, History command, Internet Explorer adds a History bar to the left side of the window. This bar lists the sites you've visited over the past 20 days. Just click a link to go to a site. Note that the items you see in the History bar are based on the contents of the %UserProfile%\Local Settings\History folder.

Navigating Sites Quickly and Easily Using the Address Bar

Internet Explorer's Address bar (and the Address bar that appears in any Windows XP folder window) appears to be nothing more than a simple type-and-click mechanism. However, it's useful for many things, and it comes with its own bag of tricks for making it even easier to use. Here's a rundown:

- Internet Explorer maintains a list of the last 15 URLs and UNCs you typed into the Address bar. To access this list, press F4 and then use the Up and Down arrow keys to select an item from the list.

- To edit the Address bar text, press Alt+D to select it.

- To create a shortcut for whatever object is displayed in the Address bar, drag the object's icon (it's on the left side of the text box) and drop it on the desktop or some other location.

- The Address bar's AutoComplete feature monitors the address as you type. If any previously entered addresses match your typing, those addresses appear in a list. To choose one of those addresses, use the Down arrow key to select it and then press Enter. The quickest way to use AutoComplete is to begin typing the site's domain name. For example, if you want to bring up *http://www.microsoft.com/*, start typing the "microsoft" part. If you start with the full address, you have to type **http://www.** or just **www.**, and then one other character.

- Internet Explorer assumes any address you enter is for a Web site. Therefore, you don't need to type the **http://** prefix because Internet Explorer will add it for you automatically.

- Internet Explorer also assumes that most Web addresses are in the form *http://www.something.com*. Therefore, if you simply type the "something" part and press Ctrl+Enter, Internet Explorer will automatically add the *http://www.* prefix and the *.com* suffix. For example, you can get to the Microsoft home page (*http://www.microsoft.com*) by typing **microsoft** and pressing Ctrl+Enter.

Insider Secret   One way to clear the Address bar list is to clear the History files. You do this by selecting Tools, Internet Options and, in the History section of the General tab, clicking Clear History. If you prefer to preserve the History, note that Internet Explorer stores the last 15 typed addresses in the following registry key:

```
HKCU\Software\Microsoft\Internet Explorer\TypedURLs
```

You can therefore clear the Address bar's history list by closing all Internet Explorer windows and deleting the settings url1 through url15 in this key. Here's a script that will also do this:

```
Option Explicit
Dim objWshShell, i
Set objWshShell = WScript.CreateObject("WScript.Shell")
For i = 1 to 15
    objWshShell.RegDelete "HKCU\Software\Microsoft _
    \Internet Explorer\TypedURLs\url" & i
Next i
```

Note that if there are fewer than 15 addresses in this history list, you will get a Windows Script Host error stating "Unable to remove registry key "HKCU\Software \Microsoft\Internet Explorer \TypedURLs\url*n*", where *n* is one greater than the number of history items found in the list. The message can be safely ignored; all the history items have been removed from the list.

- Some Web sites use frames to divide a Web page into multiple sections. Some of these sites offer links to other Web sites but, annoyingly, those pages appear within the first site's frame structure. To break out of frames, drag a link into the Address bar.

- To search from the Address bar (AutoSearch), first type your search text. As you type, Internet Explorer adds Search for "*text*" below the Address bar, where *text* is your search text. When you've finished your search text, press Tab to select the Search for item and then press Enter. Alternatively, precede your search text with either the words go, find, or search, or with a question mark (?), as in these examples:

```
go vbscript
find autosearch
search neologisms
? registry
```

Customizing the Links Bar for One-Click Surfing

The Links bar gives you one-click access to Web pages, and so is more convenient than even the Favorites folder (unless you have the Favorites bar displayed). To take full advantage of this convenience, you'll want to redesign the Links bar so that its links and setup are suitable for the way you work. Here's a list of a few techniques and options you can use to work with and customize the Links bar:

- **Moving the Links bar**   By default, the Links bar appears to the right of the Address bar with only the title displayed. Unfortunately, this means you have to click twice to launch a link, which defeats the purpose of the toolbar. To get the one-click access back, move your mouse over the Links label and then drag the bar just below the Address bar, where it will lock into place. Remember, if the Links label will not move, you need to select View, Toolbars, Lock The Toolbars to remove the checkmark.

- **Changing button positions**   The positions of the Links bar buttons are not permanent. To move any button, use your mouse to drag the button left or right along the Links bar.

- **Renaming a button**   Right-click the button and then select Rename. Use the Rename dialog box to edit the name, and then click OK.

- **Changing the URL for a button**   Right-click a button and then select Properties. On the Web Document tab, use the URL text box to edit the URL for the button.

- **Creating a new link button**   To add a new Links bar button for the current page, drag the page icon from the Address bar and drop it on the Links bar. To add a new button for a hypertext link, drag the link and drop it on the Links bar. If you've already saved the page as a Favorite, open the Favorites menu, drag the icon from the menu and drop it inside the Links bar. If the page title is long, you'll likely want to rename it to something shorter to avoid wasting precious Links bar space.

- **Deleting a link**   To remove a button from the Links bar, right-click it and then select Delete.

Insider Secret   The Links bar buttons are URL shortcut files located in the %UserProfile%\Favorites\Links folder. You can use this folder to work with the shortcuts directly. Perhaps most importantly, you can also use the folder to create subfolders. When you click a subfolder in the Links bar, it displays a list of the URL shortcuts that are in that subfolder.

Searching the Web

Veteran surfers, having seen a wide range of what the Web has to offer, usually prefer to tackle the Web using a targeted approach that enables them to quickly find information and do research. This means using one or more of the Web's many search engines. It's usually best to deal directly with a search engine site, but Internet Explorer also offers some default searching options. For example, you saw earlier in this chapter (see "Navigating Sites Quickly and Easily Using the Address Bar") that you can run searches directly from the Address bar.

You can also run searches from the built-in Search bar, which you can display either by clicking the Search toolbar button or by selecting View, Explorer Bar, Search. Internet Explorer adds the Search bar to the left side of the window, as shown in Figure 15-1.

Figure 15-1   Use the Search bar to quickly enter search arguments.

> **Tip** Press Ctrl+E to toggle the Search bar on and off.

Enter your search arguments in the text box and then press Enter (or click Search). When the search is complete, the right side of the Internet Explorer window shows links to the matching sites. You also have the following Web search options:

- **Automatically Send Your Search To Other Search Engines** When you click this link, Internet Explorer submits your search text to another search engine (such as HotBot) and then displays links for a few more search engines (such as MSN and Google). Click one of those links to submit the text to that search engine. You can also click Send Search To More Search Engines to see more engines.

- **Highlight Words On The Results Page** When you click this link, Internet Explorer asks which words you want to highlight in the search results. You have options for each search term as well as a Highlight Other Text option, which includes a text box in which you enter another word or phrase. Click the option you want and then click Highlight Next to highlight the first instance of the chosen term. Continue clicking Highlight Next to highlight subsequent instances.

- **Change Current Search** Use this text box to edit your search text or enter new search terms.

- **Start A New Search** Click this link to return to the original Search bar layout and start over again.

Changing the Default Search Engine

By default, Internet Explorer initially submits the search text to the MSN search engine. (The default search engine is also the one that Internet Explorer uses for the Address bar AutoSearch.) If you prefer to use a different search engine as the default, follow these steps:

1. Display the Search bar.
2. Click Change Preferences.
3. Click Change Internet Search Behavior.
4. In the Select The Default Search Engine list, click the search engine you prefer.
5. Click OK.

Setting Up Other Search Engines for Address Bar Searching

Address bar–based searching with the search text preceded by go or ? is often the quickest route for simple searches. Unfortunately, you're limited to using only Internet Explorer's default search engine. What if you regularly use several search engines depending on the search text or the results you get? In that case, it's still possible to set up an AutoSearch for any number of other search engines. Here are some example steps that create an AutoSearch URL for Google searches:

1. Run the Registry Editor and display the following key:

   `HKCU\Software\Microsoft\Internet Explorer\SearchURL`

2. Create a new subkey. The name of this subkey will be the text that you enter into the Address bar before the search text. For example, if you name this subkey **google**, then you'll initiate an Address bar search by typing google *text*, where *text* is your search text.

3. Select the new subkey and open its (Default) value for editing.

4. Enter the URL that initiates a search for the search engine, and specify **%s** as a placeholder for the search text. For Google, the URL looks like this:

   http://www.google.com/search?q=%s

5. You also need to specify the characters or hexadecimal values that Internet Explorer will substitute for characters that have special meaning within a query string: space, per cent (%), ampersand (&), and plus (+). To do this, add the following settings to the new subkey:

Name	Type	Data
<blank>	REG_SZ	+
%	REG_SZ	%25
&	REG_SZ	%26
+	REG_SZ	%2B

   Figure 15-2 shows the completed example. The text that you type in the Address bar before the search string—that is, the name of the new subkey—is called the *search prefix*. Although we used google as the search prefix in our example, ideally it should be a single character (such as *g* for Google or *a* for AltaVista) to minimize typing. Note, too, that you can also use Tweak UI to create search prefixes. Launch Tweak UI and select the Internet Explorer, Search branch. Then click Create to set up the search prefix and the search URL.

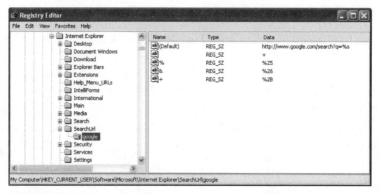

Figure 15-2 An example search prefix for the Google search engine.

Notes from the Real World

How do you know the proper URL to use for a search engine? What I do is go to the search engine site and then run a search with a single word. When the results appear, I examine the URL in the Address bar, which almost always takes the following general form:

ScriptURL?QueryString

Here, *ScriptURL* is the address of the site's search script, and *QueryString* is the data sent to the script. In most cases, I just copy the URL and substitute *%s* for my search text when I'm setting up my search prefix. Often I'll experiment with reducing the query string to the minimum necessary for the search to execute properly. For example, a typical Google search might produce a URL such as the following:

http://www.google.com/search?hl=en&lr=&ie=UTF-8&oe=UTF-8&q =mcfedries&btnG=Google+Search

In the query string, each item is separated by an ampersand (&), so what I do is delete one item at a time until either the search breaks or I'm down to the search text (q=mcfedries in the above query string). To save you some legwork, here are the minimal search URLs for a number of search sites:

All the Web   *http://www.alltheweb.com/search?query=%s&cat=web*

AltaVista   *http://www.altavista.com/cgi-bin/query?q=%s*

AOL Search   *http://search.aol.com
/dirsearch.adp?from=msxp&query=%s*

Ask Jeeves   *http://www.askjeeves.com/main/askjeeves.asp?ask=%s*

Encarta (Dictionary only)   *http://encarta.msn.com/encnet/features
/dictionary/DictionaryResults.aspx?search=%s*

Encarta (General)   *http://encarta.msn.com/find/search.asp?search=%s*

Excite   *http://search.excite.com/search.gw?c=web&search=%s*

Lycos   *http://search.lycos.com/main/default.asp?query=%s*

MSN   *http://search.msn.com/results.asp?q=%s*

NorthernLight   *http://www.northernlight.com/nlquery.fcg?qr=%s*

Overture   *http://www.overture.com/d/search/?Keywords=%s*

Teoma   *http://s.teoma.com/search?q=%s&qcat=1&qsrc=0*

Yahoo   *http://search.yahoo.com/bin/search?p=%s*

—Paul McFedries

Understanding Internet Explorer's Advanced Options

Internet Explorer has a huge list of customization features found on the Advanced tab of the Internet Options dialog box (see Figure 15-3). Many of these settings are obscure, but there are lots that are extremely useful for surfers of all stripes. This section runs through all of these settings.

Insider Secret   The advanced options can be set for users via the Group Policy Editor. Run the program and open the User Configuration, Windows Settings, Internet Explorer Maintenance branch. Right-click Internet Explorer Maintenance and then select Preference Mode. Click the Advanced branch that is added to the Internet Explorer Maintenance section. Double-click the Internet Settings item to work with the advanced options.

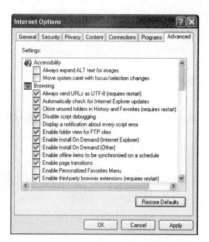

Figure 15-3   In the Internet Options dialog box, the Advanced tab contains a long list of Internet Explorer customization settings.

The Accessibility branch has two options:

■ **Always Expand ALT Text For Images**   Most Webmasters provide a text description for each image they include on a page. If you configure Internet Explorer not to show images (see the discussion of the Show Pictures check box on page 353), all you see are boxes where the images should be, and each box contains the text description (which is known as *alt text*, where *alt* is short for alternate). Selecting this check box directs Internet Explorer to expand the image box horizontally so that the alt text appears on a single line, which makes it easier to read.

■ **Move System Caret With Focus/Selection Changes**   Selecting this check box configures Internet Explorer to move the system caret whenever you change the focus. (The *system caret* is a visual indication of what part of the screen currently has the focus. If a text box has the focus, the system caret is a blinking, vertical bar; if a check box or option button has the focus, the system caret is a dotted outline of the control name.) This is useful if you have a screen reader or screen magnifier that uses the position of the system caret to determine what part of the screen should be read or magnified.

Here are the options in the Browsing branch:

■ **Always Send URLs As UTF-8 (Requires Restart)**   When selected, this check box indicates to Internet Explorer to send Web page addresses using the UTF-8 (Universal character set Transformation Format 8) standard, which is readable in any language. If you're having trouble accessing a page that uses non-English characters in the URL, the server may not be able to handle UTF-8, so clear this check box. You need to restart Internet Explorer if you change this setting.

■ **Automatically Check For Internet Explorer Updates**   When selected, this option flags Internet Explorer to check (approximately every 30 days) to see whether a newer version of the program is available. This is a useful and easy method for keeping up with the latest Internet Explorer updates and security patches.

■ **Close Unused Folders In History And Favorites (Requires Restart)**   When this check box is selected, Internet Explorer keeps unused folders closed when you display the History bar and the Favorites bar. That is, if you open a folder and then open a second folder, Internet Explorer automatically closes the first folder. This makes the History and Favorites lists easier to navigate, so it's usually best to leave this option selected. You need to restart Internet Explorer if you change this setting.

■ **Disable Script Debugging**   This check box toggles the script debugger (if one is installed) on and off. You should need to select this option only if you're a page designer and you have scripts in your pages that you need to debug before uploading them to the Web.

■ **Display A Notification About Every Script Error**   If you select this check box, Internet Explorer displays a dialog box to alert you to JavaScript or VBScript errors on a page. If you leave this option cleared, Internet Explorer displays an error message in the status bar. To see the full error message, double-click the status bar message. Again, only script programmers will want to enable this option, and only when they're debugging scripts. Many Web sites are poorly programmed and contain script errors, so enabling this option means you'll have to deal with lots of annoying dialog boxes as you surf.

- **Enable Folder View For FTP Sites** When this option is selected and you access a File Transfer Protocol (FTP) site, Internet Explorer displays the contents of the site using the familiar Windows folder view. This makes it easy to drag-and-drop files from the FTP site to your hard disk (and possibly perform other file maintenance chores, depending on what permissions you have at the site).

- **Enable Install On Demand (Internet Explorer)** When this check box is selected, Internet Explorer examines each Web page for elements that require a specific browser feature. If that feature isn't installed, and that feature comes with setup instructions in a cabinet information file, Internet Explorer asks if you want to install the feature. If you find that a page doesn't appear to work properly, a missing component could be the problem, so try enabling this option.

> **Note** For a list of the features supported by Install On Demand, see the following Web page:
>
> *http://msdn.microsoft.com/workshop/author/behaviors /reference/methods/installable.asp*

- **Enable Install On Demand (Other)** This is similar to the Enable Install On Demand (Internet Explorer) option, except that selecting this check box flags Internet Explorer to prompt you to install features that come with their own installation program. Only the Windows Virtual Machine (Java support, which is not installed by default in Windows XP) can be installed this way.

- **Enable Offline Items To Be Synchronized On A Schedule** This check box toggles the synchronization updates on and off. Clearing this check box is a good idea if you're going out of town for a few days and don't want offline pages updated while you're away.

- **Enable Page Transitions** This check box toggles Internet Explorer's support for page transitions on and off. Web sites that use a server that supports FrontPage extensions can define various page transitions (such as wipes and fades). However, these transitions often slow down your browsing, so we recommend turning them off.

- **Enable Personalized Favorites Menu**   When this check box is selected, Windows XP's "personalized" menu feature gets applied to Internet Explorer's Favorites menu. This means that Internet Explorer hides favorites that you haven't visited in a while. To see the hidden favorites, click the downward-pointing arrow at the bottom of the menu. Personalized menus reduce the command clutter that can confuse novice users, but they just slow down experienced users. We recommend leaving this option turned off.

- **Enable Third-Party Browser Extensions (Requires Restart)**   When this check box is selected, Internet Explorer supports third-party extensions to its interface. For example, the Google Toolbar is a third-party extension that integrates the Google search engine into Internet Explorer as a toolbar. If you clear this check box, these third-party extensions don't appear and can't be displayed. Clearing this check box is a good way to turn off those annoying third-party toolbars that install themselves without permission. You need to restart Internet Explorer if you change this setting.

- **Enable Visual Styles On Buttons And Controls In Web Pages**   When this check box is selected, Internet Explorer applies the current Windows XP visual style to all Web pages for objects such as form buttons. If you clear this check box, Internet Explorer applies its default visual style to all page elements.

- **Force Offscreen Compositing Even Under Terminal Server (Requires Restart)**   If you select this check box, Internet Explorer performs all *compositing*—the combining of two or more images—in memory before displaying the result on the screen. This avoids the image flashing that can occur when running Internet Explorer under Terminal Services, but it can reduce performance significantly. We recommend keeping this option cleared. You need to restart Internet Explorer if you change this setting.

- **Notify When Downloads Complete**   If you leave this check box selected, Internet Explorer leaves its download progress dialog box on the screen after the download is complete (see Figure 15-4). This enables you to click Open to launch the downloaded file or to click Open Folder to display the file's destination folder. If you clear this check box, Internet Explorer closes this dialog box as soon as the download is over.

> **Tip** You can also force Internet Explorer to close the Download Complete dialog box automatically by selecting the Close This Dialog Box When Download Completes check box in the download progress dialog box.

Figure 15-4 When Internet Explorer completes a file download, it leaves this dialog box on the screen to help you deal with the file.

- **Reuse Windows For Launching Shortcuts** When this check box is selected, Windows looks for an already-open Internet Explorer window when you click a Web page shortcut (such as a Web address in an Outlook Express e-mail message). If such a window is open, the Web page is loaded into that window. This is a good idea because it prevents Internet Explorer windows from multiplying unnecessarily. If you clear this option, Windows always loads the page into a new Internet Explorer window.

- **Show Friendly HTTP Error Messages** When this check box is selected, Internet Explorer intercepts the error messages (for, say, pages not found) generated by Web servers and replaces them with its own messages that offer more information as well as possible solutions to the problem. If you clear this option, Internet Explorer simply displays the error message generated by the Web server. However, we recommend clearing this option because the Web server error messages are often customized to be more helpful than the generic messages reported by Internet Explorer.

- **Show Friendly URLs** This check box determines how URLs appear in the status bar when you hover the mouse over a link or image map. Select this check box to see only the file name of the linked page; clear this check box to see the full URL of the linked page. We prefer to see the full URL so that we know exactly where a link will take us (particularly if the link will take us to a different site).

- **Show Go Button In Address Bar** When this check box is selected, Internet Explorer adds a Go button to the right of the Address bar. You click this button to open whatever URL is shown in the Address bar. The usefulness of this button is dubious (it's usually easiest just to press Enter after entering an address), but it doesn't hurt anything.

- **Underline Links** Use these options to specify when Internet Explorer should format Web page links with an underline. The Hover option means that the underline appears only when you position the mouse pointer over the link. Many Web sites use colored text, so it's often difficult to recognize a link without the underlining. Therefore, we recommend that you select the Always option.

- **Use Inline AutoComplete** This check box toggles the Address bar's "inline" AutoComplete feature on and off. When inline Auto-Complete is on, Internet Explorer monitors the text that you type in the Address bar. If your text matches a previously typed URL, Internet Explorer automatically completes the address by displaying the matching URL in the Address bar. It also displays a drop-down list of other matching URLs. When inline AutoComplete is off, Internet Explorer only displays the drop-down list of matching URLs.

> **Note**   If you want to prevent Internet Explorer from displaying the drop-down list of matching URLs, select Tools, Internet Options and then click the Content tab's AutoComplete button to display the AutoComplete Settings dialog box. Clear the Web Addresses check box. Note, too, that Internet Explorer's AutoComplete feature also applies to Web forms. That is, AutoComplete can also remember data that you've typed into a form—including user names and passwords—and then enter that data automatically when you use the form again. You can control this Web form portion of AutoComplete by using the other check boxes in the Use AutoComplete For section of the AutoComplete Settings dialog box.

- **Use Passive FTP (For Firewall And DSL Modem Compatibility)**
  In a normal FTP session, Internet Explorer opens a connection to the
  FTP server (for commands) and then the FTP server opens a second
  connection back to the browser (for the data). If you're on a network
  with a firewall, however, incoming connections from a server aren't
  allowed. With *passive FTP*, the browser establishes the second (data)
  connection itself. So if you're on a firewalled network (or are using
  a DSL modem) and you can't establish an FTP connection, select this
  check box.

- **Use Smooth Scrolling**   This check box toggles a feature called
  smooth scrolling on and off. When you select this check box to
  enable smooth scrolling, pressing Page Down or Page Up causes the
  page to scroll down or up at a preset speed. If you clear this check
  box, pressing Page Down or Page Up causes the page to instantly
  jump down or up.

> **Insider Secret**   When reading a Web page, you can scroll
> down one screenful by pressing Spacebar. To scroll up one
> screenful, press Shift+Spacebar.

The check boxes in the HTTP 1.1 Settings branch determine whether
Internet Explorer uses the HTTP 1.1 protocol:

- **Use HTTP 1.1**   This check box toggles Internet Explorer's use of
  HTTP 1.1 to communicate with Web servers. (HTTP 1.1 is the standard protocol used on the Web today.) You should clear this check
  box only if you're having trouble connecting to a Web site. This signals Internet Explorer to use HTTP 1.0, which may solve the problem.

- **Use HTTP 1.1 Through Proxy Connections**   This check box toggles on and off the use of HTTP 1.1 only when connecting through
  a proxy server.

The check boxes in the Microsoft VM branch are related to Internet Explorer's Java Virtual Machine:

- **Java Console Enabled (Requires Restart)**   This check box toggles the Java console on and off. The Java console is a separate window in which the output and error messages from a Java applet are displayed. If you select this option (which requires that you restart Internet Explorer), you can view the Java console by selecting the View, Java Console command. You should need to use the Java Console only if you're debugging a Java application.

- **Java Logging Enabled**   This check box toggles Internet Explorer's Java logging on and off. When it's on, Internet Explorer logs Java applet error messages to a file named Javalog.txt in the %SystemRoot% \Java folder. This is useful for troubleshooting Java problems.

- **JIT Compiler For Virtual Machine Enabled (Requires Restart)** This check box toggles Internet Explorer's internal "just-in-time" Java compiler on and off. This compiler is used to compile and run Java applets using native Windows code. In many cases, this causes the Java applet to run much faster than the regularly compiled code. However, it may break some applets, or cause them to run slower than normal. You need to restart Internet Explorer if you change this setting.

The options in the Multimedia branch toggle various multimedia effects on and off:

- **Don't Display Online Media Content In The Media Bar**   If you select this check box, Internet Explorer doesn't display online media content (such as streaming audio or video) in the Media toolbar. Instead, it plays the content in the application associated with the media file type (such as Windows Media Player). Using the dedicated media application usually gives you more options for playing the media, so we recommend selecting this option.

- **Enable Automatic Image Resizing**   If you select this check box, Internet Explorer automatically shrinks large images so that they fit inside the browser window. This is useful if you're running Windows XP with a small monitor or a relatively low resolution, and you're finding that many Web site images don't fit entirely into the browser window.

> **Tip** If Enable Automatic Image Resizing is selected, you can restore an image to its normal size by first hovering the mouse point over the image. After a couple of seconds, Internet Explorer displays the Automatic Image Resizing icon in the lower right corner of the image (see Figure 15-5). Click that icon to expand the image to its normal size.

- **Enable Image Toolbar (Requires Restart)** When this check box is selected and you hover the mouse pointer over an image, Internet Explorer displays a toolbar in the upper left corner of the image, as shown in Figure 15-5. You can use this toolbar to save or print the image, send the image via e-mail, or open the My Pictures folder.

Figure 15-5 When you hover the mouse pointer over an image, Internet Explorer can display the Image toolbar in the upper left corner of the image and the Automatic Image Resizing icon in the lower right corner.

- **Play Animations In Web Pages** This check box toggles animated GIF images on and off. Most animated GIFs are unwelcome annoyances, so you'll probably greatly improve your surfing experience by clearing this check box. If you turn this option off and you want to view an animation, right-click the animation icon in the image and then select Show Picture.

- **Play Sounds In Web Pages**   This check box toggles Web page sound effects on and off. Since the vast majority of Web page sounds are extremely bad MIDI renditions of popular tunes, turning off sounds will save your ears.

- **Play Videos In Web Pages**   This check box toggles Internet Explorer's support for inline AVI files on and off. If you turn this setting off, the only way to view a video is to turn the option back on and then refresh the page.

- **Show Image Download Placeholders**   If you select this check box, Internet Explorer displays a box that is the same size and shape as the image it is downloading.

- **Show Pictures**   This check box toggles Web page images on and off. If you're using a slow connection, turn off this option and Internet Explorer will show only a box where the image would normally appear. (If the designer has included alt text, that text will appear inside the box.) If you want to view a picture, right-click the box and then select Show Picture.

- **Smart Image Dithering**   This check box toggles image dithering on and off. Dithering is a technique that slightly alters an image in order to make jagged edges appear smooth.

In the Printing branch, the Print Background Colors And Images check box determines whether Internet Explorer includes the page's background when you print the page. Many Web pages use solid colors or fancy images as backgrounds, so you'll print these pages more quickly if you leave this setting cleared.

The options in the Search From The Address Bar branch control Internet Explorer's Address bar searching:

- **Display Results, And Go To The Most Likely Site**   Select this option to display the search engine's results in the Search bar and to display the best match in the main browser window.

- **Do Not Search From The Address Bar**   Select this option to disable Address bar searching.

- **Just Display The Results In The Main Window**   Select this option to display in the main browser window a list of the sites that the search engine found.

- **Just Go To The Most Likely Site**   Select this option to display the search engine's best match in the main browser window.

The Security branch has many options related to Internet Explorer security. We discuss these options in Chapter 14, "Implementing Internet Security and Privacy."

Insider Secret   You can "brand" your version of Internet Explorer by setting up a custom window title, a custom browser logo, and custom toolbar buttons. You can do all of this via the Group Policy Editor. Run the program and select User Configuration, Windows Settings, Internet Explorer Maintenance, Browser User Interface. Use the Browser Title, Custom Logo, and Browser Toolbar Customizations settings to perform the customizations.

16

Setting Up and Administering a Small Network

In this chapter, you'll learn how to:

■ Put together the hardware requirements for a network.

■ Configure each network computer.

■ Set up Internet Connection Sharing.

■ Access network resources.

■ Connect to a remote computer's registry.

■ Safely share your computer's resources on the network.

If you have multiple computers in your home or small office, you've probably run into one or more of the following problems:

■ In many cases, it's just not economically feasible to supply each computer with its own complete set of peripherals. Printers, for example, are a crucial part of the computing equation—when you need them. If someone needs a printer only a couple of times a week, it's hard to justify shelling out hundreds of dollars so that a user can have his or her own printer. The problem, then, is how to share a printer (or some other peripheral) among several machines.

- These days, few people work in splendid isolation. Rather, the norm is that colleagues and coworkers share data and work together on the same files. If everyone uses a separate computer, though, how are files shared efficiently?

- Most offices now standardize with particular software packages for word processing, spreadsheets, graphics, and other mainstream applications. Does this mean copies of expensive software programs or suites must be purchased for each machine? As with peripherals, what about the person who uses a program only sporadically?

- Everyone wants to be on the Internet, of course, but paying a subscription for each user seems wasteful. What's needed is a way to share a single Internet connection.

All of these problems are readily overcome by setting up a small network. Printers and other peripherals can be attached to one machine and used by any other machine on the network; files can be transferred along the cables from one computer to another; an Internet connection may be set up on one machine and the connection shared with other machines on the network; a user can access applications, disk drives, and folders on network computers as though these were part of his or her own computer.

A network can solve many problems, but it can also create a few of its own: you have to set it up and you have to administer it. In large corporate networks, these tasks require specialized knowledge, most of which is well beyond the scope of this book. However, setting up and maintaining a network for a small office or home office is within the grasp of anyone willing to learn a few concepts and techniques. It's our goal in this chapter to give you the know-how to do just that.

Setting Up a Peer-to-Peer Network

Networks appear in two guises: client/server and peer-to-peer. In general, a *client/server network* splits the computing workload into two separate, yet related, areas. On one hand, you have users working at intelligent "front-end" systems called *clients*. In turn, these client machines interact with powerful "back-end" systems called *servers*. The basic idea is that the clients have enough processing power to perform tasks on their own, but they rely on the servers to provide them with specialized resources or services, or access to information that would be impractical to implement on a client (such as a large database).

In a *peer-to-peer network*, no computer is singled out to provide special services. Instead, all the computers attached to the network have equal status (at least as far as the network is concerned), and all the computers can act as both servers and clients. On the server side, each computer can share any of its resources with the network *and* control access to these shared resources. For example, if a user shares a folder with the network, he or she also can set up passwords to restrict access to that folder. On the client side, each computer can work with the resources that have been shared by the other peers on the network (assuming they have permission to do so, of course).

We discuss peer-to-peer networks in this chapter. We'll concentrate mostly on the software side: the networking programs and features that are part of the Microsoft Windows XP package. However, the next couple of sections discuss the all-important hardware side: the devices and equipment without which networking isn't possible. We look at the two main network types: Ethernet and wireless.

Understanding Ethernet Network Hardware Requirements

The most popular network type, particularly when it comes to small networks, goes by the generic name of *Ethernet*. Although there are many different Ethernet network configurations, the easiest one to set up and maintain requires three physical components:

- **Network interface card (NIC)**   This is an adapter that, usually, plugs into an expansion bus slot inside a client computer (although some NICs are external and plug into USB ports or PC Card slots). The NIC's main purpose is to serve as the connection point between the PC and the network. The conventional NIC's backplate (that is, the portion of the NIC you can see after the card is installed in the computer) contains one or more ports into which you plug a network cable. These are the three main types of NIC:

    - **Ethernet**   This type of NIC provides 10 Mbps throughput.

    - **Fast Ethernet**   This is a relatively new iteration of the Ethernet architecture that supports 100 Mbps throughput. Because of this speed, Fast Ethernet is rapidly becoming the networking standard (if it isn't already). Note, too, that many NICs are "10/100" cards that support both Ethernet and Fast Ethernet.

    - **Gigabit Ethernet**   This type of card features 1 Gbps throughput. This is impressive speed, to be sure, but it's probably overkill on a small network.

> **Note**   If you have a broadband Internet connection, you'll need two NICs for the computer hosting that connection: one for the Internet connection and a second one for the network connection.

- **Network cable**   To set up a communications pathway between network computers, you need to install cables that connect the various network nodes together. The vast majority of Ethernet NICs provide an RJ-45 port that supports *unshielded twisted-pair* (UTP) cable, which in Ethernet circles is also often referred to as *10Base-T cables*. If you're using Fast Ethernet NICs, be sure to get at least Category 5 cable.

- **Network hub**   A *hub* (also known as a *concentrator*) is a central connection point for network cables. That is, for each computer, you run a twisted-pair cable from the computer's NIC to an RJ-45 port on the hub. Hubs range in size from small boxes with four to eight RJ-45 ports, to large cabinets with dozens of ports for various cable types. If you're using Fast Ethernet NICs, be sure to get a hub that also supports 100 Mbps. There are also 10/100 hubs available if you're using a mix of Ethernet and Fast Ethernet NICs.

Understanding Wireless Network Hardware Requirements

The cabling requirements of a standard Ethernet setup, and the restrictions these requirements impose upon a client, have led an increasing number of network users to consider the cable-free configuration of a wireless network. Using the IEEE 802.11b (or *Wi-Fi*) standard, wireless network connections can be established using radio frequencies in the 2.4-GHz range to achieve speeds up to 11 Mbps, though some manufacturers are using signal-processing chips that allow an effective rate of 22 Mbps. Wireless networks require two device types:

- **Wireless NIC**   This is a special NIC that includes (or has built into its circuitry) a small antenna that receives and transmits data using radio frequencies. If your network consists of only computers with wireless NICs, you don't need any other equipment (although you will have to set up your NICs to use *ad hoc* mode for direct NIC-to-NIC communication; see the operating manual that came with each wireless NIC).

- **Wireless access point**   If your network consists of both wireless and cable connections, you need an access point to combine them. An access point is a switch or router that enables you to connect the wireless portion of your network with the Ethernet portion. Access points typically have an "uplink" port that connects via cable to the Ethernet hub.

> **Caution**   Wireless networks are less secure than wired ones because the wireless connection that enables you to access the network from afar can also enable an intruder from outside your home or office to access the network. Microsoft has a nice collection of wireless network security tips in the following Knowledge Base article:
>
> *http://support.microsoft.com/?scid=kb;en-us;309369*

Running the Network Setup Wizard

In previous versions of Windows, setting up a network usually involved working with obscure settings. These are still available in Windows XP, but there's also a less perplexing route to network connectivity: the Network Setup Wizard. Even if you enjoy working with TCP/IP settings and network protocols, using the Network Setup Wizard is the best way to ensure trouble-free network operation.

Windows XP has a feature called Internet Connection Sharing (ICS) that enables you to share one computer's Internet connection with other computers on the network. How you start setting up your network depends on whether you'll be using ICS:

- If you'll be using ICS, run the Network Setup Wizard on the computer that will be sharing its connection. This machine is called the *ICS host*. Make sure this machine's Internet connection is active before running the wizard. When you're done, you can run the Network Setup Wizard on the other clients, in any order.

- If you won't be using ICS, run the Network Setup Wizard on any computer, in any order.

Configuring the ICS Host

Here are the steps to follow to run this wizard on the ICS host computer:

1. Launch Control Panel's Network Connections icon.

2. In the Network Tasks section of the dialog box, select Set Up A Home Or Small Office Network.

3. In the initial Network Setup Wizard dialog box, click Next, and then click Next again. The wizard prompts you to select an Internet connection method.

4. Make sure the This Computer Connects Directly To The Internet option is selected, and then click Next.

5. Select the Internet connection and click Next.

6. Run through the rest of the Network Setup Wizard's steps, as described below (see "Completing the Network Setup Wizard").

Configuring Other ICS Machines

Here are the steps to follow to run the Network Setup Wizard on the other computers in an ICS network:

1. Launch Control Panel's Network Connections icon, select Set Up A Home Or Small Office Network, and in the initial Network Setup Wizard dialog box, click Next, and then click Next again.

2. The next wizard dialog box tells you it found the shared Internet connection. Make sure the Yes, Use The Existing Shared Connection For This Computer's Internet Access option is selected, and then click Next.

3. Run through the rest of the Network Setup Wizard's steps, as described below (see "Completing the Network Setup Wizard").

Configuring a Network Without ICS

Follow these steps to run the Network Setup Wizard to configure a network without ICS:

1. Launch Control Panel's Network Connections icon, select Set Up A Home Or Small Office Network, and in the initial Network Setup Wizard dialog box, click Next, and then click Next again.

2. Select the Other option and click Next.

3.   You now have three choices (click Next when you've made your choice):

   ❏   **This Computer Connects To The Internet Directly Or Through A Network Hub**   Choose this option if your computer is attached to a hub that also has a DSL or cable modem attached to it.

   ❏   **This Computer Connects Directly To The Internet. I Do Not Have A Network Yet**   Choose this option if you computer has an Internet connection that you won't be sharing with the network.

   ❏   **This Computer Belongs To A Network That Does Not Have An Internet Connection**   Choose this option if you computer doesn't have a network connection and no other computer on the network will be sharing an Internet connection.

4.   If your computer has an Internet connection, select the appropriate connection from the first two options and click Next. Otherwise, select the third option and click Next.

5.   Run through the rest of the Network Setup Wizard's steps, as described below (see "Completing the Network Setup Wizard").

Completing the Network Setup Wizard

The rest of the Network Setup Wizard's steps are common to all configurations:

1.   If you have more than one connection on your computer, the wizard offers to bridge the connections for you. (In Windows XP, a *network bridge* is software component that enables the computers on two different networks—both connected to the bridging computer—to see each other. Note that any connection that has Internet Connection Sharing or Internet Connection Firewall enabled cannot be added to the network bridge.) If you want to enable the bridge, select Let Me Choose The Connections To My Network and click Next. Now select the check box beside the connection that you use to access the network and click Next.

2.   Enter a computer description and a computer name (which must be unique among the networked computers) and click Next.

3.   Enter a workgroup name (which must be the same for all the networked computers) and click Next.

4. Click Next to apply the network settings.

5. The wizard asks how you want to run the Network Setup Wizard on your other computers. You have four choices (click Next when you're done).

   ❏ **Create A Network Setup Disk**   Choose this option if you'll be including Windows 9x or Windows Me computers in the network. This creates a floppy disk that includes a version of the Windows XP Network Setup Wizard. You insert this disk into a Windows 9x or Windows Me client and run the wizard on that computer.

   ❏ **Use The Network Setup Disk I Already Have**   Choose this option if you've already created a Windows XP Network Setup Disk.

   ❏ **Use My Windows XP CD**   Choose this option to run the Network Setup Wizard on the Windows 9x or Windows Me computers using the Windows XP CD. In this case, you insert the CD in the other computer. When the Welcome window appears, click Perform Additional Tasks and then click Set Up A Home Or Small Office Network.

   ❏ **Just Finish The Wizard**   Choose this option if you don't need to run the wizard on Windows 9x or Windows Me computers.

6. Click Finish.

Working with Network Settings

You can change your network settings by launching Control Panel's Network Connections icon. The configuration of the resulting Network Connections window depends on the computer's role in the network. For example, if the computer is the ICS host, you'll see a configuration similar to the one shown in Figure 16-1. Three items are shown in that figure, though yours may vary:

- **DSL Internet Connection**   This icon represents the ICS host's Internet connection—a broadband connection via a DSL modem, in this case. That is, it's the connection that runs from the DSL modem out to the Internet.

- **To Local Area Network**   This icon represents the connection to the network. That is, it's the connection that runs from one NIC to the network hub.

- **To DSL Modem**   This connection represents the connection to the modem. That is, it's the connection that runs from the second NIC to the DSL modem.

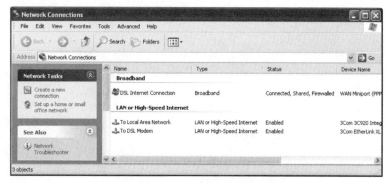

Figure 16-1   This is the Network Connections window for a typical ICS host.

Contrast this with the Network Connections window for a client machine on the same network, shown in Figure 16-2. In this case, there are only two items:

- **DSL Internet Connection on PAUL**   This is the Internet gateway that connects this computer to the DSL Internet Connection on the ICS host, a computer named PAUL in this example.

- **Local Area Connection**   This icon represents the connection to the network. That is, it's the connection that runs from the computer's NIC to the network hub.

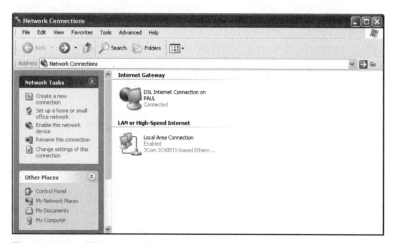

Figure 16-2   This is the Network Connections window for a client computer that uses a shared ICS connection.

From the Network Connection window, you can modify your network settings in the following ways:

■ **Running the Network Setup Wizard** If you want to make major changes to the network configuration, these are most easily accomplished by running the Network Setup Wizard again. Click the Set Up A Home Or Small Office Network link.

> **Note** If you want to change your computer or workgroup name, you can either run the Network Setup Wizard or change these values directly. To do the latter, launch Control Panel's System icon and select the Computer Name tab. Click Change, enter the computer name and/or workgroup, and then click OK.

■ **Renaming a connection** Windows XP supplies connections with generic names such as "Local Area Connection." To assign a more descriptive name to a connection, select the name of the connection, press F2, type the new name, and press Enter.

■ **Installing a networking client, service, or protocol** You shouldn't need extra networking components in a small peer-to-peer network. Just in case you do, you can install them by right-clicking the network connection, selecting Properties, and then clicking Install.

■ **Disabling a connection** If you have multiple NICs and want to disable one that you don't use, right-click its connection and then select Disable. You can enable this connection in the future by right-clicking it and then selecting Enable.

Administering Your Network

Once your network is set up, you can start using it immediately to share resources, including files, folders, programs, and peripherals. Your starting point for all of this is the My Network Places folder, discussed next.

Using My Network Places

You can get to My Network Places using any of the following methods:

- Select Start, My Network Places. (If you don't see My Network Places on the Start menu, launch Control Panel's Taskbar And Start Menu icon, select the Start Menu tab, click Customize, select the Advanced tab, select the My Network Places check box, and click OK. Now you can select My Network Places from the Start menu.)

- In Windows Explorer, click My Network Places in the Folders list.

- In the Network Connection window, click My Network Places in the task list.

- In most Open and Save As dialog boxes, click the My Network Places icon.

In Windows XP, a *network place* is a shared folder or drive on a network computer. (It can also be a location on a Web or FTP server.) When you set up a network place, you can access its files as though they resided on your own computer (subject to any restrictions that the owner of the network place may have imposed). By default, the My Network Places folder shows the network places that were defined when you set up your computer for networking. The name of each network place uses the following format:

ShareName on (`Description ComputerName`)

Here, *ShareName* is the name that the owner of the network place gave to the shared resource; `Description` is the description of the computer where the network place resides; and `ComputerName` is the name of that computer (see step 2 in the "Completing the Network Setup Wizard" section, earlier in this chapter). Figure 16-3 shows some examples.

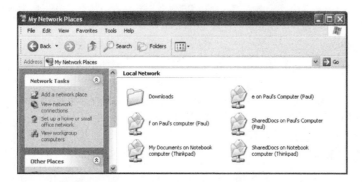

Figure 16-3 My Network Places contains icons for shared network resources.

Besides viewing the contents of the shared resources (by double-clicking a network place's icon), My Network Places also enables you to do the following:

- See the other computers in the workgroup. In the task list, select View Workgroup Computers to see a new window that contains an icon for each computer in your workgroup that is currently online (see Figure 16-4). Double-click a computer's icon to see all the resources shared by that computer. For example, Figure 16-5 shows a computer that's sharing a hard drive, a DVD drive, a fax, a printer, and several folders. (Use the Details view to see the Comments column.)

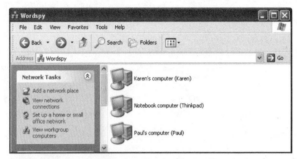

Figure 16-4   Each computer in the workgroup has its own icon.

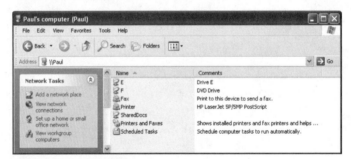

Figure 16-5   Open a workgroup computer to see the resources that computer is sharing with the network.

- See all the workgroups in your network. In the task list, select View Workgroup Computers and then click Microsoft Windows Network, also in the task list. This displays a window that contains an icon for each workgroup in your network. Double-click an icon to see that workgroup's computers.

Adding a Network Place

Whenever a workgroup computer shares a folder, Windows XP detects the new share and adds it automatically to your My Network Places folder. To add another folder (such as a subfolder of a shared resource) as a network place, follow these steps:

> **Tip**   You can tell Windows XP not to add new shared resources to My Network Places window automatically. To do this, launch Control Panel's Folder Options icon, select the View tab, and then clear the Automatically Search For Network Folders And Printers check box.

1.   In the task list, click Add A Network Place to launch the Add Network Place Wizard.

2.   Click Next. If your computer has an Internet connection, the wizard will access the Internet and retrieve a list of online storage providers.

3.   Click Choose Another Network Location and click Next.

4.   Either use the Internet Or Network Address text box to enter the network address of the resource, or click Browse to select the resource using the Browse For Folder dialog box. Click OK, and then click Next.

> **Note**   Network addresses use the Universal Naming Convention (UNC), which uses the following format:
>
> `\\ComputerName\ShareName`
>
> Here, *ComputerName* is the name of the computer, and *ShareName* is the name given to the shared resource. For example, the following UNC path refers to a shared resource named E on a computer named PAUL:
>
> `\\PAUL\E`
>
> If the UNC refers to a drive or folder, you can then use the regular path conventions to access subfolders on that resource. For example, if the resource E on PAUL is a drive and if that drive has a DOWNLOADS subfolder, you can refer to that subfolder as follows:
>
> `\\PAUL\E\DOWNLOADS`

The UNC offers you several alternative methods of accessing shared network resources:

■ In the Run dialog box, enter the UNC for a shared resource to open the resource in a folder window.

■ In a 32-bit application's Open or Save As dialog box, you can use a UNC name in the File Name text box.

■ At the command prompt, enter **START** followed by the UNC path. Here's an example:

```
START \\PAUL\E
```

■ At the command prompt, you can use a UNC name as part of a command. For example, to copy a file named DRIVER.ZIP from \\PAUL\E\DOWNLOADS to the current folder, you'd use the following command:

```
COPY \\PAUL\E\DOWNLOADS\DRIVER.ZIP
```

5. Modify the name in the Type A Name For This Network Place, if desired, and then click Next.

6. To open the network place in a folder window, leave the Open This Network Place When I Click Finish check box selected.

7. Click Finish.

Mapping a Network Folder to a Local Drive Letter

Network places are useful, but they're not as convenient as they could be, because you can't reference them directly (in, say, a script or command). UNC paths can be referenced directly, but they're a bit unwieldy to work with. To avoid these hassles, you can *map* a shared network drive or folder to your own computer. Mapping assigns a drive letter to the resource so that it appears to be just another disk drive on your machine.

To map a shared drive or folder, follow these steps:

1. Use Windows Explorer or My Network Places to display the resource you want to map.

2. Select the shared resource and then select Tools, Map Network Drive. Windows XP displays the Map Network Drive dialog box, shown in Figure 16-6.

Figure 16-6   Use the Map Network Drive dialog box to assign a drive letter to a network resource.

3. The Drive drop-down list displays the last available drive letter on your system, but you can open the list and select any available letter.

4. If you want Windows XP to map the resource each time you log on to the system, leave the Reconnect At Logon check box selected.

5. If you prefer to log on to the resource using a different account, select the Different User Name link, enter the user name and password in the Connect As dialog box, and click OK.

6. Click Finish, Windows XP adds the new drive letter to your system and opens the shared resource in a new folder window.

> **Tip**   For easier network drive mapping, Windows XP enables you to add a Map Drive button to the Windows Explorer toolbar. To do so, right-click the toolbar and then select Customize. In the Available Toolbar Buttons list, double-click Map Drive. Note, too, that there's also a Disconnect button that you can use to easily disconnect mapped resources (as described in the next section).

Disconnecting a Mapped Network Folder

If you no longer need to map a network resource, you should disconnect it by following these steps:

1. Use Windows Explorer to display the drive letter of the mapped resource.

2. Right-click the drive and then select Disconnect.

3. If there are files open from the resource, Windows XP displays a warning letting you know that it's unsafe to disconnect the resource. You have two choices:

    ❑   Click No, close all open files from the mapped resource, and then repeat steps 1 and 2.

    ❑   If you're sure there are no open files, click Yes to disconnect the resource.

Connecting to a Remote Registry

The Registry Editor enables you to work with some portions of the registry on a remote machine. First, log on as a member of the Administrators group on both machines. Then, on the remote Windows XP machine, you need to do two things:

1. Disable Simple File Sharing. To do this, launch Control Panel's Folder Options icon, select the View tab, and then clear the Use Simple File Sharing check box.

2. Enable remote access. To do this, launch Control Panel's System icon, select the Remote tab, and select the Allow Users To Connect Remotely To This Computer check box.

On the local Windows XP computer, follow these steps:

1. In the Registry Editor, select the File, Connect Network Registry command. The Select Computer dialog box appears.

2. In the Enter The Object Name To Select text box, enter the name of the remote computer.

> **Insider Secret**   If you're not sure of the correct name for the remote computer, click Advanced and then select Find Now to see a list of the workgroup computers. Select the remote computer and then click OK.

3.   Click OK. The Registry Editor adds a new branch for the remote machine's registry, although you see only the HKLM and HKU root keys.

When you've finished working with the remote registry, select File, Disconnect Network Registry, select the remote computer's name in the Disconnect Network Registry dialog box, and click OK (or right-click the remote computer's name in the Registry Editor and then select Disconnect from the shortcut menu).

Connecting to a Remote Desktop

Windows XP enables an Administrator to connect to a workgroup computer's Windows XP desktop and use the machine just as though you were sitting in front of it. This is handy if you can't leave your desk but need to troubleshoot a problem on the remote machine. On the remote machine, make sure the Remote Desktop feature is activated:

1.   Launch Control Panel's System icon.

2.   Select the Remote tab.

3.   In the Remote Desktop section of the dialog box, make sure the Allow Users to Connect Remotely To This Computer check box is selected, and then click OK, twice.

On the local computer, follow these steps:

1.   Select Start, All Programs, Accessories, Communications, Remote Desktop Connection. The Remote Desktop Connection dialog box appears.

2.   Use the Computer text box to enter the name of the remote computer.

3.   To customize the remote desktop, select Options to expand the dialog box to the version shown in Figure 16-7. You now see five tabs:

❑   **General**   Use this tab to enter the user name and password of an account on the remote machine. You can also use the Save As button to save your connection settings for later use.

❑   **Display**   Use this tab to set the size of the remote desktop and the number of colors.

❑   **Local Resources**   Use this tab to customize your access to the remote computer's sound effects, keyboard, and local devices.

❑   **Programs**   Use this tab to configure a program to run automatically when you connect.

❑   **Experience**   Use this tab to choose the connection speed. Because you're connecting over a network, you should choose LAN (10 Mbps or higher).

Figure 16-7   Clicking the Options button expands the dialog box so that you can customize your interaction with the remote desktop.

4.   Click Connect.

5.   If you didn't enter a password in step 3, the Log On To Windows dialog box appears. Enter the password and click OK.

6.   If another user is already logged on to the remote computer, Windows XP lets you know that you'll disconnect that user if you continue. Click Yes to complete the logon to the remote system.

7. At this point the remote computer displays a message to the local user saying that a remote user is attempting to log on. If the local user doesn't want to allow the remote connection, he or she can click No. Otherwise, he or she clicks Yes to allow the connection. The user is then logged off and the remote user is logged on.

The remote desktop then appears full-screen on your computer, except for a *connection bar* at the top of the screen. If you need to work with your own desktop, click the Minimize or Restore button on the right side of the connection bar. When you've finished with the remote desktop, select Start, Disconnect. When Windows XP asks if you're sure, click Disconnect.

Sharing Resources with the Network

In a peer-to-peer network, each computer can act as both a client and a server. So far you've seen how to use a Windows XP machine as a client, so now let's turn our attention to setting up your system as a peer server. In Windows XP, that means sharing individual drives, folders, printers and other resources with the network.

Clearing Simple File Sharing

The first thing you need to do is clear Windows XP's simple file sharing feature. This feature is designed for novice users who, understandably, don't want (or need) to learn about technical topics such as maximum users and file permissions. So Windows XP activates simple file sharing by default, even on Windows XP Professional installations. To help you understand the difference between simple and classic file sharing, Figure 16-8 shows the property sheet for the My Music folder on a system using simple file sharing. Notice the following on the Sharing tab:

■ In the Local Sharing And Security section of the dialog box, you select Make This Folder Private to prevent other users from accessing the folder.

■ In the Network Sharing And Security section of the dialog box, you select Share This Folder On The Network to share the folder, and you enter a name in the Share Name text box. If you want network users to be able to modify the files, you select the Allow Network Users To Change My Files check box.

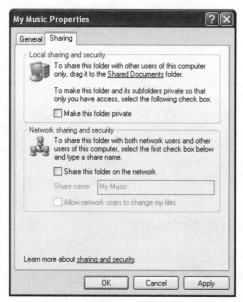

Figure 16-8 The Sharing tab on a system using simple file sharing.

As you can see, what this approach adds in ease-of-use it takes away in power and flexibility. It's an all-or-nothing, one-size-fits-all-users approach. To regain the power and flexibility to share your resources properly, you need to turn off simple file sharing by following these steps:

1. Launch Control Panel's Folder Options icon (or, in Windows Explorer, select Tools, Folder Options).

2. Select the View tab.

3. Clear the Use Simple File Sharing (Recommended) check box.

4. Click OK.

Creating User Accounts

You need to set up an account for each user that is to have access to a shared resource. We discussed creating user accounts in Chapter 5, "Managing Logons and Users," so we won't repeat the details here. Here are some notes to bear in mind for creating users who will access your computer over a network:

■ Windows XP does not allow users without passwords to access network resources. Therefore, you must set up your network user accounts with passwords.

- The user names you create do not have to correspond with the names that users have on their local machines. You're free to set up your own user names, if you like.

- If you create a user account that has the same name and password as an account of a user on his or her local machine, that user will be able to access your shared resource directly. Otherwise, a Connect To dialog box appears so that the user can enter the user name and password that you established when setting up the account on your computer.

Sharing a Resource

With simple file sharing turned off, follow these steps to share a resource:

1. In Windows Explorer, right-click the drive or folder and then select Sharing And Security. Windows XP displays the object's property sheet with the Sharing tab selected, as shown in Figure 16-9.

Figure 16-9   The Sharing tab on a system using classic file sharing.

2. Select the Share This Folder option.

3. Enter the share name and a comment (the latter is optional).

4. In a small network, it's unlikely you'll need to restrict the number of users who can access this resource, so leave the Maximum Allowed option selected. (The maximum number is 10.) If you'd prefer to restrict the number of users, select Allow This Number Of Users and then use the spin box to set the maximum number.

5. Click Permissions to display the Permissions dialog box (see Figure 16-10).

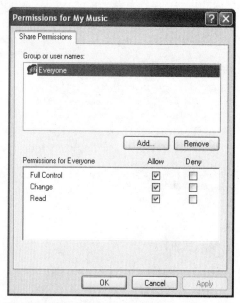

Figure 16-10   Use the Permissions dialog box to specify file permissions for the shared resource.

6. Select the Everyone group in the Group Or User Names list and then click Remove.

7. Click Add to display the Select Users or Groups dialog box.

8. In the Enter The Object Names To Select text box, type the name of the user or users to whom you want to give permission to access the shared resource. (Separate multiple user names with semicolons.) Click OK when you're done.

9. Select a user in the Group Or User Names list.

10. Using the Permissions list, you can allow or deny the following permissions:

   ❑ **Read**   Gives the group or user the ability to only read the contents of a folder or file. The user can't modify those contents in any way.

   ❑ **Change**   Gives the group or user Read permission and allows the group or user to modify the contents of the shared resource, or even delete it.

   ❑ **Full Control**   Gives the group or user Change permission and allows the group or user to take ownership of the shared resource, which enables that user to change permissions on the shared resource.

11. Repeat steps 7 through 10 to add and configure other users.

12. Click OK to return to the Sharing tab.

13. Click OK to share the resource with the network.

Insider Secret   If you want even more control over how your shared resources are used over the network, you should also set NTFS security permissions on the folder. (Ideally, you should do this before sharing the resource.) To do this, right-click the folder, select Sharing And Security, and then select the Security tab. This tab is similar to the Permissions dialog box shown in Figure 16-10, except that you get a longer list of permissions for each group or user.

Index

About the Authors

Paul McFedries is president of Logophilia Limited, a technical writing company based in Toronto. Paul has played with computers since he was a teenager in the mid-1970s; although primarily a writer now, he also has worked as a consultant, Microsoft Windows programmer, and Web site developer. Paul has written more than 40 books that have sold nearly 3 million copies worldwide.

Scott Andersen is a service-line architect with Microsoft Consulting Services, Indianopolis. He has more than 10 years of IT professional experience and has been involved in many aspects of building and deploying Windows XP desktop solutions.

Austin Wilson is a service-line architect with Microsoft Consulting Services, Kansas City. He has been involved with Windows NT deployments since version 3.1, including Windows XP early-adopter programs. He has been in the IT industry for 15 years.

Geoff Winslow is a service-line architect with Microsoft Consulting Services, Chicago. He has more than 10 years of professional field experience that includes designing and deploying Windows infrastructure solutions from Windows NT 3.51 to the present.

The manuscript for this book was prepared and galleyed using Microsoft Word. Pages were composed using Adobe FrameMaker+SGML for Windows, with text in Garamond and display type in Helvetica Condensed. Composed pages were delivered to the printer as electronic prepress files.

Cover Designer:	Patricia Bradbury
Cover Illustrator:	Todd Daman
Interior Graphic Designer:	James D. Kramer
Principal Compositor:	Barbara Levy, Stepping Stone Graphics
Principal Copy Editor:	Marilyn Orozco, Stepping Stone Graphics
Indexer:	Shane-Armstrong Information Systems

Get a **Free**
e-mail newsletter, updates,
special offers, links to related books,
and more when you

register on line!

Register your Microsoft Press® title on our Web site and you'll get a FREE subscription to our e-mail newsletter, *Microsoft Press Book Connections.* You'll find out about newly released and upcoming books and learning tools, online events, software downloads, special offers and coupons for Microsoft Press customers, and information about major Microsoft® product releases. You can also read useful additional information about all the titles we publish, such as detailed book descriptions, tables of contents and indexes, sample chapters, links to related books and book series, author biographies, and reviews by other customers.

Registration is easy. Just visit this Web page and fill in your information:

http://www.microsoft.com/mspress/register

Microsoft®
